The Worst Movies of All Time

THE WORST MOVIES OF ALL TIME

or

WHAT WERE THEY THINKING?

Michael Sauter

A CITADEL PRESS BOOK

Published by Carol Publishing Group

A Citadel Press Book

Published by Carol Publishing Group

Citadel Press is a registered trademark of Carol Communications, Inc.

Editorial Offices: 600 Madison Avenue, New York, N.Y. 10022

Sales and Distribution Offices: 120 Enterprise Avenue, Secaucus, NJ 07094

In Canada: Canadian Manda Group, One Atlantic Avenue, Suite 105, Toronto, Ontario M6K 3E7
Queries regarding rights and permissions should be addressed to:
Carol Publishing Group, 600 Madison Avenue, New York, N.Y. 10022
Carol Publishing Group books are available at special discounts for bulk
purchases, sales promotion, fund-raising, or educational purposes. Special editions can
be created to specifications. For details, contact: Special Sales Department, Carol Publishing Group,
120 Enterprise Avenue, Secaucus, NJ 07094

Manufactured in the United States of America

10 9 8 7 6 5 4 3 2 1

Library of Congress Cataloging in Publication Data

Sauter, Michael.
    The worst movies of all time; or, what were they thinking? / by
Michael Sauter.
        p.   cm.
    "A Citadel Press book."
    ISBN 0-8065-1577-5 (paper)
    1. Motion pictures—Evaluation.   2. Motion pictures—Humor.
I. Title.
PN1995.9.E9S28   1995
791.43′75′0207—dc20   94-46289
                                                   CIP

D e d i c a t i o n

For Judy,
for everything

A c k n o w l e d g m e n t s

My special thanks go to Arnie Schorr at Rhino Video, Norman Scherer at Video Oyster, Chris Nunnally and Alan Bazin at FilmFest Video, Steve Beale and Frank Linkh at The Video Room, everyone at Kim's Video and the New York Public Library for the Performing Arts. Without them all, I'd never have known how bad movies can be.

CONTENTS

INTRODUCTION

Face it: in your lifetime, you're going to see more bad movies than good ones. So you'd better find a way to appreciate them if you don't want your time spent in movie theaters to be a total waste. It may take some work at first, but inside every cloud you will find a silver lining. You just have to know where and how to look. That's what this book is for: to light the light. To show the way. To bend and twist your mind until you, too, can appreciate bad movies. Even when they hurt.

Of course, some bad movies are easy to have fun with. You don't have to be a bad-film buff to appreciate the awesome ineptitude of *Reefer Madness* or *Plan 9 From Outer Space*. You don't have to look hard to find the yuks in a badly dubbed Godzilla movie, or a hopelessly dated Beach Party movie, or a fatally cliched disaster epic. Movies like these are amusingly bad, often hilariously bad. And you feel cooler by looking down your nose at them.

But there are also movies that are agonizingly bad, so utterly, painfully impossible to sit through that, while trying, you realize you'd rather be having root canal—without anesthetic. This book is about them too, because part of appreciating bad movies is knowing how to identify a lost cause, an absolute waste of time and effort, a movie with no redeeming entertainment value whatsoever. On the occasion when you have to sit through such a film, you can consider yourself a better person for it because you've survived a supreme test of endurance. You've stared into the void. Though you may have blinked, you did not break, and you can proudly proclaim to the world, "I survived *Hudson Hawk!*" That which does not kill you only makes you stronger.

Even so, you don't want to sit through *too* many movies that bad. Thankfully, even today, there aren't that many that bad. Most bad movies, even those at the bottom of the barrel, have some sort of entertainment value. Even if you have to laugh *at* them instead of *with* them. Even if sitting through them amounts to an exercise in perverse curiosity, even if to enjoy them, you have to give in to your basest instincts. Admit it. Sometime in your life you've slowed down for a car wreck. You've paid good money to venture into a carnival sideshow. You may have watched O. J. Simpson lead the L. A. police on a low-speed car chase, even though it wasn't as good as *Natural Born Killers*. Well, watching a bad movie can be a lot like that. Face it. The experience is frequently vivid and memorable, something you think and talk about afterward, much more than you would a merely mediocre film—or even a pretty good one.

There are all kinds of ways to appreciate bad movies because there are so many kinds. There are probably more kinds of bad movies than there are kinds of good ones. This book is about all of them: the numbingly bad, the annoyingly bad, the insipidly bad, the insidiously bad, the revoltingly bad, the ridiculously bad, the historically, hysterically bad, ambitiously bad, the amateurishly bad, the amazingly bad, the abysmally bad. You won't find *every* bad movie in this book. After all, it's not an encyclopedia. Think of it instead as a "greatest hits" collection—one that covers the spectrum from Grade A big-budget bombs to Grade Z no-budget duds. Chances are you will find you favorite bad movie lurking in these pages. If not, don't think it wasn't considered. But even in a *bad* movie book, one has to draw the line somewhere. If not, there'd be no bad movies left for the sequel. . . .

THE WORST MOVIES OF ALL TIME

P A R T I

The
Megaton Bombs

WHICH BAD MOVIES ARE THE WORST? That depends on who you ask. Badness is in the eye of the beholder. For some there's nothing worse than a Burt Reynolds, good ol' boy car chase movie, especially if it costars Charles Nelson Reilly and Dom DeLuise. For others, a Douglas Sirk tearjerker is the ultimate slop, especially if it stars Rock Hudson and Jane Wyman. Still others can't abide biblical epics, whether they're solemn or silly. And others consider *Porky's* the absolute pits of the art form. Ask enough people and you'll also get votes for slasher movies, spaghetti Westerns, Japanese monster movies, Italian he-man epics, anything directed by Ed Wood, anything starring Madonna, and anything with a Roman numeral in its title. Yes, all these are bad and most are represented here. But the worst? That's tough to call. Sure there's something to be said for Grade Z, cheesy movies. That's why they have their own section in this book. There's also something to be said for the *oeuvre* of Jerry Lewis. That's why he's in here too. But there's probably the most to say about the really big Hollywood bombs, the movies that set out to be better than the rest and wound up being worse. You know the ones. They have the biggest budgets, the biggest hype, the grandest ambitions, and the greatest expectations—all of which allows them to fail on the biggest scale. They're the Hindenburgs of Hollywood, the Titanics of Tinseltown. They crash with a boom heard 'round the world. They're the Megaton Bombs.

What is it about these bombs that makes them the worst? After all, they're not as inept as say, *Plan 9 From Outer Space*, nor as insulting as *Friday the 13th: The Final Chapter*, nor as imbecilic as *Earnest Goes to Camp*. But on some level, they are the biggest failures. The bigger they are, the harder they fall. Of course, there is much more to it than that. After all, anyone with no money or talent can make a bad movie. But when you've assembled the best cast, crew, costumes, and sets that money can buy and still produce a bomb, well, that's an achievement.

Now, granted, making a good movie *is* a very hard thing to do. A movie is such a complicated, cumbersome, accident-prone thing to make that it usually has two strikes against it going in. Still, there are strikeouts and then there are *strikeouts*. And when it comes to whiffing with gale-force wind, there's nothing like the full-of-himself film-maker who hitches up his pants, puffs out his chest, swings for the fences—and misses by a mile. Ironically, moviemakers are missing by a mile more than ever. Despite all the advances in technology, technique, and all around technical know-how, the movie industry hasn't improved its product. It's sort of like the candy bar business—except movies aren't getting smaller in size, they're only getting smaller in taste.

The old folks are fond of saying, "They don't make movies like they used to." And that's true. Back in Hollywood's Golden Age, you didn't see moguls going off half-cocked, throwing big money at just any old blockbuster notion. They only made blockbusters when they had suitably big ideas. As we shall see, those big ideas weren't always brilliant. And when they weren't, the results were every bit as bad as modern day Megaton Bombs. But these misfires came fewer and farther between, simply because the old-time moguls picked their spots more carefully. They didn't mortgage their studios unless they were reasonably certain it was worth the investment.

So what happened to change all this? In a word—television. When television came along and changed the country's twice-a-week, moviegoing habit, Hollywood had to change the kinds of movies it made. At one time a movie only had to be a nice little slice of light entertainment—you know, like a TV sitcom. But when television started providing that in our own homes—free of charge—the movies had to come up with something you couldn't see on a nineteen-inch tube. Thus began the era of Cinema-Scope and Cinerama, of rampant Technicolor and stereophonic sound. And as the fifties unbuttoned into the sixties and beyond, the very content of movies changed. Suddenly there was more sex, violence, special effects, more—everything!

But especially there was more money. No longer so discerning in their blockbuster ambitions, the studios, now mostly corporate owned, began throwing money at all sorts of ideas. They threw it at good ideas, bad ideas, in-between ideas, and out-to-lunch ideas. Somehow they've managed to hit the jackpot just often enough to justify throwing all that money around.

Over the years it has only gotten harder to hit the jackpot. Having first lost their monopoly on movie theater chains (thanks to a 1948 Supreme Court ruling), then having lost their in-house stables of under-contract stars (thanks to the fifties collapse of the studio system), the major movie companies have also lost the power to succeed—or fail—on their own terms. No longer do studio honchos call the shots. Now the A-list actors do. The hot directors do. But most of all, the actors' and directors' agents do. In their greedy little hands, the art of the deal has become the most creative angle of the movie business, and this is *not* a healthy development. When superagent Michael Ovitz can be perennially anointed the most important man in Hollywood, where does that leave the next generation's Orson Welles?

Yes, folks, more than ever movies have become a complicated, cumbersome, accident-prone endeavor. And they're not helped by the fact that today's Hollywood honchos haven't much of a clue about what audiences really want to see. Nowadays the studios are run by accountants and lawyers, whose idea of a good movie is one that makes a lot of money. These men don't have instincts like the old moguls did. They judge movies by weekend grosses and preview-screening score cards, then throw their money at reasonable facsimiles of last year's hit. How *much* money depends on which A-list actors and directors they hire. And with all that high-priced talent pushing budgets ever upward, it often takes blockbuster box-office success before a studio sees a profit on that big summer popcorn movie, or that year-end Oscar contender.

That's why studio honchos have almost no choice but to swing for the fences. But with ever-inflating budgets, they can only afford to swing away a few times a year. This means they must play it that much safer with the rest of the production slate, and that's why we're seeing so many sequels, remakes, and movies made from old television shows. With their tried-and-true formulas and built-in audiences, these rehashes help insure against big-budget gambles. They also help spruce up a schedule that's probably padded with Jean Claude Van Damme action movies and throwaway comedies starring Jim Belushi. Given such competition, a movie like *The Flintstones* can turn out to be the highest grossing movie its studio has all year. *The Fugitive* can be so successful its studio will drive itself crazy trying to dream up a viable sequel. A sequel to *The Fugitive*! Kind of sad, isn't it?

And as the nineties drag on and studio honchos become increasingly uninspired, we'll no doubt see increasingly uninspiring bad movies. The Age of the Extravagantly Bad has probably peaked. However, there will always be throwbacks. There will always be studios that will back a bank-breaking ego trip like *Last Action Hero*—if the ego involved belongs to someone like Arnold Schwarzenegger. And there will always be producers who will overpay for schlock screenplays by people like Shane Black, who somehow acquired a reputation as a hot screenwriter even though his biggest produced script to date was the forgettable *The Last Boy Scout*. There will always be such aberrations in a town that throws together agents who only have eyes for percentages, directors whose visions are bigger than their budgets, and studio heads who ultimately need to succeed even more than they need *not* to fail.

So no, they *don't* make movies like they used to. But they'll probably always make

Megaton Bombs the same way. The biggest bombs will always be born of self-importance, self-indulgence, and self-delusion. They'll always be the result of runaway egos, runaway ambitions, and runaway costs. They have been since Cecil B. De Mille made his first bombastic biblical epic, since David O. Selznick tried to top his own *Gone With the Wind* only to bite the dust with *Duel in the Sun*, since Howard Hughes set out to reconquer Hollywood with *The Conqueror*—starring John Wayne as Genghis Khan. In spirit and deed, these master builders set the standard for Francis Coppola (*One From the Heart*), George Lucas (*Howard the Duck*), and even Steven Spielberg (*1941*). All of them have been men of enormous movie-making might who made the mistake of thinking they could make any movie worth doing—even if it wasn't. When such monster talents squander untold millions on misbegotten ideas, there is only one way it can end: with the sonic boom of a Megaton Bomb. Get out your earmuffs.

■

THE SIGN OF THE CROSS

1932 ⭢ Paramount

Produced and directed by Cecil B. De Mille. Screenplay by Waldemar Young and Sidney Buchman, based on the play by Wilson Barrett.

CAST: Fredric March (*Marcus Superbus*); Elissa Landi (*Mercia*); Claudette Colbert (*Empress Poppaea*); Charles Laughton (*Emperor Nero*); Ian Keith (*Tigellinus*); Vivian Tobin (*Dacia*); Harry Beresford (*Flavius*); Tommy Conlon (*Stephanus*).

CECIL B. DE MILLE DIDN'T INVENT the biblical epic. It only seems that way. That's partly because he made so many of them, but also because he made them so *big*. *The Sign of the Cross* was his first talkie epic, and thus deserves to be singled out as the prototype it is. *Cleopatra* (1934) might be equally silly, *The Crusades* (1935) might be even sillier, but *The Sign of the Cross* was first. It defined the De Mille formula, not just for C. B.'s future epics, but also for countless imitators. After this, the genre would never be the same.

To be truly De Millean, an epic must be more than big. It must be over the top. Seas must part. Cities must topple. Casts of thousands must perish in massive battles. Sex and sin must be punished—but only after being allowed to flourish in all their divine decadence. According to the C. B. credo, you could wallow in all the depravity you wanted as long as decency triumphed in the end. That, of course, was how he sneaked so much risqué business past the censors. "You can't show triumph over sin unless you show the temptation," he argued. Obviously agreeing, decent Americans showed up in legions, paying reserved seat prices to be awed and titillated by outrageous orgies of excess. And they could do it with a clear conscience, for they knew that whatever evil De Mille might depict, God would always win in the final reel.

To C. B. De Mille, the Bible wasn't just the greatest story ever told. It was the greatest show on earth!

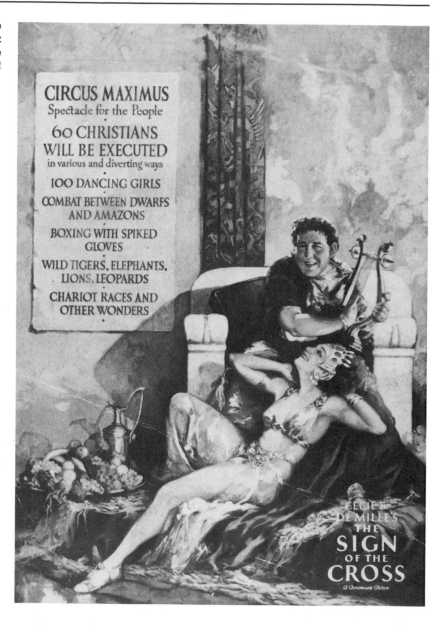

And in *The Sign of the Cross,* there is plenty for God to be wrathful about. Right from the start, the orgies of excess come hot and heavy. The epic begins with Charles Laughton as Emperor Nero literally fiddling while Rome burns. "Burn, Rome, burn," he sings, while his great city lights up the night sky in flames below. Laughton has a gay old time as the "queenly" emperor, flouncing around the palace with slave boys at his feet. But he's not the only one having fun. The film is replete with decadent Roman royalty indulging in forbidden pleasures. There is Empress Poppaea (Claudette Colbert), who languishes naked in a tub of asses' milk, calling to her handmaiden, "Take off your clothes and get in here." There is the sultry Ancaria (Joyzelle Joyner), who does her "Dance of the Naked Moon" while wrapping herself around virtuous Christian girls. There are Roman interrogators who take an inordinate pleasure in torturing captive Christian boys. And finally there are Rome's ruling aristocrats, who gather at the Colosseum to witness all manner of mayhem and mutilation. But thank God for every one of these sinners, for without them this film would be one long, sumptuously appointed snore.

That's because the good guys are *so* damn good. Fredric March plays the hero, Marcus Superbus (no kidding), a Roman officer torn between his loyalty to the empire and his love for a Christian girl. Elissa Landi plays that Christian girl, Mercia, a devout and humble maiden, even if she does wear her hair in a curly blond bob more fitting for a goldigger of 1933. On Mercia, somehow, the hairdo works.

The hero and heroine's romance develops more or less on the run. The Christians, you see, are being strenuously persecuted, having been blamed by Nero for setting fire to the city. When not being arrested or massacred, they skulk in alleys scribbling down the Scriptures, or gather secretly to talk about how to spread the Word. The problem is that, coming from their mouths, the Word sounds awfully contemporary. If De Mille is to be believed, the streets of ancient Rome don't sound much different from New York's Lower East Side, circa 1932. Bit players shout "Hey!" and "Look out, will ya?" just like they would in a gangster movie. Accosting Mercia and her friends in the marketplace, one soldier says to his buddy, "Aw, she's lyin'. They're Christians. Arrest 'em."

But all this romance and religious persecution is merely a buildup to the movie's grand finale, in which scores of Christians are gathered together, marched off to the Colosseum and thrown to the lions, among other beasts. The movie's climax is a regular cavalcade of eye-popping atrocities—gladiators brain each other with clubs, elephants trample and maim, crocodiles chow down on screaming women, apes and bears maul men tied to stakes, and to top it off, Amazon women battle a tribe of pygmies in a gory free-for-all. (One poor pygmy gets speared by an Amazon, who then holds him

up and shakes him in triumphant glee.) Meanwhile, in the box seats, Romans yawn and peel grapes. Talk about cheap thrills.

In what almost seems an afterthought, Marcus and captive Mercia pledge their eternal love—and their faith in an afterlife—before going out together to be eaten by lions. It's an uplifting ending to a barbaric tale, but old C. B. isn't fooling us. The real show was over the moment he took his cameras out of the Colosseum. Minutes after the movie ends, you can't remember a word of Mercia's brave farewell. It's hard enough just to remember Elissa Landi. But Amazons skewering pygmies? That's another story. That's the kind of thing that "sticks" with you forever.

2

RASPUTIN AND THE EMPRESS

1932 ⋅ MGM

Produced by Bernard Hyman. Directed by Richard Boleslavsky. Screenplay by Charles MacArthur.

CAST: John Barrymore (*Prince Chegodieff*); Ethel Barrymore (*Czarina Alexandra*); Lionel Barrymore (*Rasputin*); Ralph Morgan (*Czar Nicholas*); (*Natasha*); Tad Alexander (*Alexis*); C. Henry Gordon (*Grand Duke Igor*).

PITY POOR IRVING THALBERG. The great producer must have thought he had the casting coup of the decade when he signed all three Barrymores for their only appearance together on the big screen. Little did Thalberg realize that *no* screen was big enough for all three Barrymores. Thrashing around in the same frame, the siblings tried so voraciously to upstage each other it's a wonder there was any scenery left without teeth marks. *Rasputin and the Empress* may have been intended as a serious history lesson, but onscreen all you can see is serious histrionics.

In this case, however, thank heavens for big egos, because if it wasn't for the Barrymores' spirited competition, there would be very little happening here. Set in the last days of czarist Russia, the film is a pretentious palace intrigue that seems infinitely more concerned with costume and decor than with anything remotely dramatic, and it moves at a pace so stately that it's static. Director Richard Boleslavsky confines himself to a handful of opulent sets, and whenever he feels the absolute need to throw in an exterior crowd scene, he splices in some badly worn newsreel footage of huddled masses or marching armies. Despite such cost-cutting maneuvers, the movie set a new standard for pomp and circumstance. There are so many banquets, balls, and ceremonies that fully half the budget must have gone to dressing the extras.

Lionel Barrymore *is* Rasputin.

It's all sashes and robes and shiny helmets with pointy tops—but the people wearing those clothes make a less memorable impression.

Except for the Barrymores, of course. Ethel is the empress who reigns with her husband, the czar (Ralph Morgan), over all of Russia. John is Prince Chegodieff, a nobleman who makes a royal pain of himself with his warnings that the peasants are about to rise in revolt. And Lionel is Rasputin, the mysterious "Mad Monk," who turns up at the palace when the empress's son is deathly ill, performs a miracle cure, and is given the run of the place by an eternally grateful royal family. Having gotten his foot in the door, Rasputin quickly starts wheeling, dealing, blackmailing, brainwashing, and murdering his way into control of the empire. With lip-smacking relish, Lionel does pretty much the same thing with the movie.

Draped in black robes, with a stiff, phony beard stuck on his chin, Lionel hogs the spotlight, using the other actors like props. He strokes his whiskers, rolls his eyes, cackles, chortles, and rants like a nut. "I've got Russia right where I want her, d'ya hear me?" goes one typical outburst. "I am the czar of all the Russias!" For her part, Ethel plays the grand empress to the hilt, striking imperial poses, holding her head aloft, warbling her lines in a way better suited to her beloved Broadway stage. She invests a simple, "Please . . . leave us" with more dramatic weight than all the film's other actresses can wring out of a script's worth of dialogue. But Ethel is taking the high road, and that's no way to win the battle of the Barrymores. John, on the other hand, goes toe-to-toe with Lionel, and after getting blown off the screen in their first few scenes, he fights his brother to a virtual standoff.

But oh, how they spar! When Lionel belches during a banquet scene, John's eyes bug out in mock shock. When Lionel launches into a long soliloquy, spitting out food and wiping his feet on the furniture, John arches his eyebrows, purses his lips, and nonchalantly slices the air with his glistening sabre. And when Lionel smirks at having poisoned the mind of the czar's young son, John bellows "You filthy swine!" and tries to strangle his brother—all too convincingly.

But the boys save the best for last. In a desperate attempt to rid Russia of Rasputin, the prince tries poisoning him during yet another banquet. In retaliation, the Mad Monk forces the prince into the cellar, where he taunts him at gunpoint, flashing a maniacal grin that would put Ivan the Terrible to shame. Not to be outdone, John lets loose an equally maniacal laugh. "I've poisoned you, ha-ha-ha!" he taunts back. The standoff ends with the two of them flailing around the cellar, *throwing* the scenery for a change instead of chewing it. "Get back in hell!" John roars at Lionel, beating him with a fireplace poker. Refusing to take this lying down, Lionel showily staggers to his feet, whereupon John grabs him by the hair, drags him out the door, hauls him through the snow and throws him into an icy canal. When last seen, Lionel is bobbing down under an ice floe, somehow having failed to get in the last word.

But he does have the last laugh. *He*, at least, gets to go out in style. For the others, the movie drags on. Palace life returns to normal, people change into new costumes, and the Romanoffs make big plans for the future, cheerfully oblivious to the fact that they're about to be overthrown. Sure enough, just before the bittersweet end, the empress and her brood are finally taken out and shot. But of course it's all anticlimatic. Even offscreen, Lionel has upstaged his sister, simply by making her grand, tragic exit seem like just another loose end to be tied up. No wonder old Ethel never appeared in a film with her brothers again.

Probably nobody asked her. As it turned out (surprise!) *Rasputin* was a hit with neither critics nor paying customers. On top of that, it became the target of a multimillion dollar lawsuit by a real Russian prince who claimed he'd been libelously portrayed by John Barrymore. All things considered, MGM was lucky that the real Rasputin and empress were long gone by the time the movie came out. If they'd seen how *they* were depicted, there would have been *serious* hell to pay!

3

SHE

1935 ⸱ RKO

Produced by Merian C. Cooper. Directed by Irving Pichel and Lan-sing C. Holden. Screenplay by David T. Chandler, based on the novel by H. Rider Haggard.

CAST: Helen Gahagan (*She*); Randolph Scott (*Leo Vincey*); Helen Mack (*Tanya Dugmore*); Nigel Bruce (*Archibald Holly*); Gustav Von Seyffertitz (*Billali*); Samuel S. Hinds (*John Vincey*).

THE ANNALS OF HOLLYWOOD are littered with the corpses of filmmakers who peaked too soon—producers or directors who made their greatest movie early on, then spent the rest of their careers trying to repeat the feat. One such producer was Merian C. Cooper, who wowed the world with the spectacular *King Kong*, only to come back a mere two years later with the seriously silly *She*. Based on the novel by H. Rider Haggard, *She* was at best (and worst) a fragrant bit of comic strip fantasy. Blown up on the big screen, with all the costumes, sets, and extras money could buy, its essential silliness is magnified many times over. And yet everyone involved treats this movie so solemnly you'd think it was a biblical epic instead of a boys' adventure yarn. It's that seriousness of purpose that pushes this picture way past ridiculous, straight to sublime.

Our story begins one foggy night in London, where a group of men sip brandy in a study while planning an expedition in search of the Flame of Life. "It's pure radiation," one man explains. "Only God can produce it," offers another. They all agree that the place to look is "the world's ultimate northern rim." Already, we're beginning to wonder if they wouldn't be better off forming a new search for the Holy Grail. But since hero Randolph Scott's

This vintage poster sings the praises of *She*.

ancestor already lost his life in a previous quest for the Flame, we know there will be no turning back. And so it's off to the northern rim.

That's the Arctic Circle to you. And it's a treacherous trip. The party consists of Scott, Nigel Bruce, a wily old guide, and a pretty tagalong named Tanya (Helen Mack). After an avalanche buries the guide, the three survivors immediately become lost and wander into a mysterious cave, where they are promptly captured by fierce-looking savages. Our friends are about to be offered to the gods (or worse) when a high priest dressed like Ming the Merciless shows up to put a stop to the tribal pep rally.

The high priest leads us through the bowels of the earth to the land of Kor, where men wear their hair like Cleopatra, women mince around in high heels, and everyone bows to the queen, who stands behind a plume of heavenly smoke atop an Art Deco staircase.

"Who are you?" asks Nigel Bruce, properly awed.

"I am yesterday, today, and tomorrow," says the voice behind the flame. "I am sorrow and longing and hope unfulfilled. I am She Who Must Be Obeyed!" Just call her *She* for short.

She doesn't look that tough, but her subjects seem to buy her act, so we do too. Yet once She gets Randolph Scott alone behind closed doors, she reveals her softer side. Practically throwing herself on him, She explains that she's been waiting for him for hundreds of years and now that he's finally here they can live happily ever after. But how can that be? Randolph Scott wants to know. As heroes go, he's a tad dim. He hasn't caught on that She is the keeper of the Flame of Life, that his ancestor was here hundreds of years before him, that the two of them look exactly alike, or that She has decided that Scott is the reincarnation of his ancestor—whom she killed in a fit of jealousy when he refused her offer of everlasting life. "But who *are* you?" Scott asks, still confused. She just smiles, demurely.

If She is a softie around Randolph Scott, she's a regular demon around everyone else. "How you try my patience," she sniffs at some captive savages before having them tossed in the fire pit. Suddenly it's clear why they call her She Who Must Be Obeyed.

"She's wicked, I tell you," Tanya declares, back in the guest quarters. "Aw, don't be too hard on her," Randolph Scott says. "She's strange—and wonderful." Whatever She is, as played by Helen Gahagan, she sure has a way with florid dialogue. Whether expressing anger, anguish, or adoration,

Gahagan's technique involves tilting her head back, thrusting her chin forward, and widening her eyes—but never unclenching her jaw. Gahagan was a theatrically trained actress, yet somehow she seems never to have learned basic breath control. On one mouthful of air she attempts to tell Scott, "Oh my love, take away my eyes, let darkness utterly shut me in and still my ears would know the sound of your unforgotten voice." At the end she's literally breathless.

Dialogue like that will do that to a girl, especially when she has to explain everything two or three times to her leading man. Gahagan fares far better when she's snapping at her minions or ordering the sacrifice of her rival, tagalong Tanya.

The sacrifice itself is the movie's camp centerpiece, with dozens of dancers encircling a flaming pyre, photographed from above as if in a primitive Busby Berkeley number. Eventually, the whole chorus line parades down a sprawling staircase, forming a seemingly endless string of bizarre costumes and weird tribal rites. As this underground Mardi Gras boogaloos past the camera, everyone tries to gyrate like a pagan without dislodging topheavy masks and headdresses. Meanwhile drums are pounding, horns are sounding, and torches are blazing. As the entire cast gathers before the throne of She to offer up the sacrificial lamb, the film turns into such a big production that even our dim hero has time to figure out that the lamb being sacrificed is Tanya.

Rushing to the rescue, Randolph Scott grabs Tanya from the brink of the fire pit, then takes off on a wild chase through caverns, over chasms, and down more marble staircases. It all ends up in front of that much-talked-about Flame of Life, where She offers Scott another chance at everlasting happiness: "If you refuse, the girl will die," She warns. "You mean if I refuse to go in the Flame, you'll have her killed?" he asks, seeking clarification. It really makes you wonder what She sees in this dope.

But he's what she wants. Impatient to get on with the rest of her eternal life, She steps once more into the Flame, crowing so obnoxiously about her youth and beauty that you just know she's in for big trouble. Sure enough, the Flame flares and She ages fifty years. Then the Flame flares again, and she ages another fifty. This goes on until she's roughly two hundred years old and practically mummified. Staggering out of the Flame, She delivers a final soliloquy that lasts so long we *all* age another fifty years. Then she collapses in a pile of dust.

Helen Gahagan sits pretty;
Randolph Scott obeys.

Safely back in foggy old London, Nigel Bruce surmises that She's second bath in the Flame resulted in "overexposure." "Maybe we just weren't meant to be immortal," he says. "Maybe some higher power reached down and decided her fate." Yeah, right, Nigel. Or maybe old H. Rider Haggard didn't give a hoot about plot logic and was just making it up as he went along.

Amazingly, the story of She has been filmed six times, including three silent versions. But not even a 1965 remake, starring Ursula Andress, could top the absurd extremes of this 1935 version. Nor is any future remake likely to do so either. In order to surpass this *She*, you'd have to take it even more seriously than these people did. You'd have to instill it with the sheer conviction that would guarantee the sheerest camp. And after this *She*, who could ever take it that seriously again? No, folks, this *She* is still the queen, destined to reign eternally.

4

THE ADVENTURES OF MARCO POLO

1938 ⁜ United Artists

Produced by Samuel Goldwyn. Directed by Archie Mayo. Screenplay by Robert E. Sherwood, from a story by N. A. Pogson.

CAST: Gary Cooper (*Marco Polo*); Sigrid Gurie (*Princess Kukachin*); Basil Rathbone (*Ahmed*); Ernest Truex (*Binguccio*); George Barbier (*Kublai Khan*); Binnie Barnes (*Nazama*); Alan Hale (*Kaidu*); Lana Turner (*Maid*); H. B. Warner (*Chen Tsu*).

GARY COOPER AS MARCO POLO? Now there's a casting decision that takes some getting used to. In fact, after nearly two hours of trying, one still has trouble picturing him in the role. Coop has somewhat the same problem. He wears his period costumes as if afraid of getting them wrinkled. He struggles with scads of supposedly silver-tongued dialogue. He forces the hearty chuckles of a swashbuckling hero. Coop just doesn't seem to be having much fun. He seems acutely aware that, with one wrong move, he could make an absolute fool of himself. And he has reason to worry. Even without a major misstep, he still looks pretty foolish.

But even if the part fit him like a glove, it hardly would have mattered. Though the movie had all the trappings of an epic adventure (including a then-unheard-of-two-million-dollar budget) the finished product is a pretty paltry affair. Marco and his trusty sidekick (Ernest Truex) journey from Venice to the Orient in search of romance, adventure, and trade agreements. What they get instead is a set-bound sojourn with all the sophistication (but little of the action) of a Saturday matinee serial. Everybody talks a blue streak in this movie, but except for the usual "I present you with these fair maidens" proclamations, most of the dialogue sounds like everyday chitchat circa

Gary Cooper looks askance at Sigrid Gurie, who was dubbed "The Norwegian Garbo" by producer Sam Goldwyn.

1938. "Cozy, isn't it?" Marco remarks during a tour of a torture chamber. Did I mention that much of the movie is played for laughs?

Too bad it isn't funny, because there are plenty of times when the draggy proceedings could use some comic relief. They may call it *The Adventures of Marco Polo*, but Marco's adventures are few and far between. On what should be an epic odyssey across the Old World, he and his sidekick brave stormy seas, blazing deserts, and blinding mountain blizzards—but the whole voyage unfolds in one two-minute blur. Arriving in Peking, hardly the worse for wear, they discover spaghetti, gunpowder, and coal on their first night. By their second night they are already the guests of the Emperor Kublai Khan and Marco is already wooing Khan's drop-dead exotic daughter Kukachin (Sigrid Gurie). It all comes so easily to Marco Polo!

Ah, but nevertheless, there is trouble ahead. Like all great explorers from our high school history books, Marco is nearly undone by his womanizing ways. It all starts innocently enough, with Marco off in a comfy corner of Khan's palace teaching the willing princess how they kiss in Venice. But while you're giggling at the camp value of this cutesy-poo puckerfest, get ready for a revelation: It's the movie's pivotal scene—or at least it would have been had Shakespeare written it. As it is, the script was written by Robert E. Sherwood, a respected New York playwright shanghaied by Samuel Goldwyn to give this gaudy production a touch of class. Goldwyn should have known better. So should Sherwood.

But back to our story: A palace tattletale sees Marco and Kukachin smooching and runs off to tell the emperor's treacherous adviser Ahmed (Basil Rathbone). Already feeling threatened by Marco's presence, Ahmed gladly spills the beans to the emperor, who angrily sends Marco on a suicide mission into the wilderness. Marco is immediately captured by the emperor's rebel enemies, and all looks bleak. But wait! Instead of executing Marco, the rebel warlord (Alan Hale) decides to keep him around, as a plaything for his horny wife. Meanwhile, back in Peking, Kublai Khan has gone off to war in Japan, leaving evil Ahmed to seize the empire and put the moves on princess Kukachin.

But never fear—it's Marco to the rescue! Discovering a new use for gunpowder, he blows down the walls of Khan's castle, battles with the evil Ahmed, and wins the princess's heart. And though she has already been promised to the King of Persia . . . Well, where there's a will, there's a way. Marco, you see, has been appointed to escort the bride to her arranged marriage, but as he and the princess gaze conspiratorially into each other's eyes, you just know that this time Marco's voyage will last longer than two minutes.

Nineteen thirty-eight was not a vintage year for Sam Goldwyn. His other big movie was the aptly titled *Goldwyn Follies*, a misconceived musical comedy cavalcade that attempted to merge highbrow appeal (ballet and opera) with lowbrow belly laughs (the Ritz Brothers). But as bad as that was, *Marco Polo* was Goldwyn's true folly. Never mind that Goldwyn could never decide whether it was a costume epic, a comic romp, or a haphazard history lesson. Never mind that he struck Gary Cooper in a role that should have been played by Errol Flynn. Never mind that he hired a starlet named Lana Turner and shaved off her eyebrows to make her look more exotic and they never grew back! The real symbol of Goldwyn's folly was his "discovery," Sigrid Gurie, whom the producer alternately promoted as "the Norwegian Garbo"

and "the Siren of the Fjords." It's hard to know if the girl had any talent behind the inscrutable mask of makeup she wore in this film. If she did have
talent, she never got to show it. *Marco Polo* died a quick death at the box office, as did Sigrid Gurie's career. Of course, it didn't help when the press sub-
sequently discovered that "the Norwegian Garbo" was really born and raised
in Brooklyn. All things considered, the world of Marco Polo turned out to
be a very small place indeed.

SIGNS OF THE TIMES

Jeanette MacDonald and Nelson Eddy

They were the darlings of the Depression. That'll give you an idea of how depressing the
Depression was. But even in their heyday, Jeanette MacDonald and Nelson Eddy were,
at best, an acquired taste. Middlebrow matinee ladies and dreamy-eyed adolescents might
have fallen for their hopelessly high-flown romantic operettas, but critics and other
cynics weren't nearly as susceptible. "Jeannette MacDonald and Nelson Eddy are like
tapioca," the *New York Times'* Frank Nugent once said. "You either like them or you
don't." But even if you liked *them*, there was still the matter of their *movies*. Individually,
these vehicles might be dismissed as silly, frilly artifacts of the day. Taken together, their
silly frilliness ceases to be amusing. In fact, it's damn near insufferable.

Naughty Marietta (1935) Jeanette plays a runaway French princess who disguises herself as a scullery maid, hops a ship full of mail-order brides, and winds up in the
clutches of colonial pirates. To the rescue comes wooden woodsman Nelson, with a
coonskin cap on his head and a song in his heart. "I'm falling in love with someone,"
he warbles, while rowing Jeanette down a romantic river. No sooner does he finish his
serenade than he sings it again—all the way through. A winning formula is born.

Rose Marie (1936) "Here come the Mounties to get the man we're after!" sings stiff-
backed troop leader Nelson. The man they're after is escaped con Jimmy Stewart, but
that doesn't keep Nelson from wooing Jimmy's sister Jeanette in a north-woods courtship
that culminates with the infamous "Indian Love Call." ("When I'm calling you-ou-ou-
ou-ou-ouu . . .") This duet is, of course, historic camp, but the movie's unsung highlight
is a tribal celebration that is part *Mondo Cane* and part Super Bowl halftime show. How
else would you describe a chorus line of fancy-feathered Indians doing a fertility dance

**MacDonald and Eddy, in a
mutual serenade . . .**

around a blazing bonfire—to a tune by Oscar Hammerstein? That's entertainment!

Girl of the Golden West (1938) MacDonald and Eddy go West! Jeanette runs a saloon where miners and gamblers swoon when she sings "Ave Maria." Meanwhile, Nelson's out robbing stagecoaches as a dashing bandit who dresses like the Cisco Kid and talks like Ricky Ricardo. Since Nelson wouldn't be Nelson without a uniform, he also gets to disguise himself as a dashing cavalry officer. Suddenly, he sounds like Nelson Eddy again. How could Jeanette resist?

New Moon (1940) Sailing from Paris just before the Bastille is stormed, aristocrat Jeanette has a brief shipboard romance with rebel outcast Nelson. When next they meet, he's reporting for New World duty as her private servant. Can a haughty mademoiselle be happy with a commoner who sings while shining her shoes? She can when he highjacks a ship and sweeps her off to the Caribbean. Still caught up with revolution fever, Nelson will later march through a swamp singing, "Give me some men who are stouthearted men." For a change he isn't wearing a uniform—but you get the picture.

5

ONE MILLION B.C.

1940 ⁊ United Artists

Produced by Hal Roach Sr. Directed by Hal Roach Sr. and Hal Roach Jr. Screenplay by Mikell Novak, George Baker, Joseph Frickert, and Grover Jones.

CAST: Victor Mature (*Tumak*); Carole Landis (*Loana*); Lon Chaney (*Akhoba*); Conrad Nagel (*archaeologist/narrator*); John Hubbard (*Ohtao*); Mamo Kent (*Nupondi*); Mary Gale Fisher (*Wandi*).

WHEN MOST PEOPLE HEAR the title *One Million B.C.*, they think of Raquel Welch in a fur bikini. But that was *One Million Years B.C.*, and as ridiculous as it was, it was nothing more than a remake. The original *One Million B.C.* is the one we're talking about here, both because it's a ridiculous film in its own right and because it's the granddaddy of all caveman movies: the one that set the tone for all future distortions of our distant past.

Here, for the first time, we learn that cavemen coexisted with dinosaurs, that woolly mammoths were just elephants draped in ratty shag rugs, and that some Neanderthals were clean shaven, especially if they had strong chins like Victor Mature. No doubt about it, this is prehistory—Hollywood style. But as if he were afraid the public still wouldn't buy his story, producer Hal Roach—better known for his Our Gang comedies—decided to add a preposterous prologue. In it, Mature and Carole Landis play members of a modern day mountain-climbing party who stumble upon a strange archaeologist while exploring a cave. The archaeologist has found some cave drawings, and explains to our happy wanderers that the art is prehistoric. "Say, do you mean that at some time a primitive people made this cave their home?" asks one of the party's brighter members. Compared to these boneheads, the cavemen aren't going to seem so primitive at all.

Victor Mature shows a pet-
store iguana who's boss.

Like all good caveman movies, this one is the tale of two tribes. The rock people live in the hills and seem to be Neanderthals. The shell people live by the sea and seem to be more advanced. Mature belongs to the rock tribe— or at least he does until his dad, the chief, throws him off a cliff in a dispute over some freshly killed Triceratops. Dazed and lost, Mature floats down a river, right into the camp of the more peaceful shell people. There he quickly attracts the attention of Landis, whose permed blond hair and Max Factor makeup make her a perfect match for our pre-Maturely beardless hero.

Warily, welcomed, by this elite tribe, Mature learns to use stone-age forks and spoons and sing prehistoric lullabies. In turn, he earns his keep by saving some women and children from a rampaging Tyrannosaurus rex. Briefly, he's a hero. But after clubbing a jealous rival in a tug-of-war over Landis, Mature is once again an outcast. Taking Landis with him, he makes the dangerous trek back to his own territory, where he reclaims his rightful position as chief.

Mature proves to be a strong, wise leader, while his new mate teaches her adopted tribe how to grow fruits and vegetables and use Cro-Magnon table manners. All is idyllic until—wouldn't you know it—the local volcano blows.

Carole Landis models the fashions of a million years ago. Or thereabouts.

The cataclysm splits the earth, floods it with flaming lava, and sets up Mature's big acting challenge: the moment when he finds Landis's sandal and naturally assumes she's dead. Eegah! Imagine his joy when he learns that she's alive and well and back with the shell people. But don't ask how she got there. It doesn't really matter. The important thing is she's already in danger again. She and her tribe are trapped in their cave by an iguana the size of Godzilla. Of course, Mature and his fellow rockers rally to the rescue, raising the movie's most profound question: If the shell people are truly superior, why are they so wimpy?

Maybe this doesn't really matter either. Once the monster is conquered, the two tribes strike up a chorus of prehistoric lullabies, decide to stick together, and presumably live happily ever after—or at least until the next ice age. As for those mountain climbers in the cave, we never do learn what happened to them. Like many an extinct Hollywood species, their fate was left on the cutting room floor.

From what's onscreen alone, this caveman myth earns a permanent place among all-time movie misfires. But what gives it added stature is the fact that its original director was none other than D. W. Griffith! At the time Griffith hadn't made a movie in ten years—yet considering that, except for some grunts and groans, this was essentially a silent picture, it really wasn't such an unlikely choice for a comeback vehicle. Alas, at some point during production Griffith decided *not* to come back. It's never been clear exactly what went wrong. Maybe the idea of filming pet shop lizards on miniature sets struck him as beneath his dignity. Or maybe he and Roach encountered the proverbial "artistic differences." Or maybe his hiring was never anything more than a Hal Roach publicity stunt. Whatever happened, the fact remains that for posterity Roach is the man whose name is imprinted on this project. From the looks of what's on the screen, the right man got the credit.

6

The Outlaw

1943 ∢ RKO

Produced by Howard Hughes. Directed by Hughes and Howard Hawks. Screenplay by Jules Furthman.

CAST: Jack Buetel (*Billy the Kid*); Jane Russell (*Rio*); Thomas Mitchell (*Pat Garrett*); Walter Huston (*Doc Holliday*); Mimi Aguglia (*Guadalupe*); Joe Sawyer (*Charley*).

INVENTOR, IDEA MAN, and all-around big-business titan, Howard Hughes packed more accomplishment into his life than any other billionaire who ever died a recluse. But when it came to making movies he had the *minus* touch: everything he put his hands on turned into the Spruce Goose.

Hughes just didn't back the wrong projects; he imposed himself on everyone and worried his projects to death. He'd hire the best directors and give them the best technology money could buy, then he'd tinker with what they turned out, sometimes for years. For *Jet Pilot*, he convinced the U.S. Air Force to let him use their state-of-the-art fighter planes, then sat on the movie, playing around with it until its military hardware was obsolete. For *Underwater* he built the whole adventure around a new invention called scuba, then got so bogged down with the equipment that the movie sank like a stone. But these projects pale next to this most fanciful folly: a highfalutin horse opera known simply as *The Outlaw*.

The most famous thing about *The Outlaw*, then and now, was Hughes's hyped-up ad campaign—specifically, the striking poster of teenage discovery Jane Russell languishing come-hither style in a haystack, her legendary breasts barely concealed, but still dominating the shot. No wonder the poster is what endures from the film. It's the only lucid aspect of the whole endeavor.

Jane Russell captures the essence of Howard Hughes's *The Outlaw.*

This is another of those producer-driven projects that started with a famous director who quickly got tired of interference from above and vamoosed into the hills. In this case the director was Howard Hawks. He stayed with the picture just long enough to leave a trace of himself here and there, but it's obvious that the bulk of his oddball film is the work of someone far more off-the-wall.

At heart, this is the old Pat Garrett–Billy the Kid story, except this version adds old Doc Holliday to the mix. Doc rides into town to visit his pal Sheriff Pat (funny, we always thought he was Wyatt Earp's friend), and what do you know—Billy the Kid shows up the very same day! When the two gunslingers form a mutual admiration society, Sheriff Pat starts to worry about public safety. Accompanied by a small army of deputies (most of whom wind up dead), Garrett runs the outlaws out of town. They get as far as the desert shock where Doc's girlfriend Rio lives. Here Doc drops off wounded Billy before riding into the sunset. This leaves the Kid (and the movie) in the hands of Miss Russell's Rio, a hot tamale whose taste in blouses matches her taste in men: low-down.

Rio started this movie hating Billy the Kid because he once gunned down her brother, but that was before she tried to shoot Billy in a stable and ended up rolling in the hay with him instead. Now she's had a change of heart. Boy, has she ever! No sooner has Doc deposited Billy on her doorstep than Rio is curing his fever and chills by jumping into bed with him. As soon as he can stand up, she marries him!

Unfortunately, we don't actually see much of this activity. Hughes has an annoying habit of portentously implying what's about to happen, then pointing his camera at the nearest wall. He does throw in one colossal close-up of Russell's impassioned face coming straight at the camera, while the orchestra swells and cymbals crash. But most of the time his style is an ostentatious tease. He sets up everything in lurid detail, then looks the other way. Take that, censors!

Anyway, the romance doesn't last. As soon as he's back on his feet, Billy is itchin' to join Doc on the lam. Oh, he's grateful to Rio for everything she has done—he even offers to pay her. Putting a price on love! The Kid's just no damn good. Making matters worse is Doc, who comes back to find that the Kid has stolen his woman. Doc graciously offers to step aside with a so-what shrug. He even gives the Kid a choice between his roan horse and Rio, while the poor girl stands there speechless. Don't worry, she gets her revenge. After Doc and Billy saddle up and ride out, Rio sics Sheriff Pat on their trail.

The rest of this fortified oater is a curious game of cat and mouse in which the three cowpokes take turns hog-tying each other, and changing their allegiances at every bend in the trail. Doc can't decide where his loyalties lie; Sheriff Pat can't decide whether to take Doc in or let him go; Rio can't figure out which cowpoke really loves her—and Hughes can't figure out how to make it all coherent. There are increasing indications that he means this movie to be funny—a sort of knockabout comedy about four people who love to hate each other. Indeed, as the characters bicker around various campfires, stage clunky fistfights while wearing handcuffs, and take headlong plunges into watering holes, *The Outlaw* briefly threatens to become an all-out burlesque. But wait! That's smoke on the horizon. There are Indians on the warpath. Suddenly, we're off on a desperate chase across the open plains, a grand-scale action scene that ultimately does nothing except kick up a lot of dust. Once it settles, our four friendly enemies go back to gently kidding the genre. Or at least the three men do. Miss Russell, for the most part, just stands there heaving her chest, which, after all, is the real star of the movie.

Naturally, it all comes down to a final showdown. So who's the fastest,

Billy the Kid (Jack Beutel), Pat Garrett (Thomas Mitchell), and Rio (Jane Russell) attend to dying Doc Holliday (Walter Huston).

Doc or the Kid? Never mind, it's just another Howard Hughes tease. Billy can't bring himself to draw on his new friend. But Doc won't take no for an answer. "Do you want to fight or do you want me to nick your ears?" Doc shouts. Then he proceeds to do just that, firing away with his six-shooter until little notches start appearing in Billy's earlobes. But Billy still won't draw. "You're the only real partner I ever had," he gushes to Doc. "Gosh, do you really feel that way, son?" Doc gushes back. They're about to ride off into the sunset together when jealousy rears its ugly head. But it's not Rio. It's Sheriff Pat! "You used to be *my* best friend," poor neglected Pat bitches to Doc. Then he forces him into the showdown we *didn't* want to see.

So what's the real subtext of all this cowboy bitching and bonding? Maybe we don't really want to know. Suffice it to say that justice prevails (or does it?), that crime doesn't pay (or does it?), and that a cowboy's only true friend is his horse (or is it?). Actually, by the time Hughes pulls his final plot twist, we no longer have a clue what the point was supposed to be. The only thing reasonably clear is that Hughes is putting us on. (Or is he?) Intentional or not, *The Outlaw* is a joke. If you listen closely, you can hear Howard Hawks, somewhere out on the prairie, laughing all the way to Red River.

7

DUEL IN THE SUN

1946 ⤻ Selznick International

Produced by David O. Selznick. Directed by King Vidor. Screenplay by Oliver H. P. Garrett and Selznick, based on a novel by Niven Busch.

CAST: Jennifer Jones (*Pearl Chavez*); Joseph Cotten (*Jesse McCanles*); Gregory Peck (*Lewt McCanles*); Lionel Barrymore (*Senator McCanles*); Lillian Gish (*Laura Belle McCanles*); Walter Huston (*The Sin Killer*); Herbert Marshall (*Scott Chavez*); Charles Bickford (*Sam Pierce*); Butterfly McQueen (*Vashti*).

TALK ABOUT GRAND AMBITION. When David O. Selznick started on this picture, he dreamed it could be another *Gone With the Wind*. And as was his custom, he spared no expense or extravagance to make that dream come true. To create the proper milieu for this epic Western, he laid miles of railroad track, built a sprawling ranch from scratch, and stocked it with a cast of thousands, including horses and cows. Then, to make sure he captured every possible moment of cinematic magic, he let the cameras roll for nearly three hundred hours of footage. He literally tried to will this movie to be great. But in the end all he got for his trouble was an overblown sagebrush soap opera that plays like a parody of itself. About the only thing it has in common with *Gone With the Wind* is Butterfly McQueen.

At least we know right from the start what kind of movie we're in for. Through narrator Orson Welles, we get a quick introduction to the "wild young lovers who found heaven and hell in the shadow of the Rockies." That would be Pearl Chavez (Jennifer Jones), "the half-breed girl from down along the border," and Lewt McCanles (Gregory Peck), "the laughing outlaw" who loves her. Jones wears dark brown body makeup, the better to set off her flashing eyes and teeth; Peck wears a sinister sneer spilling out the side of his mouth. As hot-blooded caricatures, they more than live up to Welles's pretentious introduction. However, it takes some real huffing and puffing to throw them together.

Half-breed Pearl needs a new place to live after her gambler Pa (Herbert Marshall) shoots her trampy Indian Ma in a jealous rage. Sentenced to hang, he sends his only daughter to the home of his old flame, Laura Belle Mc-Canles (Lillian Gish), now the wife of ruthless cattle baron Senator McCanles (Lionel Barrymore). Arriving at Paradise Flats, the "Paris of the Pecos," Pearl soon becomes embroiled in the McCanles clan melodramas. Gentle Laura Belle is the sort of sweet old soul who sips sherry and sings "Beautiful Dreamer" at her piano. The tyrannical senator has no patience for such niceties; he walks all over his wife, even though he's stuck in a wheelchair. Nor does the senator have much use for older son Jesse (Joseph Cotten), an Eastern-educated lawyer who disapproves of his father's feudal ways. Ah, but younger son Lewt (Gregory Peck) now he's the apple of Pa's eye: rowdy, randy, and rotten to the core. "What a boy!" the senator says whenever Lewt gets himself in a scrape. The senator gets to say it a lot.

Pearl, of course, is overripe for lusty Lewt's picking. On her first night at the ranch he swaggers into her room looking for love—but she throws him out, slamming the door and spitting for good measure. What a little hellcat! Yet when it becomes clear that gentleman Jesse has no romantic interest in her, Pearl's willpower weakens. "Resistin's gonna be a darn sight harder for you than for females protected by the shape of sows," observes local preacher Walter Huston. How right he is! With Lewt hanging around like a horny dog, it's only a matter of time before resistin' becomes too hard.

"Guess I'm just trash, like my ma," Pearl moans. But the girl can't help it; it's in her hot blood. So she gives in to Lewt, then curses him, then runs after him, then rejects him, then hangs onto his pants leg, then gives in again, hating herself the whole way. "Trash!" she says, pulling at her hair. "Trash, trash, trash, trash, trash!" Really, the lady protests too much. After a while we get the feeling she's fishing for compliments. So imagine her surprise when Lewt douses her fire, telling her, "No woman can tie onto me, least of all a bob-tail little half-breed like you."

All of this unfolds against widescreen vistas and Technicolor skies. Every so often, seeking to justify their broad canvas, the filmmakers give us a snort of the senator's ongoing war against the encroaching railroad: a conflict that drives away Jesse and turns Lewt into a self-styled Robin Hood. Already

"I'm trash!" says Jennifer Jones. "You're a bobtail little halfbreed," says Gregory Peck. Stop already! You're both right!

wanted for gunning down a rancher Pearl planned to marry on the rebound, Lewt takes to hiding in the hills and dynamiting freight trains while singing "I've Been Working on the Railroad." But even with a price on his head he can't resist Pearl. And even though she wants to kill him, Pearl can't resist him either.

Along the way, Laura Belle dies of heartbreak, the senator sees the light about both of his sons, and Lewt shoots his own brother—because that's what low-down laughing outlaws do. This, however, is the last straw for his love-hate affair with Pearl. When next the fated couple meet, it's at godforsaken Squaw's Head Rock for one of the most memorably ludicrous climaxes in movie history. Firing away from opposite cliffs, Pearl and Lewt blast each other out of the sky only to end up crawling across the canyon floor, bleeding, dying, and bellowing each other's names. We don't know if they want to finish each other off or die in each other's arms, and neither do they. After bellying across acres of sand and stone, they finally crash together in one last embrace. Then it's all over but the credits . . . and the blame.

Though King Vidor was the director of record, he had plenty of unsolicited help from the meddling Selznick, who brought in such giants as Josef von Sternberg to "consult," and, of course, was always on hand to offer his own input. Ad nauseam. Eventually, after some twenty months of shooting, Vidor got fed up and quit, leaving Selznick to do what he wanted to do all along: direct the movie himself. The result was far from the great film Selznick envisioned, but, hey, it was a hit. It garnered Jennifer Jones an Oscar nomination, and fifty years later it is still being watched, albeit for all the wrong reasons. Had it been just another puny passion play taking place on a couple of ranch-house sets—which is all the material warranted—*Duel in the Sun* would now be just a dim, dusty footnote in the Hollywood archives. For better or worse, Selznick made it what it is today. Wherever he is, he's probably beaming with pride.

THE BABE RUTH STORY

1948 ⵏ Monogram/Allied Artists

Produced by Joe Kaufman. Directed by Roy Del Ruth. Screenplay by Bob Considine and George Callahan, based on the book by Considine.

CAST: William Bendix (*Babe Ruth*); Claire Trevor (*Claire*); Charles Bickford (*Brother Mathias*); Sam Levene (*Phil Conrad*); William Frawley (*Jack Dunn*); Fred Lightner (*Miller Huggins*).

A FEW YEARS AGO, John Goodman played Babe Ruth in a warts-and-all portrait of baseball's greatest slugger. Most people agreed that Goodman made a pretty good Bambino, but that the rest of *The Babe* was pretty bad. Still, that made it a considerable improvement over the last movie based on the Babe's life and times. Starring William Bendix, who wasn't even a good Bambino, *The Babe Ruth Story* is a blot on the memory of the Hall of Fame legend. Released the same year that Ruth died, it might even qualify as sacrilege. But since it tries so earnestly to sanctify its subject, let's give it the benefit of the doubt. Let's just call it sentimental tripe—of truly Ruthian proportions.

What makes this so significantly bad is the example it set for the baseball movies that followed. *The Babe Ruth Story* is a virtual blueprint for all those bogus biopics featuring whitewashed baseball heroes in G-rated versions of their careers. You know the lineup: Jimmy Stewart as Monty Stratton in *The Stratton Story*; Ronald Reagan as Grover Cleveland Alexander in *The Winning Team*; Tony Perkins as Jimmy Piersall in *Fear Strikes Out*. They all owe a debt to *The Babe Ruth Story*. Yet all of them together couldn't lay it on as thick as this treacly tribute to the Sultan of Swat.

The movie starts hitting us with hokum right away. Led by an annoying narrator who sounds like Heywood Hale Broun, we are taken on a brief tour of

William Bendix, all decked out in pin stripes as the legendary Babe. At least he got the shape right.

the Baseball Hall of Fame, stopping at last at Ruth's plaque so we can reflect for a moment on the greatness of the man. From there we flash back to the Babe's humble beginnings, when he was just George Herman Ruth, an incorrigible kid spending most of his childhood at St. Mary's School for Boys. Indeed, he's still there at age nineteen as a sort of unofficial school mascot. Since George spends most of his time hitting baseballs through church windows, kindly Brother Mathias (Charles Bickford) arranges a tryout with the Baltimore Orioles. The rest is sugarcoated history.

Now, the real Babe Ruth was a coarse kind of a guy who had a soft spot for kids (and women, and food, and booze). This movie's Babe is more like an overgrown kid. "You mean I'm gonna get *paid* to play baseball?" he says, looking at his first contract. "Boy, a hundred dollars! There's not that much money in the whole world!" Yes, sports fans, according to this movie, the Bambino was a bumpkin, a regular babe in the woods. And Bendix plays the role for all it's worth.

At the rate this biopic has been going, we're grateful when Babe gets to the majors and the years start whizzing by. Sometimes the movie even throws in a little baseball, although there are precious few scenes of on-the-field action. Most of Ruth's feats are depicted in close-ups in the batter's box, with newspaper headlines that tell us what the decidedly dumpy Bendix couldn't hope to demonstrate: BABE RUTH STRIKES OUT TY COBB! trumpets one headline, while elsewhere on the front page World War I is raging. RUTH

HAMMERS 59 HOME RUNS! blares another banner, as if he had hit them all in yesterday's doubleheader.

Yes, sports fans, Babe Ruth *was* the center of the universe. And why not, with all the good deeds he did between dingers? In fact, this movie would have you believe that every home run (and even some of the foul balls) was accompanied by a sappy human interest story.

The bathos just keeps coming. In one heartwarming interlude, the Babe accidentally beans a young fan's dog, then rushes the pooch to the nearest people hospital, where he talks the chief of surgery into performing a lifesaving operation. In another poignant highlight, Babe visits "awful sick" Johnny in the hospital, promising to sock a home run for the nearly comatose kid. You know how this one goes: Babe steps up to the plate. His wife Claire shouts, "Remember Johnny!" from the stands. Babe says, "I'm ridin' this one out of the park. Me and a young pal of mine." Then he points to centerfield, not once, not twice, but three times, takes a mighty William Bendix swing and—whammo! It's gone! Back in the hospital, Johnny comes out of his coma, on the miracle road to recovery.

But the movie's just warming up. Years later an over-the-hill Babe is playing out the string with the Boston Braves. After hitting three home runs in a final blaze of glory, he walks away from the game into the front office job he thinks is awaiting him—only to be fired on a contract technicality. "You oughta sue," a friend tells him. "Sue baseball?" says Babe, ever the bumpkin. "Naw. That'd be like suing the church."

It's an ignoble end for the Sultan of Swat, but at this point we'd take it. Unfortunately, the film has other plans, dragging on interminably while Babe spends his final years refereeing women's wrestling and getting underfoot at home. If this *had* been a warts-and-all biography, Babe's slow fade might have provided some bittersweet food for thought. As shown here, however, it just gives us another chance to wallow in schmaltz while waiting for the inevitable fatal illness to strike the Babe down.

Finally it does. The great Babe now lies flat on his back, while wife, Claire, reads him tear-stained get-well notes and a heavenly chorus of fans stands outside his window singing a hymn-like version of "Take Me Out to the Ball Game." As the violins on the sound track pick up the refrain, we find ourselves going into insulin shock. We just know the end is near—for Babe, for the movie, and for us.

Bendix does his version of
Babe Ruth's mighty swing.

But no. Seems there's this untested serum that just might prolong Babe's life. Claire tells the doctor, "Get it." We cry "No! Let him die like Gehrig, with a little dignity!" Too late. The doctors prepare the Babe to be a human guinea pig, and he gets to do one more sappy scene before getting wheeled down the hospital corridor to that big stadium in the sky.

As the heavenly chorus builds to another crescendo, the annoying narrator returns to proclaim Babe a hero for giving his body to medical research. But wait—wasn't he going to die anyway? Oh, never mind. There's no stopping this movie now. Lifting his voice, the narrator intones, "Babe's name will live on, as long as there's a ball, a bat . . . and a boy." He forgot to say a candy bar, but we get the point. Babe Ruth was such a great ballplayer that he could even survive *two* bad movies about him. Jimmy Piersall and Grover Alexander should be so lucky.

9

THE FOUNTAINHEAD

1949 ⭢ Warner Bros.

Produced by Henry Blanke. Directed by King Vidor. Screenplay by Ayn Rand, adapted from her novel.

CAST: Gary Cooper (*Howard Roark*); Patricia Neal (*Dominique*); Raymond Massey (*Gale Wynand*); Kent Smith (*Peter Keating*); Robert Douglas (*Ellsworth Tooey*); Henry Hull (*Henry Cameron*); Ray Collins (*Enright*).

AMONG THE WORST MOVIES ever made, *The Fountainhead* is a special case. It's guilty by reason of insanity. It takes a radical philosophy by an out-to-lunch author, boils it down to oversimplified pulp, then pumps itself back up with so much self-importance that it seems to have been erected as a monument to itself. It might have been a real controversial picture—if anyone had understood it.

Still, the film is fascinating, in a weird sort of way. Directed by King Vidor (yes, again) and adapted from the cult novel by Ayn Rand, it is strikingly stylized, dramatically delirious, and as emotionally cold and hard as galvanized steel. We watch its idealistic hero standing tall and fighting for what he believes in, but we're never the least bit stirred. That's because the film never lets us inside his head—and even if it did, we wouldn't want to be there.

The hero is Howard Roark (Gary Cooper), a brilliant architect at odds with the rest of the world. Roark is always out of work because he's so far ahead of his time, because he's so aesthetically pure, and because he will not compromise. Don't you just hate him already?

Since Howard can't make ends meet, he has to take menial jobs, like operating a drill in a Connecticut rock quarry. This is where he meets Dominique (Patricia Neal), who just happens to be an architecture critic whose father just happens to own the quarry. Dominique rides up on her stallion,

Patricia Neal and Gary Cooper go over the top (when they aren't on the floor) in _The Fountainhead._

takes one look at Howard and his drill, and goes home to smash her marble fireplace so that Howard can come up and fix it. When Howard elects not to fix her too, she gets very upset. The next day at the quarry she gallops up again and slashes him across the face with her riding crop. Later, he barges into her bedroom and they throw each other off the walls. This is Ayn Rand's idea of foreplay. And if all the movie were as campy as this sequence, it might have been a lot more fun.

Unfortunately, _The Fountainhead_ soon settles into a grim pursuit of truth, honor, and individualism, as defined by Ayn Rand. Howard Roark eventually becomes a ground-breaking architect, and Dominique eventually marries ruthless newspaper publisher Gail Wynand (Raymond Massey), who has always gone out of his way to bury Roark in print. Over the years, the trio's paths keep crossing, as less honest, less honorable, less _manly_ men conspire to make Roark conform and compromise. But Howard Roark will not compromise!

It all comes to a head (in more ways than one) when Roark dynamites a public housing project because the builders had the gall to modify his design.

It doesn't seem to matter that investors' millions have gone up in smoke, that hundreds of people have lost their homes, or that soulmate Dominique has been dragged in as an accomplice. Howard Roark *does not compromise!* With former nemesis Wynand rallying to his cause ("This is my chance to redeem myself," Wynand claims), Roark weathers a storm of public outrage that would wither a lesser man. And indeed it does destroy Wynand, who sells Roark out to save his paper, then shoots himself in shame. Alone against the world, Roark delivers an astonishing courtroom diatribe defending his right to stick to his principles no matter what the cost to everyone else. In case you hadn't guessed, Howard Roark wins his case, becomes a wealthy builder, and marries Dominique. The last scene finds the new Mrs. Roark riding an outdoor elevator to the top of the world's tallest skyscraper, where Mr. Roark stands erect, in triumph, head literally in the clouds. What world are these people living in anyway?

The answer is the world according to Ayn Rand, as translated for the mass-movie audience. The trouble is, her neo-Nietzschean theories of "objectivism" don't sum up easily in twenty-five words or less. And poor Gary Cooper, once again miscast, is far from the ideal man to be mouthing a lot of mumbo jumbo about how superior individuals don't have to live by the same rules as everybody else. His speeches seem literally wrenched from clenched teeth. Trying to strike noble poses, he instead comes off solemn, rigid, and self-righteous. He's a man standing alone against the crowd just like in *High Noon*, except that here his only cause is himself. Cooper isn't helped by a supporting cast that drives home the high seriousness of it all with icily theatrical performances. Drop them all in ultramodern sets, set them off with expressionistic lighting, and you've got one hell of an oppressive experience.

This was the second late-forties lost cause for director King Vidor. He had signed on late in the project, never had much say over the script or casting, and reportedly never felt Cooper was right for the role. But then, who would have been? Howard Roark was never meant to be *played*. *The Fountainhead* was never meant to be a *movie*. The fact is that some books are just plain unfilmable. Unfortunately, Hollywood never seems to know which ones they are until after it has tried to film them. *The Fountainhead* is a classic case, perhaps the quintessential example. Rarely has so much pretentious drivel come out sounding like . . . so much pretentious drivel.

10

BEYOND THE FOREST

1949 ⁴ Warner Brothers

Produced by Henry Blanke. Directed by King Vidor. Screenplay by Lenore Coffee, from a novel by Stuart Engstrand.

CAST: Bette Davis (*Rosa Moline*); Joseph Cotten (*Dr. Lewis Moline*); David Brian (*Neil Latimer*); Ruth Roman (*Carol*); Minor Watson (*Moose*); Dona Drake (*Jenny*).

THE FORTIES WERE A BAD TIME for King Vidor. First there was the David O. Selznick donnybrook with *Duel in the Sun*, then the impossible challenge of deciphering Ayn Rand's *The Fountainhead*. But if Vidor had his hands full with those two misbegotten projects, it was nothing compared to the hell he must have endured with Miss Bette Davis, his temperamental star in *Beyond the Forest*. Always a terror on the set, Davis was at the end of a long association with Warner Bros., and the studio was doing its best to hasten her departure. On top of that, she reportedly hated the character she was playing, which only made her angrier—at Jack Warner, at the world, at *everyone*. Under the circumstances, Vidor might have been forgiven had he walked out on this no-win assignment. But he stuck with it, and proved himself to be the right man for the job. He knew better than to try to control Miss Davis—so he encouraged her!

As Rosa Moline, a low-rent Madame Bovary pining to run off to Chicago, the star puts on a show that could hardly be embellished by even the best Bette Davis impersonator. Hair and skin darkened to look vaguely half-caste (à la Pearl Chavez), Davis keeps her lip perpetually curled, opening her mouth only to cut off men at the knees and then bite their heads off for good measure. Right from the start, she's over-the-top. On a fishing trip with her husband (Joseph Cotten), the town doctor, she perches on the riverbank, plucking her eyebrows and snorting in utter contempt of his boring Bohunk

Bette Davis seduces David Brian in a rare tender moment. So why does he look like a fly in a spiderweb?

hobbies. A little later she spots a porcupine in a tree, grabs the nearest gun, and blasts the animal to kingdom come. "I don't like porkies; they irritate me," she sniffs. Still later, she sashays down the stairs of her all-too-humble home, surveys the decor and utters her immortal assessment: "What a dump!" Why the good doctor puts up with this one minute is a mystery. But of course, if he didn't there'd be no movie.

As all low-rent Madame Bovarys must, Rosa has an affair with a man who raises her hopes. In this case it's rich, handsome Neil Latimer (David Brian), a big-city businessman who loves her, leaves her, and goes back to Chicago. Eventually she can't stand it and takes off after him, only to have the big lug inform her that he's going to marry a society girl. Rejected, Rosa spends a luridly nightmarish night on the street, where she's accosted by cackling crones, manhandling winos, and sinister-looking cops. Left with no other option, she goes crawling back to her husband, who of course welcomes her, no questions asked. She has just about resigned herself to life in her small town purgatory when her handsome lover returns to take her away with him. He truly loves her, he says. He doesn't care what kind of slut she is.

Bette Davis matches slatternly scowls with the hired help (Dona Drake).

Ah, but not so fast. Seems that dear Rosa has gotten herself pregnant. Even worse, a kindly old caretaker knows her secret and is threatening to tell everyone and ruin her getaway plans. Does that stop Rosa? Not a chance. She shoots the caretaker during a hunting trip and gets herself acquitted at the murder trial. Then, when her husband won't let her run to her lover, she throws herself down a mountainside to kill her unborn child. Unfortunately, she also succeeds in bringing on a high fever, which gives Davis the license to turn it up yet another notch, playing the rest of the movie in a state of sheer delirium. As she sits at a vanity table smearing her face with makeup, we get a glimpse of the Bette Davis who will go on to play Baby Jane. It isn't a pretty sight.

But it gets worse. In a last-ditch attempt to reach Chicago, Rosa wobbles off toward the train station, face still painted like Baby Jane. We pray that Vidor will show mercy and kill her off quickly, but no such luck. Like a dying elephant making its way to the graveyard, Davis takes forever to drag herself to the depot. Once there, she collapses beside the railroad tracks as the train to Chicago pulls out. What a dump, indeed.

Aware that it was presenting an unpleasant bunch of characters, Warners prefaced the film with a moralistic disclaimer to help patrons understand why they should wade through this swill. Such disclaimers weren't uncommon during Hollywood's Golden Age, before moviegoers knew what to make of antiheroines like Rosa. Still, *Beyond the Forest*'s preface was quite a mouthful, wrapping up the movie's themes and schemes in a proverbial nutshell. To wit: "This is the story of evil. Evil is headstrong—is puffed up. For our soul's sake it is salutary for us to view it in all its naked ugliness once in a while. Thus we may know how those who deliver themselves over to it end up like the Scorpion, in a mad fury, stinging themselves to eternal death."

That about said it all concerning Davis and her contract breaker at Warners. She stung herself in the nose, to spite her face.

■ ■

THE GREATEST SHOW ON EARTH

1952 ⁙ Paramount

Produced and directed by Cecil B. De Mille. Screenplay by Federic M. Frank, Barre Lyndon, and Theodore St. John. Story by Frank, St. John, and Frank Cavett.

CAST: Betty Hutton (*Holly*); Cornel Wilde (*Sebastian*); Charlton Heston (*Brad*); Dorothy Lamour (*Phyllis*); Gloria Grahame (*Angel*); James Stewart (*Buttons*); Lyle Bettger (*Klaus*); Emmett Kelly (*himself*).

WHO SAID ALL OSCAR-WINNING MOVIES had to be great? Who said they even had to be *good*? Let's get serious: Some of them were really quite bad, and none more flamboyantly so than this big-top epic from—who else?— C. B. De Mille.

The Best Picture winner for 1952, *The Greatest Show on Earth* must have bowled over the competition with sheer mass. It's hard to imagine what the Academy voters saw in it; even then it was considered a surprise winner. But they did nominate it, right? Like somebody once said, there's no accounting for taste. In Hollywood, lots of people really do believe that bigger is better.

They don't come much bigger than this. Filmed with the cooperation of Ringling Bros. Barnum & Bailey Circus, the film captures all the razzle-dazzle of a big-time, star-spangled, three-ring circus. Accompanied by De Mille's newsreel-style narration, the movie not only piles on animal acts, aerial feats, and full-dress parades; it also shows us the animals being fed, the big top being set up, the circus breaking camp, the whole show hitting the road. We learn everything we'll ever want to know about life with the circus.

We also get a plot that's so creaky it leaks sawdust and a handful of subplots that play like so many sideshows. In the center ring there's boss man

Charlton Heston, who is trying to keep the circus solvent while still playing all those small towns that form the backbone of this great country. The owners, however, want to play only the big cities. "Times have changed," they tell him. "Kids haven't," he snaps. Heston is sort of partial to perky trapeze star Betty Hutton, but that doesn't stop him from hiring another aerial attraction—a European import played by Cornel Wilde with a hard-to-pin-down accent. His character's name is Sebastian, but is he French? Italian? Spanish? Who knows? Half the time he sound like Maurice Chevalier, the other half like Ricardo Montalban. But *all* the time he's such a ham we fear he'll get fed to the big cats by mistake.

But when it comes to overacting Wilde can't shout down all-time champ Chuck Heston, who has never been more of a pompous gasbag than he is here. Somehow, bouncy Betty winds up torn between these two men. Given the possibilities of that triangle, we welcome the development of subplots. But we'll be sorry.

It's hard to decide which sideshow is the most annoying. Is it the crooked midway hustler who gets booted out by Heston and swears revenge? Is it the elephant tamer and his wife who carry on a running argument like big-top Battling Bickersons? Or is it Jimmy Stewart, playing a clown who is really a doctor wanted by the police for the mercy killing of his wife? (Honest, that's really his story.) From town to town, he sneaks off into the audience to get messages from his mother(!) who gives him updates on the law's progress in tracking him down. And not once during the movie does he take off his clown makeup. Get it? He's hiding behind that mask, crying the tears of a clown.

There's more where that came from. This movie is a regular treasure trove of big-top clichés: The show must go on. He's got sawdust in his veins. Everybody loves a clown. Circus people gotta stick together. It gets so we jump for joy when C. B. switches to the action in center ring. The trouble is, he keeps cutting away from it to show us the rubes in the crowd—who are invariably scarfing up popcorn and slurping down sodas while asking stupid questions like, "How did they do that?" and "What are they gonna do next?" No doubt this is meant to show us the innocent joy a red-blooded, small-town American boob can have at the circus. Hurry, hurry folks! Step right up!

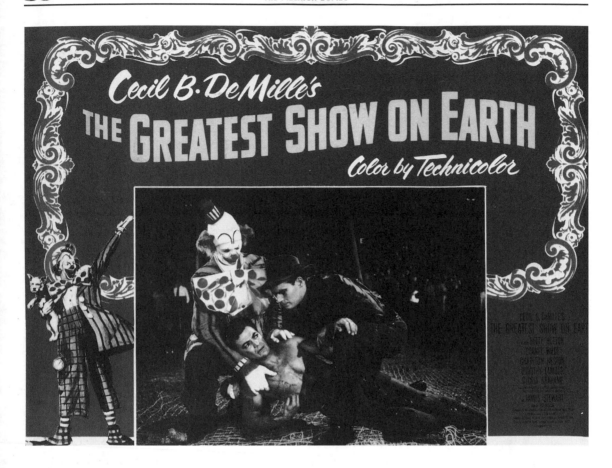

Big Top Spectacle! High-Wire Tension! Clownish Comic Relief! All that, plus a corny love triangle *and* a colossal train wreck. Ladies and gentleman: *The Greatest Show on Earth!*

Shameless showman that he is, De Mille leaves no trick unturned. He even throws in a few full-blown musical numbers, including one on a trampoline, featuring Hutton, Stewart, and some midgets—all singing! Just often enough, C. B. gives us a dramatic jolt, like toppling Cornel Wilde off the trapeze without a net (*every* circus movie has an aerialist who plummets to disaster, and this is the one that started it). And just when the movie is running out of steam, with no grand finale in sight, C. B. engineers a massive train wreck that sets up all sorts of heart-tugging moments of truth, as these brave troupers pull together to save each other and the circus. Like the man said, the show must go on. And on, and on, and on. But did it have to take us with it? By the end, we feel like we've spent an entire season with this circus—and that's about two and one half hours too long.

Betty Hutton is torn between high-wire hotshot Cornel Wilde left and high-minded ramrod Charlton Heston.

SIGNS OF THE TIMES
Esther Williams

Esther Williams was a champion swimmer. A gorgeous champion swimmer. In Golden Age Hollywood, that made her star material. But Esther wasn't just any star. She was property of MGM. That meant great big musicals. That meant splashy Technicolor. That meant Busby Berkeley. When you were an MGM star, the sky was the limit—except that Esther's element was water. As an actress, she was a good swimmer. As a singer, she was a good swimmer. As a dancer, she was a good swimmer. And besides, she looked so good in bathing suits that Louis B. Mayer simply had to put her in them as often as possible. Esther's movies always found a way to get that beautiful body near a body of water. Sometimes the setting was a natural, like the Hawaiian environs of *On an Island With You*. Sometimes it was a real leap, like the Sun Valley ski resort in *Duchess of Idaho* (paging Sonja Henie!). But wherever Esther went you could be sure the place at least had a pool. Laugh if you will, but that formula held water for over a dozen movies, and inspired synchronized swimmers for generations to come.

Pagan Love Song (1950) Esther finds an ideal setting, on the sun-splashed isle of Tahiti. But as a plantation owner's daughter she's just not satisfied. "I've had my fill of

Esther Williams rises to the
occasion in a typically
splashy Busby Berkely
number from *Million Dollar
Mermaid.*

spearfishing and moonlit beaches," she declares, making plans to head for the mainland.
Then along comes handsome Howard Keel with his great big voice. Civilization can
wait! Amazingly, even with the ocean all around her, the studio still had to dream up
some native-girl fantasy numbers in the lagoon. Meanwhile, Keel remains on dry land,
singing happy-go-lucky songs against rear-projection backdrops. The MGM backlot
never looked more like Tahiti.

Texas Carnival (1951) What's a mermaid like Esther doing in a two-bit carny deep
in the heart of Texas? She's a "Dunk Me" girl, what else? Since this is no place for an
MGM star, she soon moves on to a desert resort (with a big pool, of course), where
everyone mistakes her for a millionairess. For comic relief, frequent costar Red Skelton
sticks his head in the pool and makes funny faces underwater (just like he did in
Bathing Beauty). Esther, meanwhile, does her big swim number in yet another fantasy
sequence—dressed in a billowy nightgown! The lady did not live by bathing suits alone.

Million Dollar Mermaid (1952) Esther gets her dream role as real-life swimming star
Annette Kellerman. But this version of Kellerman's life story is pretty much all wet. The
movie's idea of drama is to take us on a twenty-six-mile stunt swim down the Thames,

and boy is it ever a marathon! "I'll make it," she glubs, around mile twenty-five, "I know I can." Sure *she* can, but can we? Still to come are diving exhibitions, skimpy swimsuit scandals and Busby Berkeley production numbers at New York's Hippodrome. To see Esther emerge on a rising platform surrounded by spurting fountains and torch-sized sparklers is to know where Bette Midler got her inspiration for *Clams on the Half Shell.*

Skirts Ahoy (1952) Esther joins the navy, where she sings more than she swims. Fine kettle of fish for a WAVE* to be in. Eventually she does get an underwater routine, with a couple of tots in water wings. Later, she leads the other girls in aquatic calisthenics. Still later, somewhat desperate, she does a splash-dance duet with an inflatable pool toy. For once she fares better out of the water, breezing through boot camp, romancing officer Barry Sullivan, and even brawling with some wiseacre WACs. *Dames at Sea* it ain't.

*WAVEs were lady sailors.

12

THE SILVER CHALICE

1954 ⁍ Warner Brothers

Produced and directed by Victor Savile. Screenplay by Lesser Samuels, based on a novel by Thomas B. Costain.

CAST: Virginia Mayo (*Helena*); Jack Palance (*Simon*); Pier Angeli (*Deborra*); Paul Newman (*Basil*); Alexander Scourby (*Luke*); Joseph Wiseman (*Mijamin*); E. G. Marshall (*Ignatius*); Lorne Greene (*Peter*); Natalie Wood (*the young Helena*).

THE AD CAMPAIGN PROCLAIMED IT "The Mightiest Story of Truth and Temptation Ever Produced." Star Paul Newman called it "the worst film of the 1950s." It doesn't take long to determine who was closer to the truth. Perhaps the dullest (and dumbest) of all religious epics, *The Silver Chalice* meanders all over the Middle East to tell the story of Basil (played by Newman in his film debut), a young Greek sculptor who rises up from slavery to engrave the cup Christ used at the Last Supper. Watching him do the dinner dishes might have been more fun. Not even Jack Palance, as a magician with messianic delusions, and Lorne Greene, as the apostle Peter, can uplift this dud to camp glory.

However, they *do* help. Dressed like Mickey Mouse in *The Sorcerer's Apprentice*, Palance couldn't look more ridiculous if he were doing one-arm pushups. Delivering his lines as if he were playing God himself, Green couldn't have been a more pompously pious Peter. Unfortunately, this isn't really their story. This is the story of Basil, and so it's sort of obligated to follow him around. As we shall see, that becomes an arduous task.

After being adopted as a boy by a wealthy Roman (E. G. Marshall), Basil grows up cultivated and content. Then his guardian dies and Basil's greedy relatives sell him into slavery. Gaining some local fame as a sculptor, Basil is eventually freed by Christians who bring him to Jerusalem to work on the

Paul Newman gazes into the seven-veiled orbs of temptress Virginia Mayo.

sacred chalice. Meanwhile, in another part of the movie, the evil Simon the Magician (Palance) has been recruited by a rebel group who want to pass him off as the new Messiah. They hope he'll inspire new disciples to their cause and build a strong enough following to overthrow Rome. It doesn't seem to have occurred to anyone to look for a simpler plan.

But why complain? Simon is by far the movie's most interesting character, especially when accompanied by beautiful helper Helena (Virginia Mayo). Helena used to be a slave girl who befriended Basil as a boy. Now she's so coiffed and painted that she looks like Rita Hayworth in *Salome*. Basil still loves her anyway. And she still wants him.

Complications arise when Pier Angeli shows up as a Christian girl named Deborra, who also has a thing for Basil. But just when it looks like some sparks might fly, the movie slows down for one of its marathon talkfests, during which the characters stand around spouting generalities about religion and revolution while dust collects on the chalice. As if aware that they're on the

The Silver Chalice didn't win the Oscar for Best Costume Design. Jack Palance shows you why.

verge of converting us to Satan worship, the filmmakers periodically veer off in various odd directions, searching for some action to shake things up. Thus we get a big party scene in which Helena prances among drunken Roman soldiers purring such endearments as, "my curly-headed ram" and "my vestal virgin in armor." We also get some obligatory chase scenes and skirmishes, as Romans try to round up Christians and rebels try to grab the chalice.

The whole road show finally ends up in Nero's Rome, where Basil has come to find the apostle Peter. For added tension Simon is also in town seeking an audience with the emperor. While Basil is achieving a state of grace in Peter's humble home, Simon makes a terminal fool of himself, trying to prove to Nero that he is, indeed, the Messiah. Contriving an elaborate hoax—all hooks and wires and invisible rods—the magician plans to simulate flight from a tower high above the Colosseum. At the last minute, however, his delusions of divinity get the best of him. "I shall fly by the power of my own will," he proclaims, just before splattering on the Colosseum floor.

"He didn't fly," yawns the easily distracted Nero. But not wishing to send the restless throngs home disappointed, the emperor decrees that Helena, too, should be tossed from the top of the tower. Granted, this is a pretty titillating turn of events, but it doesn't happen until almost the end of the movie.

The silver chalice ends up being stolen by rioting Romans, but all is not lost. The wise and holy Peter sonorously foresees that the cup will someday be returned to its rightful place. Thus reassured, Basil and Deborra float away on a barge, and the movie floats away with them.

After this dubious debut, Newman must have wondered if he'd ever work in Hollywood again. Or New York. Or Rome. And yet, he's really not bad here, just extremely *earnest*. Certainly no one else in the film comes off much better. With the exception of Palance and Mayo, who seem to have wandered in from another soundstage, most of this ensemble is simply overwhelmed by tons of didactic dialogue and theatrically styled sets. Under all that weight, the performances aren't so much flat as *flattened*. Under these circumstances, what could any one actor have done? *The Silver Chalice* was beyond redemption.

13

LAND OF THE PHARAOHS

1955 ⁴ Warner Brothers

Produced and directed by Howard Hawks. Screenplay by William Faulkner, Harry Kurnitz, and Harold Jack Bloom.

CAST: Jack Hawkins (*Pharaoh*); Joan Collins (*Princess Nellifer*); Dewey Martin (*Senta*); Alexis Minotis (*Hamar*); James Robertson Justice (*Vashtar*); Luisa Boni (*Kyra*); Sydney Chaplin (*Treneh*); Kerima (*Queen Nailla*).

HOWARD HAWKS DIRECTED this movie, and William Faulkner helped write the screenplay. But if not for the campy, vampy performance of a starlet named Joan Collins, *Land of the Pharaohs* would be the most boring, big-budget blockbuster ever made about ancient Egypt.

What's so boring about this costume pageant? For one thing, the pageantry. There's the opening return of the Pharaoh's army from war, which takes as long as Macy's Thanksgiving Day parade, but isn't as colorful. There's the forced march of thousands of slaves who come from all over Egypt to build the Pharaoh's new pyramid. And that's only half the slog. Nearly as dull is the step-by-step, stone-by-stone demonstration of how a pyramid gets put together. Admittedly, this involves some pretty impressive engineering, and some of it even figures in the film's ironic finale. But a little of this stuff could last a lifetime (and seems to). You could've just given us the basics, fellas. We'd have trusted you on the rest.

But no, they have to show us *everything*. And when they're not showing they're telling us about it. The Pharaoh (Jack Hawkins) is especially in love with the sound of his own voice. He talks about building a monument to himself. He reflects that conquests and riches mean little without a male heir to pass them on to. He negotiates with his slave engineers, who will be granted their freedom once they've finished his pyramid. When there is noth-

ing else to talk about, he complains about the sand. "Why can't we do away with the desert?" he asks his advisors. All this talk is the usual costume epic dialogue: a "What say you?" here, a jarringly modern "Whaddya know?" there. Having fought all their battles before the movie began, the Pharaoh and his people have become a long-winded crowd. The only excitement we get is incidental. Like when a bunch of branded cowards are thrown to the crocodiles, or when a pyramid stone falls and crushes some slave labor, or when a group of priests who've had their tongues cut out hum together as one, in response to the Pharaoh's inquiries.

Finally, sultry Joan makes her entrance as Princess Nellifer, the new ambassador from Cyprus. Right way, the Sahara starts heating up. The princess is so insolent in her very first scene that the Pharaoh has her taken out and whipped, which sets the tone for the rest of their relationship. At their second meeting he commands, "In the presence of the Pharaoh you will kneel." In reply, she bites him. Something bout her spirit compels him to spare her life. While he's at it he makes her his second-string wife. That is the Pharaoh's fatal mistake.

Once she feasts her eyes on the Pharaoh's vast treasure (which he intends to take to his tomb for use in future lives), the princess starts plotting to make herself very rich. She seduces a handsome young palace guard and forces him to become her accomplice. She tricks the Pharaoh into taking a long trip. She sucks up to the Pharaoh's first wife to set her up for foul play. Then she teaches the Pharaoh's son to play the flute. Little does he know that the song he's playing is the one snake charmers use to lure cobras out of their baskets. The next thing you know, the kid's tootling way, and his mom is dead meat. Now queen of Egypt, Nellifer sends her personal slave to kill off the Pharaoh. When the assassination backfires, she blithely blames the whole plot on her palace guard paramour, setting up a sword fight that leaves both the Pharaoh and the palace guard dead—and scheming bitch Queen Nellifer with the keys to the kingdom. The finale finds this dragon lady deep inside the Pharaoh's Great Pyramid preparing to dig her fingernails into all that delicious treasure. And if you can't guess what happens next, you deserve to sit through this everlasting epic just for the privilege of finding out.

If the Joan Collins portion of *Land of the Pharaohs* sounds like fun, it is—providing you can endure the ongoing lessons in Pyramid Building 101. The problem is that by the time she shows up, the numbness has already set into your extremities, and has begun to creep toward your cerebral cortex. Collins can't do much to alleviate the condition. She can only make it bearable. Barely.

The question, however, remains: Where do Hawks and Faulkner fit in? The answer is, they don't. You'd be hard pressed to find a trace of either man's

creative input here. Adapting to the conventions of the costume epic, both were all too successful in sublimating their own voices. The presence of two such legends as mere hired hands is yet another reminder that in Hollywood commerce has always come before art. But at least Hawks and Faulkner were paid in full for their dusty desert sojourn. The studio, on the other hand, spent six million bucks on this glorified construction project and only made back two. Leave it to Hollywood to hold up the Great Pyramid as a symbol of human folly and greed—only to drop the damn thing squarely on its foot.

14

SINCERELY YOURS

1955 ⁂ Warner Brothers

Produced by Henry Blake. Directed by Gordon Douglas. Screenplay by Irving Wallace, based on the play *The Man Who Played God* by Jules Eckert Goodman.

CAST: Liberace (*Anthony Warrin*); Joanne Dru (*Marion Moore*); Dorothy Malone (*Linda Curtis*); Alex Nicol (*Howard Ferguson*); William Demarest (*Sam Dunne*); Lori Nelson (*Sarah Cosgrove*); Lurene Tuttle (*Mrs. McGinley*).

THOSE WHO KNOW LIBERACE only as a Las Vegas oddity ought to know that he was also a movie star. Once. Back in the fifties, when he was selling out stadium concerts and reaching millions with his weekly TV show, some studio decision-makers got the brilliant idea to bottle all that magic and put it on the big screen. Liberace was getting thousands of fan letters a week! How could he not sell tickets?

Well, he didn't. *Sincerely Yours* was so sincerely bad that even Liberace's loyalest fans—mostly middle-aged, middlebrow matrons—couldn't bring themselves to support it. Even they had more taste than that; even they had enough sense to know that just because someone is a star in one field doesn't mean he'll shine in another.

But oh how he does twinkle! Playing—what else—a concert pianist, Liberace seems beside himself with joy just to be *in* a movie. He's so happy, in fact, that he can't stop smiling, even in serious scenes. And there you have it. *Sincerely Yours* is insipidly sentimental, hopelessly hokey, stiflingly hothouse-flowery. But what takes it from bad to worst is the star. The man. The movie's whole reason for being.

Liberace plays Anthony Warrin, a fellow so much like himself that, well, it's scary. He's a concert pianist all right, but not just any old concert pianist. He's the kind who will dazzle you with Chopin, then play "Chopsticks" for

Ladies' man Liberace serenades Dorothy Malone (*seated*) and Joan Dru (*on piano*).

the little girl in the balcony. A concert pianist who plays requests! No wonder highbrow critics don't take him seriously.

But Anthony craves critical validation. He wants to be taken seriously. He's Richard Clayderman who wants to be Van Cliburn, and he won't be happy until he plays Carnegie Hall. Eventually this movie will give him that chance. But first it gives him a sterner challenge. It takes him way from his piano bench and makes him play actual scenes. And Liberace can't play actual scenes. When he does there's nothing *actual* about them. Whether flirting with a pretty girl, joking with a friend, or talking serious business, he plays every scene the same—like Liberace. He wrinkles up his nose, smiles that simpering smile, speaks in that soft little bleat—and everything sounds alike. When the scene calls for sweetness and light, that's one thing. But when it calls for sarcasm . . . well! Listen to what he says when he first meets Dorothy Malone, who's been plinking away on his precious piano: "My dear young lady, what are you doing to my piano? Teasing it? Flirting with it? Where did you practice your scales? Reaching for a martini?" Just imagine that coming from the mouth of Liberace.

No wonder he spends half the movie behind his piano. But even here he can't escape the drama—for it is during his long-awaited Carnegie Hall concert that Anthony Warrin starts going deaf! It's a horrible moment. Liberace widens his eyes in an attempt to express profound fear while the sound track fades in and out, making us wonder if the rest of the film will be silent. Even more horrible, however, is the realization that this movie has been going on forever and it's just getting started!

Fortunately, Anthony's deafness is an on-and-off affair. Sometimes he can her, sometimes he can't. His only chance is a delicate operation that, if it fails, could leave him totally, permanently deaf. What to do?

While deciding, Anthony learns to lip read. He gets so good at it he starts using his binoculars to spy on people in Central Park from his terrace. It becomes such a pastime that he hardly goes out anymore. Once in a while, for a change of pace, he reads books about Beethoven. (Old Ludwig was deaf too, remember?)

The people close to Anthony start to worry about him. His manager (William Demarest) worries. His fiancée (Dorothy Malone) worries. His loyal secretary (Joanne Dru), who secretly loves him, worries. (How *does* Liberace get these girls? The movie never tells.) But of them all, only his secretary will be straight with him. And when he becomes suicidal, she's right by his side. "I won't let you quit," she says.

And by God he doesn't. Using his newfound lip-reading talent, he seeks out the unhappiest people in Central Park, then swoops down to help them. First, it's a little crippled boy whose family can't afford an operation. Then it's a lonely old lady whose rich married daughter is ashamed of her. There are a million sad stories down there in the city, and Anthony wants to give them all a sappy ending. So he gives the little boy the money he needs for his operation, and he treats the old lady to a shopping spree that will make her presentable to her snotty in-laws. Helping people in need is so deeply satisfying that Anthony stops feeling sorry for himself. And when his gorgeous shallow fiancée falls in love with another man, well that's okay too. Anthony Warrin is now big-hearted enough to wish her a Merry Christmas and send her off with a big, brave Liberace smile. All this makes him realize that he can take whatever happens, so he courageously submits to the operation that could result in all or nothing. Guess how it turns out.

The movie closes with Liberace back onstage, leading the orchestra in rousing renditions of "Beer Barrel Polka" and the "Notre Dame Fight Song." The message, of course, is that all those Carnegie Hall aspirations were just a lot of pride and vanity. Playing for the people is what's closest to his heart,

Liberace gets tough, while William Demarest tries to keep a straight face. *Somebody* had to.

and now that he can hear gain he's going to keep taking requests. All well and good. But at the very end, when he gets up and does a little tap dance to the tune of "Tea for Two," we realize it really might have been better if he had gone stone deaf and stayed that way—if not for him, then at least for us. Ah, but let's not get carried away. This movie's dismal failure ensured that we wouldn't have Liberace to laugh off the screen anymore. After this, he'd never hear from Hollywood again.

SIGNS OF THE TIMES
Dean Martin and Jerry Lewis

Once upon a time, when they were still speaking to each other, Dean Martin and Jerry Lewis were an inseparable team, sort of an Abbott and Costello, only with music. Dean was the straight man, Jerry the comic contortionist. Dean got the girls, Jerry got the laughs. Dean sang the songs, Jerry squawked them. Somehow this formula lasted eight years and sixteen movies, even though Jerry's singing voice never improved. Come to think of it, neither did Dean's. Looking at their movies, you've got to wonder how this partnership endured, or, for that matter, how these guys were able to go straight from this into successful solo careers. Still, you've got to give them their place in showbiz history. For without Dean and Jerry to pave the way, there never could have been an Allen and Rossi. Let us now toast strange bedfellows.

At War With the Army (1950) "The navy gets the gravy," sings messy mess cook Jerry, "but the army gets the beans." The nuts too, it would seem. During the movie's high point of hilarity, buck private Lewis dresses up in drag and serenades unsuspecting drill instructor Mike Kellin. The rest of the time, however, these barracks-bound hijinks are a different sort of drag. When Jerry gets to sing more songs than his partner, you know the formula still needs work.

The Caddy (1953) Dean is a dapper golf pro; Jerry is his dopey caddy. Together they crash the snooty world of pro tournaments and posh country clubs. When not out on the course, Dean romances Donna Reed. When not carrying Dean's clubs, Jerry just carries on—frequently in his underwear. At his most "inspired" he sings, "I'm known as the gay continental, and I got this way quite accidental," while doing a pratfall into the pool. Not to be outdone, Dean sings the immortal "That's Amore," while standing in the kitchen of his mama's Italian restaurant. Kitsch doesn't get much kitschier than this.

Scared Stiff (1955) On the run from the mob *and* the law, the boys hop a slow boat to Cuba, accompanied by Lizabeth Scott, who's just inherited a haunted castle. During the voyage, Carmen Miranda also shows up as shipboard entertainment. You haven't seen overkill until you've seen Jerry and Carmen bumping and grinding in the same frame. But that's nothing compared to Jerry *as* Carmen—complete with fruit bowl turban. Eventually the whole overripe mess spills over at the haunted castle, where Dean and Jerry do a bad impression of Bob Hope in *The Ghost Breakers*. They never did know how to quit while they were ahead.

Artists and Models (1955) Dean's a struggling artist; Jerry's a struggling writer. What fun they have scrimping and saving (and sharing a bathtub) in their tiny New York apart-

Jerry Lewis, at the "height"
of his popularity, in a scene
from *Scared Stiff.*

ment. Just when the relationship is starting to get *too* cozy, we get several ambitious production numbers, including a few so strange they'll make you blink twice: Like when Dean does a sidewalk song-and-dance number surrounded by kids who seem to be having epileptic fits, and when Shirley MacLaine serenades Jerry while climbing up and down a staircase like a horny orangutan. Jerry couldn't have done it any better himself.

Hollywood or Bust (1956) Teaming up one last time, Dean and Jerry drive a red convertible on a cross-country trip to Hollywood. Dean's on the run from gangsters again, while Jerry just wants to meet Anita Ekberg. Along the way, they wave to bevies of beauties, who pose like calendar girls on the side of the road. Then along comes real girl Patricia Crowley, who gives Dean someone to sing to. For his part, Jerry tries to milk an angry bull and gets chased up a tree. Finally, he does meet Anita Ekberg—and promptly knocks her into a swimming pool. Hey, when a joke works, it works.

15

THE CONQUEROR

1956 ⋅ RKO

Produced and directed by Dick Powell. Screenplay by Oscar Millard.

CAST: John Wayne (*Temujin*); Susan Hayward (*Bortai*); Pedro Armendariz (*Jamuga*); Agnes Moorehead (*Hunlun*); Thomas Gomez (*Wang Khan*); John Hoyt (*Shaman*); William Conrad (*Kasar*); Lee Van Cleef (*Chepei*).

OBVIOUSLY FEELING HIS OATS as America's number one box-office draw, John Wayne decided it would be a worthy challenge to play Mongol warrior Genghis Khan. As career moves go, it wasn't a very smart one. But the dumbest decision on this movie was made by Howard Hughes. Proving that he hadn't lost his "minus touch," the RKO honcho gladly hired Wayne for the one role in a long career that he was absolutely, positively wrong for. Then Hughes poured six million dollars into producing the Megaton Bomb that would dash his delusions of mogulhood once and for all.

Hughes and Wayne must have been the only two people in Hollywood who didn't think the Duke would look idiotic in a Fu Manchu mustache and forcibly slanted eyes. But even worse than how Wayne looked was how he *sounded*, wrapping his tongue round *The Conqueror's* pseudo-classical dialogue. This is one of those movies where warriors greet their mothers with "I greet you, my mother" and wealthy chieftains heartily proclaim, "Come, let there be music and a feast." Even the relatively eloquent supporting players had their mouths full with this fruity verbiage. For the laconic Wayne, it may as well have been a foreign language, and as the star, he was burdened with the lion's share of overripe oration. The results are sometimes side-splitting, and sometimes surreal, as is the case when he draws a deep breath and drawls: "Send swiftly and in secret to your clans to mobilize and join with me in

The movie itself is every bit as silly as the poster makes it look.

wiping out the Tartars and Merkits. Thus my father will be avenged, and much stock and grazing land added to our own. I depart with the first light."

To make things even more surreal, director Dick Powell cast creamy-com-

John Wayne stars as
Genghis Kahn. So why does
everyone call him Temujin?
No matter. The Duke by any
other name is still the
Duke. Even when he's
wearing a Fu Manchu.

plexioned redhead Susan Hayward as the Tartar princess who stirs the conqueror's loins. Placing this lily-white leading lady in the midst of the yellow hordes swept away any lingering hope of the movie being taken seriously. As if her mere presence wasn't distraction enough, Hayward's prominent role as romantic interest seriously played against Wayne's strength as a two-fisted man of action.

After kicking off the film by abducting the Tartar princess, Mongol Wayne wastes an awful lot of time wearing down her resistance, finally winning her over with what would now politely be called date rape. When his trusted lieutenant (Pedro Almendariz) warns him about her "perfidy," the Duke draws another deep breath and explains, "She is a woman—much woman. Should her perfidy be less than that of other women?"

Hard to argue with that. Yet when the retaliating Tartar tribes threaten the Mongol's reign of terror, even feisty Hayward can't keep her man from getting back in the saddle. Yes, war lovers, at long last the movie stirs up some big battle scenes, mostly consisting of many men on horses charging down slopes to meet many other men on horses, whereupon they try to knock each other off. But when they're all done and the dust has settled this story still comes down to the Duke, his perfidious woman, and too many pages of dialogue. As he poses on the edge of a cliff delivering one last lungful to the heavens, we find ourselves thinking wistfully of his movies with John Ford and Howard Hawks, when the Duke could deflate a rival's threat with a simple, "That'll be the day" or "Bring your lunch." Of course, "Bring your lunch" would have sounded kind of funny coming from a man with a Fu Manchu. Then again, would it really have been any funnier than his philosophical discourse on the perfidy of women?

The Conqueror is one John Wayne film in which his words speak louder than his actions, and that, even more than the Fu Manchu, explains why Hughes lost a bundle on it. Perhaps the best thing that can be said about this complete failure is that it drove Hughes out of Mogulhood forever. After a couple of decades in the movie business, he finally realized he had no business making movies.

16

The Ten Commandments

1956 ⟨ Paramount

Produced and directed by Cecil B. De Mille. Screenplay by Aeneas MacKenzie, Jesse L. Lasky Jr., Jack Garris, and Frederic M. Frank, based on various works.

CAST: Charlton Heston (*Moses*); Yul Brynner (*Rameses*); Anne Baxter (*Nefretiri*); Edward G. Robinson (*Dathan*); Yvonne DeCarlo (*Sephora*); Debra Paget (*Lilia*); John Derek (*Joshua*); Sir Cedric Hardwicke (*Sethi*); Nina Foch (*Bithia*); Judith Anderson (*Memnet*); Vincent Price (*Baka*).

THE FIFTIES WERE *the* decade of the religious epic: from *Salome* to *Solomon and Sheba*, from *The Robe* to *The Silver Chalice*. But *The Ten Commandments* was something else entirely. It was a C. B. De Mille religious epic. And with this one, the granddaddy of Biblical schlockmeisters topped even himself. If *The Sign of the Cross* set the standard, *The Ten Commandments* broke the mold. After this, he would never do another. There wouldn't have been any point.

What was impressive about De Mille's ancient chronicles was how they changed with the times. With *The Sign of the Cross* and *The Crusades*, he was getting sex and sin extravaganzas past the censors because they were, well, biblical. By the time of *Samson and Delilah* (1949), he was doing the opposite—giving the public the uplifting religious parables they *thought* they wanted, while filling this pageantry full of the juiciest pulp this side of King Vidor.

But oh what a pompous package *The Ten Commandments* comes in. Before the story even starts, C. B. strolls out from behind a curtain to explain what we're going to see: "As many of you know, the Holy Bible omits some thirty years of Moses' life, from the time he was a three-month-old baby . . . until he learned he was a Hebrew and killed the Egyptians. To fill in those missing years, we turn to ancient historians. . . ." You know the ones he means—Philo, Josepha, the Holy Scriptures. Why trust Paramount scriptwriters to get it right

Charlton Heston as Moses spreads the Word with a vengeance.

when you can go to the source? But give De Mille credit; he does it with such humility. "Our intention is not to create a story," he blathers, "but to be worthy of the divinely inspired story created three thousand years ago." Then he proceeds to go out and show us just how unworthy he is.

When we first see Moses he's a baby in a basket, being pulled out of the bulrushes by the Pharaoh's daughter. She knows he might be the Hebrew child prophesized to deliver his people from her country, but she adopts him anyway. When next we see Moses, he's a handsome young prince (Charlton Heston), returning victorious from war. For his reward, he is stuck with the responsibility of building the Pharaoh's new city. While Moses is off proving himself a fair-minded slave-driver, his half-brother Rameses (Yul Brynner) is conspiring to betray him. "You adder," says sexpot Nefretiri (Anne Baxter), who's been promised to whichever brother inherits the Pharaohship. Rameses isn't *her* first choice, but just in case he's the one, she cuddles up to him, adder or not.

Smart girl. For before the next hour of the movie elapses, Moses will learn of his true heritage, and in a noble show of solidarity, join his people slaving in the mud pits. Truly, this is cause for rejoicing, because up to this point, *The Ten Commandments* has been one laborious blabfest. Oh sure, it unfolds on palatial sets. Oh sure, there are the usual De Millean mobs, hauling pyramid blocks

across sprawling landscapes in glorious Technicolor. But for what seems like an epoch this epic just plods along, as if De Mille had grown weary after decades of marshaling casts of thousands and could barely lumber through the motions anymore. But once he topples Moses from his princely life of privilege, C.B. starts getting the old spring back in his step. Suddenly the bible is sexy again!

All it really takes is one good bedroom scene in which Nefretiri, having pulled Moses out of the mud pit, is trying to seduce some sense into the big lug. "You stubborn, splendid, adorable fool," she gurgles, dousing him with perfume. "They may be your people, but do you have to wallow with them . . . *smell* like them?"

Now De Mille is starting to cook. Full of classic Heston righteousness, Moses resists Nefretiri, then rushes off to rescue Hebrew slave John Derek, by strangling his torturer, the sneeringly evil Vincent Price. By now it has dawned on the Pharaoh and Rameses that Moses isn't one of them anymore. So they cast him into the desert, where the night wind wails his name and De Mille lays on a litany of suffering: "He cannot cool the burning kiss of thirst upon his lips nor shade the scorching fires of the sun. . . . Learning that it can be more terrible to live than to die, he is driven onward through the burning crucible of desert, where holy men and prophets are cleansed and purged for God's great purpose."

Edward G. Robinson makes like Little Caesar, as the Pharaoh's right-hand man.

However, since the movie is only a couple of hours old, Moses isn't ready just yet. First, he must dally idyllically for a few years with his Bedouin bride (Yvonne DeCarlo). Then, John Derek must show up to remind him that his people are still back in Egypt, suffering worse than ever under the new Pharaoh, Rameses. Then Moses must go up the mountain, get the word from the Burning Bush, and come back down miraculously coiffed, with a magnificent new beard. *Now* he's ready. In the hours to come he will perform many miracles. He will twice more resist Nefretiri's temptations. ("Why must I be in love with the Prince of Fools?" she sighs.) He will say, "Let my people go" so many times that he drives Rameses batty. He will inspire his people to look toward the future and speak accordingly. ("We're going to the land of milk and honey," says one flip Hebrew. "Anybody know the way?")

But Moses's really big miracles are the work of a higher power. No, not God—C. B. De Mille! Divinely inspired, De Mille piles up the set pieces that make this the most awesome bad movie anyone ever directed. Staffs turn into snakes. Hailstones turn to fire. Rivers turn to blood. Twelve thousand extras stage an orderly Hebrew exodus. The Red Sea parts, then crashes back together again. And that's not even the end. Having drowned the Pharaoh's whole army with that Red Sea stunt, Moses then climbs up yet another mountain, where God appears to him in a swirl of flame to burn the commandments in stone. Meanwhile, down below, his restless followers, goaded on by the treacherous Dathan (played Little Caesar–style by Edward G. Robinson), indulge in a hilariously hedonistic orgy. Wanton women chug wine, pound tambourines, ride men like horses, and polish a golden icon with their hair and breasts. "And there was idolatry and lasciviousness," declares De Mille, disgusted. Truly, he's reached full fire-and-brimstone glory. In the best De Mille tradition, he sends Moses down to put a stop to "the noise of song and revelry," with bolts of lightning and an avalanche of boulders.

When last seen, Moses is standing on yet another mountaintop gazing toward heavenly shafts of light, having delivered his people and laid down the law. So it was written, so it was done. De Mille's last epic was history. More religious epics were still to come, including King Vidor's very De Millean *Solomon and Sheba*, but for all intents and purposes an era was over. Just as there was only one God, there was only one C.B. Chances are we'll never see his like again.

17

A SUMMER PLACE

1959 ⌃ Warner Bros.

Produced, written, and directed by Delmer Daves, from the novel by Sloan Wilson.

CAST: Richard Egan (*Ken Jorgenson*); Dorothy McGuire (*Sylvia Hunter*); Sandra Dee (*Molly Jorgenson*); Troy Donahue (*Johnny Hunter*); Arthur Kennedy (*Bart Hunter*); Constance Ford (*Helen Jorgenson*).

THE LATE FIFTIES were a precious time to be a teenager in love. The first baby boomers hadn't yet reached puberty and the sexual revolution wasn't yet on the horizon, but youth was already on its way to taking over the country: Hollywood had discovered that kids were big box office. By 1961 that would mean that Warren Beatty and Natalie Wood could go literally mad with desire in *Splendor in the Grass*, but in 1959, moviegoers weren't quit ready for that. So instead they got *A Summer Place*, a super make-out movie with a swoony hit theme song. Today the song is probably better remembered than the movie. Ah, but we should never forget the movie. As a kitsch artifact of its time it's every bit as lush as its music, and besides, it was the breakthrough for two young stars who embodied the taste and temperament of young, mainstream America, circa 1959.

Of course, we're talking about Troy Donahue and Sandra Dee, who happened to be *very* big stars in their day. Somehow, though, they're rarely remembered that way. Maybe that's because their brand of squeaky-clean-cut teenager, squeezed in between *Rebel Without a Cause* and *Beach Party*, had a relatively short reign as a role model for American youth. Or maybe it's because they never resurfaced in any other viable screen persona. Once their day was over, it was *over*. One look at them here and you'll understand why.

Troy is callow Johnny. Sandra is cutie-pie Molly. They're young and in love and they just want to be left alone. Fat chance, with the parents they've got.

The poignance! The passion! The heavy petting!

Johnny's crusty dad (Arthur Kennedy) used to be the squire of a ritzy Maine coast resort. Now he runs the weather-beaten Pine Island Inn with a martini in his hand and a long-suffering wife (Dorothy McGuire), who pines for better days. Speaking of which: Molly's dad (Richard Egan) is a former Pine Island lifeguard who used to be in love with Johnny's mom. Now he's returning to Pine Island a rich man, having made his millions as a research chemist (huh?). By his side is his self-made snob of a wife (Constance Ford), who is so stone-cold bitchy so early that we just know we'll be hissing her by the end. She's mean to Sandra Dee and she's supposed to be her *mother*! If that's not hissable, what is?

The atrocities start right away, when Mom tries to force her nubile daughter to flatten her figure with an industrial-strength bra and girdle. "She says I bounce when I walk. Do I?" Molly moans to her daddy. "Heh-heh-heh," Daddy chuckles, "only in a pleasant way." Since Molly has earlier confessed to Daddy that she used to let the boy next door spy on her when she undressed ("It gave me hot and cold flashes," she says. "Is that awful?"), we begin to wonder just how "pleasant" Daddy finds his daughter. When he lights into his wife for repressing poor little Molly, we don't quite know whose side we're on. "You insist on de-sexing her," Daddy snarls, "as though sex were synonymous with dirt."

Only for you messed up grown-ups. For these innocent kids it's as pure as the driven snow—or at least it is early on, as Johnny and Molly meet and immediately fall prey to major puppy love. The prelude to their first kiss is so prolonged we're not sure they even know *how* to do anything wrong. Johnny, especially, is so busy pointing out the sights during a stroll on the grounds that he seems oblivious to the way Molly bounces when she walks. Just in time, though, Molly gets a thorn in her thigh—and the sight of all that baby-fat flesh leads to their long-awaited first kiss. But wouldn't you know it? Mama's watching from her window. Poor Molly gets an awful earful when she gets to her room.

"She's anti-sex," Molly moans to her daddy, crawling into his bed and nuzzling her head in his bathrobe. "Whenever I have a naughty dream, do I have to feel guilty?"

"Of course not," Daddy says, clenching has jaw in defiance of whatever guilty feelings *he* might be having at the moment.

And he's got plenty to feel guilty about. Soon enough, he and Johnny's mom have rekindled their romance, sneaking off to the boathouse for mid-night meetings that add an adult subplot to this puppy-love story. But while they're flagellating themselves for their extramarital activities, the kids are fac-ing a sex crisis of their own: To do it or not to do it?

They don't, but try telling that to Molly's mom, the hissable harridan. After the kids get caught in a storm and spend the night on another island, she's so sure they've *done it* that she drags a doctor all the way out to the inn to verify her daughter's virginity. Things are coming to a head, all right. And when they erupt, the pent-up emotions blow away both marriages and send the kids kicking and screaming to private schools.

Sandra Dee, at least, kicks and screams. Troy Donahue, on the other hand, gives new meaning to the term *minimalist*. He never kicks or screams or scowls or smiles. He never does anything! Once or twice in this movie, he raises his monotone voice, and that's how you know Johnny is not loboto-mized. But what is going on in there? Is Johnny sad? Mad? Glad? Who knows?

When it's time for action, however, Johnny comes marching through. Pur-suing his beloved to the ends of the earth—or at least to Boston during Christmas vacation—Johnny meets Molly on a street corner near a church, where he asks the immortal question, "Do you care if I kiss you right here, in front of God and everybody?" Even after that they *still* don't do "it," but when Molly gets home she catches hell anyway, receiving a whack from her mother that sends her flying into the plastic Christmas tree. "Merry Christ-mas, Mama," poor Molly sobs, all decked out in colored lights.

Meanwhile, back in the adult soap opera, Johnny's mom and Molly's dad get married, with no family in attendance. It's lonely being adulterers in 1959. It's also boring, compared to the *sturm und drang* of the kids' star-crossed romance. Thankfully, in a gesture of reconciliation, the newlyweds in-vite Johnny and Molly to visit their new summer place—a little shack de-signed by Frank Lloyd Wright. Under such idyllic conditions, our two young lovers are soon exchanging heartfelt vows. "I love you so much I ache inside," Johnny proclaims. And though his expression suggests it's probably only gas, hers indicates that she loves him too. Thus, the old dilemma crops up again: To do it or not to do it? This time they do it.

Of course, Molly gets pregnant. But that is as it should be. In movies like this, virgins *must* be sacrificed, not only to dramatize the preciousness of virtue, but to underscore the importance of compassion and forgiveness. All knocked up with nowhere to turn, Molly becomes the one who pulls this splintered family back together. There are, however, casualties. By the end of this sudsy saga, the hissable harridan is alone and embittered, and Johnny's dad, squire of Pine Island, is so permanently polluted that the coast guard has to come out and cart him away. As for Johnny and Molly? Why, they get married, what else? As the ubiquitous theme from *A Summer Place* wells up for the umpteenth time, they're seen disembarking on Pine Island, where they plan to fix up the old inn and live happily ever after—or at least until they hire a handsome lifeguard.

A Summer Place was the first of several Warner Bros. weepies featuring Mr. Troy Donahue. Though he eventually grew into characters of college age and beyond, they never seemed to get much more mature, or emotional, than his classic Johnny. Through such twaddle as *Parrish*, *Rome Adventure*, and *Susan Slade*, Donahue never did learn to inflect a line of dialogue, or even smile like he meant it. Makes you wonder why Delmer Daves, who directed all these movies, kept saddling himself with the same problem. But this was 1959, big blond hunks in sloshy romances were still the order of the day. The studios still decided which blond hunks made which sloshy romances and which directors directed them. Ah, the studio system. The next time you hear someone say those were the good old days, remind them of Troy Donahue, Delmer Daves—and their *Summer Place*.

SIGNS OF THE TIMES
Beach-Blanket Bimbos

Blame it on the Beach Boys. Blame it on the bikini. Or just blame it on the baby boom, which gave birth to the Pepsi generation, which was on its way to the sexual revolution. Certainly all of this helped inspire the wave of sun-and-surf movies that washed over Hollywood during the early sixties. The genre began with *Gidget* (1959), starring Sandra Dee as the quintessential California surfer girl. Then came *Where the Boys Are* (1960), the original spring break movie, and suddenly the pipeline was open. Frankie Avalon and Annette Funicello were only riding the crest of the wave—it's who came in their wake that made this genre such a wipeout. From Edd "Kookie" Byrnes in *Beach Ball* to Tommy Kirk in *It's a Bikini World*, you've never seen so many careers crashing on the rocks.

The *Beach Party* movies. Nobody does it like Frankie and Annette—even though they never do it. They'll go steady for seven whole movies and always get stuck on the same point: Frankie wants to get into Annette's bathing suit; Annette wants to hear wedding bells first. From *Beach Party* (1963) to *How to Stuff a Wild Bikini* (1965) this song-and-dance never changes. Neither does the singing and dancing. In fact, Frankie, Annette, and friends are nothing if not consistent: They warble a few duets, hatch some romantic subplots, and invariably endure the intrusions of Eric Von Zipper (Harvey Lembeck) and his idiot biker gang. Through it all, Annette never actually wears a bikini and Frankie never actually surfs—he just fakes it in front of rear-projected waves as big as tsunamis. Yet despite the formula patness, there *are* ways of telling these movies apart. Take *Bikini Beach* (1964), which features a surfing chimp named Clyde and a Beatle-wigged rock star called the "Potato Bug" (Frankie in a stunning dual role). Or better yet, take *Beach Blanket Bingo* (1965), with an all-star supporting cast that includes Don Rickles, Paul Lynde, Buster Keaton, Linda Evans, and Marta (*Lost in Space*) Kristen as a mermaid. After all, even *Beach Party* movies have to have a high-water mark.

Ride the Wild Surf (1964) The sudsiest of all surf movies takes place in Hawaii, where all the bronze, blond beach boys treat surfing like . . . real life! Tab Hunter gives up being a beach bum to marry a pineapple heiress. Fabian conquers his fears by winning the big-surf competition. Shelley Fabares changes her hairdo as often as she changes her swimsuit. And Peter Brown jumps off a waterfall, just to impress Barbara Eden! Despite the presence of Fabian and Fabares, nobody in this cast sings. Of course, nobody actually surfs, either, but that location footage of real north shore Kahunas sure does look impressive! Cowabunga!

Frankie and Annette on the beach (or its likeness) in a publicity pose from their *Beach Party* years.

A Swingin' Summer (1965) Take the kids off the beach, dump them at a lakeside resort, and you still have fun, fun, fun—even if star William Wellman, Jr., *does* get a little bit stressed by his dance pavilion job. Picking up the slack, costar James Stacy plays a macho game of water-ski "chicken" *and* romances Raquel Welch, in her film debut as a well-rounded egghead who takes off her glasses, let's down her hair, and sings "I'm Ready to Groove." Stacy and Wellman will later reteam in *Winter à Go Go* (1965), which like the same year's *Ski Party* offers further proof, that you can take the party off the beach—but you can't take the beach out of the party.

18

CLEOPATRA

1963 ⁘ Twentieth Century-Fox

Produced by Walter Wanger. Directed by Joseph L. Mankiewicz. Screenplay by Mankiewicz, Ranald MacDougall, and Sidney Buchman, based on various works.

CAST: Elizabeth Taylor (*Cleopatra*); Richard Burton (*Marc Antony*); Rex Harrison (*Julius Caesar*); Pamela Brown (*high priestess*); George Cole (*Flavius*); Hume Cronyn (*Sosieges*); Martin Landau (*Fufio*); Roddy McDowall (*Octavian*).

THIS IS THE ULTIMATE RUNAWAY production. The quintessential big-budget bomb. The one that first proved that if you threw enough good money after bad, you could actually bankrupt a studio. Or come close, anyway. Twentieth Century-Fox came *very* close with *Cleopatra*, spending more money than had ever been spent on a movie before. The picture made some of it back simply because people were so curious about this historically *huge* production. But people weren't curious enough. Not by a long shot.

What made *Cleopatra* so expensive? Blame the usual problems in unusual abundance. Things got off to a disastrous start when Elizabeth Taylor came down with pneumonia. That caused a delay that lasted a full six months—leading to the resignation of director Rouben Mamoulian, to the departures of original costars Peter Finch and Stephen Boyd, to the change of location from London to Rome, and to various rewrites and reshoots once new director Joseph Mankiewicz took over. Then, when everything finally got underway, a robustly recovered Liz fell in love with her new leading man, Richard Burton. Since both were married to others at the time, the affair became an international scandal, leading to still more distractions and delays. The whole production dragged on for months, and when it was finally finished, Fox had a four-plus-hour spectacle that had cost over $40 million. That made it not only the most expensive movie yet made, but also the longest.

But is it bad? You bet it's bad. Like most ancient Egypt epics, *Cleopatra* is boring. And boring equals bad, especially at four-plus hours. In fact, at four-plus hours, this is probably the most boring bad movie ever made.

The boredom begins immediately, as Julius Caesar (Rex Harrison) sails to Egypt to visit his favorite allies. Upon arriving, he finds himself in the middle of a power struggle between Cleopatra and her brother. Forced to chose sides, Caesar chooses Cleo. He knows she's tougher than she looks. To quote one of Caesar's advisers: "In attaining her objectives, Cleopatra has been known to employ torture, poison, and even her own sexual talents, which are said to be considerable." Who could say no to a girl like that?

Eventually we'll get to see this Nile cobra in action. Initially, however, we've got to be content with displays of her leadership qualities—which

Wars, assassinations, love affairs, and more! It's all there in the poster for *Cleopatra*. And it doesn't take four hours to take them all in.

means endless negotiations, strategies, and games of verbal one-upmanship, as Taylor and Harrison sink their teeth into Mankiewicz's mouthfuls of dialogue. *Cleopatra* is one of the more literate ancient epics, but at two hundred forty-six minutes, it still gets old in a hurry. "You talk too much," Caesar tells Cleopatra before the first hour is up. Amen, brother.

Still, she does have her moments. "You have such bony knees," she tells Caesar, tossing him a pillow so he may kneel before her. Later, finally ready to reveal her renowned sexual talents, she still can't seem to shut up. "My breasts are full of love and life," she says, seducing Caesar. "My hips are round and well apart. Such women, they say, have sons." What emperor could resist?

But oh, that Cleo! What she really wants is to merge with Rome. Caesar and Cleopatra, together in one big empire, bearing sons! "You have a way of mixing politics and passion," notes the everastute Caesar. "Where does one begin and the other leave off?"

In this film the two are inseparable, which takes the edge off both. Even after they marry and merge, Caesar and Cleopatra are doomed to endless politicking (none of it passionate)—with the Roman Senate, their various advisers, and, of course, each other. Even when Richard Burton belatedly shows up as loyal but lusty Marc Antony, the added cross-currents don't cause many sparks to fly. In a livelier epic, Cleopatra's conflicting ambitions and emotions might have made for some juicy palace intrigue. Here, they just confuse the issues and drag them on forever. "Queens, queens!" Antony fumes at one point, fed up with Cleo's royal airs. "Strip them naked as any other woman and they're no longer queens."

Rest assured, it never comes to that, but if it had, at least it would have picked up the pace. Instead, it is almost intermission before Caesar is bloodily assassinated. And it's well into hour three before Cleo and Antony kiss. And it's nearly another hour before all hell finally breaks loose in climactic warfare. Between these high-water marks, the movie continues to wade in oceans of conversation. Everybody talks about alliances, betrayals, and conquests, but nobody does much about them. One begins to think back with fondness on Cecil B. De Mille's camp orgies and gory massacres. Come back, C.B., all is forgiven!

That's not to say that this too-tasteful epic doesn't have its De Millean moments. First, there is Cleopatra's arrival in Rome, in a procession that includes

Liz Taylor has Dick Burton just where she wants him in this ostentatiously intimate moment.

an exotic lead dancer in flower petal pasties, African acrobats in feathery white headdresses, beautiful slave girls flapping golden wings, an ensemble of trumpeters on white stallions, and a thousand or so extras pulling a scaled down sphinx, upon which Cleopatra sits, in glittering gold robes and a hat about four feet high. Later there's a Bacchanalian feast, in which Antony is caressed by wenches in fig leaf bikinis while a green-painted satyr chortles on the sidelines. After that, there's an actual burst of trashy emotion, in which Cleo pitches a jealous fit, slashing her bed chamber drapes and stabbing her mattress. Finally, there's a full-scale naval battle, in which entire fleets go up in flames, scores of Romans drown, and Antony abandons ship to swim after Cleo's barge.

But it's all too little, too late. Long before they lose their empire and each other, we've stopped giving a damn about Antony and Cleopatra—if we ever did. After four hours of watching them talk themselves to death, it's hard to

Top-heavy Liz sports yet another dazzling ensemble from her queenly *Cleopatra* wardrobe.

shed a tear when they finally die for real. It seems like overkill, but at least it's an ending.

   Cleopatra marked the first of eleven teamings between scandalous lovebirds Liz and Dick. Throughout the rest of the sixties they would seldom make a movie without one another. Yet maybe because love was blind, or maybe because they had no taste, or maybe because they were just in it for the money, Liz and Dick rarely teamed on a project worth their time—or ours. From *The Sandpiper* to *The Comedians* to *The VIPs* to *Boom!*, their first decade together was one wallow after another. Eventually the public got tired of their act, just as the two got tired of each other. The seventies were mercifully free of the Taylor-Burton Connection.

19

THE OSCAR

1966 ⁺ Embassy

Produced by Clarence Greene. Directed by Russell Rouse. Screenplay by Harlan Ellison, Rouse, and Clarence Greene, from a novel by Richard Sale.

CAST: Stephen Boyd (*Frank Fane*); Elke Sommer (*Kay Bergdahl*); Milton Berle (*Kappy Kapstetter*); Eleanor Parker (*Sophie Cantoro*); Joseph Cotten (*Kenneth Regan*); Jill St. John (*Laurel Scott*); Tony Bennett (*Hymie Kelly*); Edie Adams (*Trina Yale*); Ernest Borgnine (*Barney Yale*).

●JOSEPH E. LEVINE ONCE SAID, "You can fool all the people all the time if the advice is right and the budget is big enough." But as a studio chief, he never actually proved it. Maybe he never had the right advice. Certainly he had big enough budgets. Big budgets helped him fool some of the people with such splashy potboilers as *The Carpetbaggers* and *Harlow*, but when it came to *The Oscar*, no amount of money could help. *The Oscar* was so bad that *nobody* was fooled.

This bomb has it all: bad story, bad directing, bad dream sequences, bad hair. But worse than anything else—even worse than the awful dialogue—it has the absolute in bad film acting. The chief offender is Stephen Boyd, who stars as Frankie Fane, a Hollywood heel scratching and screwing his way to fame. Boyd is so hopeless that he can't even hack it as the no-talent actor Frankie is supposed to be. Tearing through the movie like the Tasmanian Devil, he snarls, sneers, makes sudden menacing gestures, snarls some more, sneers some more, and makes the cords in his neck stick out. It's a thoroughly exhausting performance—especially for the audience. But don't blame Boyd alone. The way the part is written, he'd have had trouble even if he had any talent, because Frankie Fane is too bad to be true. He's a mean, misogynistic cutthroat who steps on everyone on his way to stardom, grinding in his

Stephen Boyd escorts Elke Sommer to one more power party, on his way to *The Oscar.*

heel for good measure. And since this movie is all about his meteoric rise, he gets lots of opportunities to do what he does best.

The movie opens on Oscar night, as our hero sits in the crowd waiting to win for Best Actor. Across the auditorium sits Tony Bennett (yes, Tony Bennett) as Frankie's ex-best friend Hymie Kelly (yes, Hymie Kelly). Giving the debut performance that will end his movie career, Bennett drearily doubles as *The Oscar*'s narrator/conscience. Squinting his eyes and trying to look scornful, he sets the moralistic monotone in his very first voice-over: "Ya finally made it Frankie—Oscar night!" (Bennett's eyes start to glaze.) "Here you sit on top of a glass mountain called success." (*Our* eyes start to glaze.) "Been quite a climb, hasn't it Frankie? Ever think of it? I do, friend Frankie. I do. . . ."

Come with us now back in time as we retrace the progress of Frankie and Hymie. They start out as strip-joint hustlers teamed with Jill St. John, who plays movie history's most wholesome stripper. While shacking up with this meal ticket, Frankie sneaks off to a "swingin' party in the Village," where he meets cosmopolitan Elke Sommer and immediately puts his moves on her. "I'm not the sort of woman who uses sex as a release . . . or as a weapon," she tells him. "Do you always talk like that?" Frankie sneers. "You free thinkers confuse me." See, Frankie's a man of simple pleasures.

Accompanying Sommer to an Off-Broadway rehearsal, he jeers the actors' attempts at stage combat, then jumps onstage to teach them how to *really* knife fight. His animal passion scares everyone—except Hollywood talent scout Eleanor Parker, who thinks he has a future in pictures. Besides, she's so horny that she'll gladly let him try to sleep his way to the top.

And so, Frankie goes to Hollywood. Almost overnight he gets an agent, a multipicture contract and a swingin' pad with a swimming pool. Our boy is now on the fast track to fame and, well, let's let Hymie tell it: "Like a junkie shooting pure quicksilver into his veins, Frankie got turned on by the wildest narcotic known to mortal man—success! The parts got bigger and bigger. . . . Frankie got hungrier and hungrier. . . ." And the script gets dumber and dumber.

The Oscar was written by Hollywood pros, yet it exhibits all the insider savvy of a slush pile screenplay by two housewives from Ohio. The showbiz clichés are strictly public domain, torn from the pages of fan magazines—and from other bad movies about the movies. But that doesn't mean that a larger-than-life louse like Frankie can't drag those clichés down to new depths.

When Frankie's not causing scenes at movie premieres and restaurants, he's callously using up women and throwing them away. "Like Kleenex," comments the ever-eloquent Hymie. Among the discards is Parker. Among the recyclables is Elke Sommer, who shows up from New York to work as a costume sketch-artist. At first she wants nothing more to do with Frankie ("You represent everything I loathe," she says. "You mean everything you *love*," he snarls.) But when he throws his weight around and gets her a job as a senior costume designer, she decides she *can* stand him. In fact, she marries him.

Soon enough, she's sorry. Frankie continues to screw everyone in Hollywood (in more ways than one), until he's finally the most hated man in the business—and box-office poison to boot. Then, just when it looks like he has doomed himself to a career in television, Frankie gets an Oscar nomination. Suddenly he's hot again! But the high doesn't last. After a cheesy nightmare sequence in which everyone he's ever stomped on comes back as a talking head to haunt him, Frankie wakes up in a cold sweat, knowing he must win that Oscar or become an overnight nobody! He'll do anything to win. He even smears the name of the now deceased St. John, in a scheme to smear his own name and win sympathy votes, "Frankie used them all," says Hymie, "whether they were living or dead."

Tony Bennett does the emotional equivalent of lip-synching in this career-ending movie debut.

But every dog has his day and Frankie's comes on Oscar night. All by himself at the ceremony, he is already rising to receive his award before they even announce who won. But wait! "The winner is: Frank . . . Sinatra!" Poor Frankie stands there, naked to the world, as Sinatra strolls to the stage. Surrounded by the cheering crowd, our hero numbly starts to applaud—which inspires everyone else to join him on their feet and give Sinatra a standing ovation. Irony of ironies! And as the applause continues to thunder, Frankie then becomes the only person seated, crumpling into his chair and clapping maniacally, like some mad wind-up toy. Yes, bad movie mavens, it's another grand camp finale, ranking right up there with *Duel in the Sun* and *Beyond the Forest*. The big difference here is that Frankie doesn't die, he only fades away, before our very eyes.

Hollywood can be such a cruel town.

20

CASINO ROYALE

1967 ⤙ Columbia

Produced by Charles K. Feldman and Jerry Bresler. Directed by John Huston, Kenneth Hughes, Robert Parrish, Val Guest, and Joseph McGrath. Screenplay by Wolf Mankowitz, John Law, and Michael Sayers, from the novel by Ian Fleming.

CAST: Peter Sellers (*Evelyn Tremble*); Ursula Andress (*Vesper Lynn*); David Niven (*Sir James Bond*); Orson Welles (*Le Chiffre*); Joanna Pettet (*Mata Bond*); Woody Allen (*Jimmy Bond*); Deborah Keer (*Lady Fiona*); William Holden (*Ransome*); Charles Boyer (*Le Grand*); John Huston (*M*).

DURING THE SIXTIES, the whole movie world had 007 fever. James Bond was the western hemisphere's favorite action hero, and every producer worth his license to kill was jumping on the Bond-wagon trying to cash in. The result was a slew of very poor imitators—but more about them later. This space is reserved for a special Bond spoof, the one that thought it was above all the others, and spent millions just to prove it. It was called *Casino Royale* and it was meant to be the Bond spoof to end all Bond spoofs. At least the film-makers got *that* part right—although not in the way they intended.

Presumably, the producers realized that 007, who did a good job himself of kidding the spy genre, had pretty much been spoofed to death by 1967. So they didn't bother keeping the old tongue-in-cheek. Instead, they let it all hang out. Sent it up in grand style. Threw in everything-but-kitchen-sink realism. With five directors, at least six screenwriters (half of them uncredited), and one big all-star cast hamming it to the hilt, *Casino Royale* careened across the screen, making a lot of noise but not much sense. Ah, but that was the general idea. This was the *sixties!* Movies weren't supposed to make sense, they were supposed to be a *trip*. A *happening*. You know, like *Help!*

Ten minutes into this movie, "Help!" is what you're screaming. By then

you've stopped looking for a plot; you're just hoping to occasionally be entertained by the random chaotic events. Ten minutes later, you've given up on that, too. What's left now is to try to keep your eyeballs from rolling back in your head while this pointless exhibition collapses in a heap. To preserve your sanity, you might try counting the number of people passing themselves off as the famous 007.

First up is David Niven as the original Sir James Bond. He's living a life of luxury on his country estate, where he cultivates roses, plays Debussy at sunset, and wears a nightshirt to bed. Nevertheless, he is called out of retirement to battle the evil organization SMERSH, because even after all this time, there is still nobody who does it better.

Be that as it may, he turns out to need a lot of help. Taking over control of Her Majesty's Secret Service, he immediately hires a new batch of spies, and just to confuse the enemy (not to mention the audience) he dubs them all 007. There are 007s everywhere, and not one of them is tall, dark, or dangerous. There is Peter Sellers as a baccarat expert recruited for his gambling know-how. There is Joanna Pettet as Mata Bond, Sir James's daughter by way of Mata Hari. There is Ursula Andress, who apparently qualifies because she played the original Bond girl in *Dr. No.* And there is Woody Allen as Sir James's nephew, Little Jimmy Bond, a bumbling novice first seen dodging Latin American firing squads, only to resurface later as the evil supervillian "Dr. Noah," whose plan is to rid the world of everyone except beautiful women and men under four-feet-six. These are the jokes.

Of course, so many Bonds require many worthy adversaries. Deborah Kerr shows up briefly as a counterspy who can't bring herself to kill Niven, and becomes a nun instead. Jacqueline Bisset slinks into a hotel room, slips Sellers a mickey, and slips back out forever. And SMERSH agent Orson Welles bellies up to the baccarat table for a high-stakes game that seems to last all night. Also sticking their heads in along the way are John Huston as "M," William Holden as a CIA chief, Charles Boyer as his French counterpart, Peter O'Toole as a Scottish bagpipe player and . . . oh, you get the picture. The list goes on and on.

Lurching from one plot line to another, the film imperceptibly changes directors until all five have had a crack at the material. Who directed what and where does it begin and end? Who knows? Who cares? Together, they've assembled such a cluttered, clunky mess that the seams never show. There *are* no seams. The only thing that unites these directors is their uniform lack of self-control. Each as pretentiously onanistic as the next.

The actors, meanwhile, aren't much better. Coasting through the movie, playing down to their characters with conspicuous aplomb, they seem to have thought they could make a "happening" happen just by being there. So while they're milling around the milieu bemusedly half-engaged, sight gags fizzle, farcical bits fall flat, the satire sits there. Nothing kills comedy faster than a bunch of people just clowning around.

Eventually, because all movies must, this one comes to an end. Finally all the Bonds converge on the floor of the Casino Royale for a donnybrook that also includes the French Foreign Legion, the CIA, the U.S. Cavalry, a chimpanzee in a fright wig, two seals on a piano, a roulette wheel that turns into a flying saucer, a posse of cowboys on horseback, and a war party of Hollywood Indians who spontaneously drop their weapons and break into the watusi. Ah, the sixties! As a punch line, Woody Allen reemerges, having just gulped a cocktail spiked with explosives. With one good hiccup, he blows the whole place to smithereens, mercifully bringing the movie to an abrupt but overdue conclusion. What *was* it all about, Alfie? Not a damn thing. But whatever the joke was, it was ultimately on the producers. They spent $10 million, didn't make it back, and got bad reviews in the bargain. James Bond spoofs were dead forever—and yet Bond himself lived on. Nearly three decades later, he is still making movies and saving the world. Take that, Dr. Noah!

Ursula Andress is 007?

SIGNS OF THE TIMES
Superspies of the Sixties

Born out of Cold War paranoia—and formed by the *Playboy* Philosophy—the sixties secret agent supplied a timely new male fantasy: a suave, sexy, supremely confident hero
who could bed a beautiful girl at a moment's notice, kill an enemy spy in half that time,
tell a martini's temperature with just one sip, and single-handedly save the world from
the mass destruction that was always just a button-push away. Of course, nobody did
it better than James Bond. But what's surprising is how far short most of his imitators
fell. Or maybe you've forgotten Vince Edwards in *Hammerhead*, Stewart Granger in
Code Name Alpha, and Mike ("Mannix") Connors in *Kiss the Girls and Make Them Die*.
These are only a few of the not-so-super spies who collectively left the sixties neither
shaken nor stirred. A few more:

Boozy Dean Martin admires the view in one of his interchangeable Matt Helm movies.

The Matt Helm movies. The best known of all Bond imitators, Dean Martin's Matt Helm at least has a style of his own: Nobody does it blearier. Through four slapdash spy capers, Helm indulges in casual derring-do with a drink in his hand, a leer on his lips, and saloon songs by—who else—Dean Martin on his car radio. Slouching through towns like London and Acapulco, Helm spends most of his time putting the make on buxom blond bimbos (from Stella Stevens in *The Silencers* (1966) to Sharon Tate in *The Wrecking Crew* (1969). Every so often, however, he'll set those pursuits aside to go through the motions of saving the world from some madman who has stolen a nuclear missile or experimental death ray. And when it comes to going through the motions, no spy can top Helm's repertoire of cornball wisecracks, cheesy special effects, and clunky action scenes. In one classic clip from *Murderers' Row* (1966), he shoots it out with a bad guy in a brewery while slurping streams of beer from bullet-ridden vats. Cool, huh? But that's nothing compared to *The Wrecking Crew*, which finds him weaving from one boudoir to another, seduced by beauties whose come-ons invariably cause him to roll his eyes heavenward, as if to ask, "How much sex can one stud stand?" How this "stud" can stand at all remains the greatest mystery of the Matt Helm movies.

The Second Best Secret Agent in the Whole Wide World (1965) His name is Vine. Charles Vine. He's on the job because What's-his-name is elsewhere saving the world—

as if What's-his-name would ever be bothered with a mission so, well, second rate. Assigned to guard an antigravity formula, Vine shoots it out with faceless foes and takes equally faceless bimbos to bed—where he's second best to no man. "I met someone like you once," sighs one satisfied customer. "His name was James . . . something." Despite such flattering comparisons, Tom Adams (no relation to Don) plays Vine with all the panache of a drone from the decoding department. Later, as if by popular demand, he'll return in *Where the Bullets Fly* (1966), the *second* best Charles Vine movie in the whole wide world.

Operation Kid Brother (1967) How do you make the cheesiest Bond rip-off of all? Start with Neil Connery (brother of Sean), then completely surround him with bonafide Bond alumni: *Thunderball* villain Adolfo Celli, *From Russia With Love* Bond girl Daniela Bianchi, Bernard "M" Lee as the secret service chief, and Lois "Moneypenny" Maxwell as his assistant, who sees almost as much action as Neil. But watching Miss Moneypenny blow away enemy agents sure beats watching our hero mope through his mission, throwing stiff karate chops and making even stiffer passes at pretty girls. Does his perpetual frown have anything to do with the silly goatee he's wearing? Or is he just pouting because he's so clearly the runt of the Connery litter?

21

REFLECTIONS IN A GOLDEN EYE

1967 ⤙ Warner Brothers

Produced by Ray Stark. Directed by John Huston. Screenplay by Chapman Mortimer and Gladys Hill, from the novel by Carson McCullers.

CAST: Elizabeth Taylor (*Leonora Penderton*); Marlon Brando (*Major Penderton*); Brian Keith (*Lt. Col. Morris Langdon*); Julie Harris (*Alison Langdon*); Zorro David (*Anacleto*); Robert Forster (*Private Williams*).

ANYONE WHO WONDERS WHY Marlon Brando had to audition for *The Godfather*, or why his performance in that film was called a comeback, need only look at the movies he made in the previous decade. From *Mutiny on the Bounty* to *Morituri*, from *The Ugly American* to *The Countess From Hong Kong*, they comprise the most curious collection of ambitious underachievements that any great actor ever attempted. Most curious of all, perhaps, was this overheated helping of southern fried perversity, served up with a heavy hand by John Huston.

Carson McCullers's novel as pretty weird to begin with. Huston's film just takes that weirdness and holds it up to a magnifying mirror, making it even larger than life. Set on a postwar Georgia army base, it stars Brando as a repressed homosexual major, Elizabeth Taylor as his oversexed wife, Brian Keith as the colonel who lives in the next bungalow, and Julie Harris as Keith's fragile missus, who has been teetering on the brink of madness since she lost her baby at birth—after which she mutilated her own breasts.

"Cutting off her nipples with garden shears!" Taylor snorts. "You call *that* normal?"

"Well," drawls Keith, "the doctors say she's neurotic."

And she's not the only one! Taylor and Keith are carrying on a casual affair right under Brando's nose. But you really can't blame Liz. Her prissy prig of a

Marlon Brando, as pent-up Major Penderton, stands, er, straight and tall, before his men.

husband hasn't touched her in years—a situation that leads her to desperate acts like disrobing before dinner, then shaking her booty in his face as she sashays up the stairs. "I swear I'll kill you," Brando sputters during one such slutty display. Unfazed, she shoots right back, "Have you ever been collared and dragged out in the street and thrashed by a naked woman?" That shuts him up.

But it doesn't turn him on. Right then and there, Liz should have deduced that Brando doesn't like girls. But she's cheerfully oblivious to all the signs. She never catches him gazing at pictures of Roman centurions or fondling delicate teaspoons or plastering "rejuvenating cream" all over his face. Nor does she notice how his nostrils flare whenever buck private Robert Forster comes around to do the yard work—barechested, of course.

For that matter, she never notices how strange Private Forster is. But, boy, is he ever! At night, he lurks outside their bungalow, peering into the windows. During the day, on breaks from his stable boy duties, he rides bareback through the woods—absolutely naked! One day, out riding, Liz and the officers see Forster streaking sun-dappled through the trees. "Outrageous!" Brando sniffs, all the while ogling bug-eyed. The others don't seem to give it a second thought.

Nobody seems to notice *anything* in this movie, even when it's happening right in front of them. Let Forster sneak into Liz's room and spend the night sifting through her lingerie. Liz won't wake up. Let Julie Harris dote on her Filipino houseboy (Zorro David), who flits around the house like a ballerina and perfumes his mistress's urine samples before sending them to the hospital. He-man Keith will simply growl: "You're a rare bird, you are," and go back to his newspaper. That's what repressed sexuality does, folks—don't do it enough and it makes you blind.

Some things, however, cannot be ignored—like when Brando beats Taylor's horse ("He's a stallion," Liz is fond of pointing out,) after getting tossed from the saddle. When Liz finds out about that, she gives Brando a dose of his own medicine, whipping him with a riding crop in the middle of her annual garden party. But that's mild compared to Harris's reaction when she barges into Liz's bedroom expecting to find her husband and instead finds Private Forster, alone, with his face in one of Liz's clean nighties. After staring for a long, incredulous moment, she marches straight back home and demands a divorce, anyway—whereupon Keith has her committed to a sanitorium . . . whereupon she promptly expires. When people *do* vent their feelings in this movie, they do it in a big way.

But nobody does it bigger than Brando. His eventual eruption literally ends the movie with a bang, and like all volcanic displays, you can see it building well in advance. First, he drifts off teary-eyed while giving a lecture on leadership. The he stalks Forster around the base, picking up his discarded candy wrappers. Then he flabbergasts Taylor and Keith with a rhapsodic reverie on the joys of barracks life, where men are men, "clean as a rifle . . . living in utter simplicity. They eat and they train and they shower and they play jokes and they go to a brothel together and they sleep side by side and they're never lonely."

Yes, folks, Brando's about to come out in a blaze of glory. Spotting Forster entering his house on a stormy night, he pathetically primps in his room, under the impression that this gentleman caller has come for him. When the gentleman calls on his wife instead, well, that tears it! Brando whips out a pistol, kicks in the door, and blasts the nightie-sniffing soldier to kingdom come! Finally, Liz wakes up to the world around her, as Huston dizzyingly pans his camera from her screaming face to Forster's dead body to Brando with his head in his hands, as if to say, "What have I done?" What indeed, Marlon?

Liz Taylor plays poker with stud Brian Keith, while hubby Marlon Brando drifts off in his own little world.

All plodding pacing, blatant symbolism, and artsy camera movements, *Reflections in a Golden Eye* set the rarified standard for pretentious sixties moviemaking. There is not a single scene in this hothouse movie that lets us up for air, not a single interlude that lets us step aside from this rancid roundelay. There is, however, plenty of unintentional comic relief. As the actors chew and savor every overripe moment—while playing it absolutely straight—we can't help but wonder if, deep down inside, Huston didn't think that all these riding crops and bareback rides were just so much horse manure. But then he gives you another long close-up of Forster's feverishly voyeuristic eyes, or another turgid gurgle of Alex North's abstract music score, and we realize with dismay: Huston was serious too.

After this massive misfire, the miracle wasn't merely that Brando would regain his former eminence, but that Huston would too. As for Elizabeth Taylor . . . well, three miracles would have been an awful lot to ask, even in Hollywood. For Liz, there would be more where this came from.

22

VALLEY OF THE DOLLS

1967 ⸰ Twentieth Century–Fox

Produced by David Weisbart. Directed by Mark Robson. Screenplay by Helen Deutsch and Dorothy Kingsley, based on the novel by Jacqueline Susann.

CAST: Barbara Parkins (*Anne Welles*); Patty Duke (*Neely O'Hara*); Sharon Tate (*Jennifer North*); Susan Hayward (*Helen Lawson*); Paul Burke (*Lyon Burke*); Martin Milner (*Mel Anderson*); Tony Scotti (Tony Polar); Lee Grant (*Miriam*).

YOU KNOW A MOVIE IS BAD when it inspires a feature-length parody. You know it's beyond bad when *it's* still funnier than the movie making fun of it. Such is the case with *Valley of the Dolls*. Russ Meyer and Roger Ebert may have mercilessly spoofed it with their 1970 *Beyond the Valley of the Dolls*, but really, the original remains its own best parody. Based on the Jacqueline Susann best-seller, it takes a trashy novel and turns it into ultra-trash.

Legend has it that Miss Susann wasn't happy with what Hollywood did to her book. That's not so surprising. Yet history has shown that the movie, not the novel, has left its enduring imprint on our impressionable pop culture. That's not so surprising either. Whenever you drag three glamour puss girls through all sorts of cheap, sleazy ordeals, you're bound to attract a crowd and make an impression.

Of course, Susann's book had already guaranteed a built-in audience. And prurient interests were only further piqued by an intensive prerelease publicity campaign that included a coming attractions trailer that captured all the movie's trash appeal in high camp hyperbole:

> Barbara Parkins is Annie, a good girl with a million-dollar face and all the bad breaks. She took the green pills.

Patty Duke is Neely, who was such a nice kid. And then someone put her name in lights and turned her into a lush. She took the red pills.

Sharon Tate is Jennifer, an international sex symbol victimized by everyone. She took the blue pills.

Before they start raiding that Technicolor medicine chest, these girls could be the girls next door. The unintentional fun is in watching them rise and all so fast that whole lifetimes seem to pass through the muck in two action-packed hours. Good girl Parkins is a Radcliffe grad working for a showbiz lawyer when she suddenly gets chosen as the "Face" of a zillion-dollar cosmetics ad campaign. Nice kid Duke is a singing and dancing dynamo streaking to the top so fast that she doesn't even see the people she'll spend time with on her way back down. Sexy Tate is a dumb blonde chorus girl who doesn't want to make it on her looks alone—which is exactly what she does.

Of course, these girls have men, if only to dramatize how romance and success don't mix. Parkins's fella is a smooth but sensitive lawyer (Paul Burke) who wants to quit the rat race, "So I can write my book," but won't commit to marriage. Duke's guy is a rising young press agent (Martin Milner) who gives up his career to become her personal doormat. And Tate's Romeo is a slick saloon singer who whisks her away to Hollywood along with his big sister (Lee Grant), who watches over them like a mother hen. Make that a mother harpy.

With guys like those, the three stars hardly have to worry about having any scenes stolen—except when Susan Hayward shows up as a legendary Broadway diva. Hayward storms on early to tear up a few contracts, rip up a few agents, and toss Duke out of her show because she fears the up-and-comer will steal her thunder. (Fat chance). Then, unfortunately, she's off the screen until late in the film, when she storms back for the most memorable scene in a movie full of them.

But even without Miss Hayward to contend with, the stars stay plenty busy. Duke hits Hollywood running and keeps popping pills to keep up the pace. Eventually this takes its toll on her faithful husband, who gets tired of being underfoot. ("I'm not the butler," he complains. "You're not the bread-winner either," she reminds him.) After emasculating hubby and sending him back to New York with his tail between his legs, she takes up with an AC/DC costume designer, increases her dosage of booze and pills, and goes off the

deep end when she finds her lover splashing in the pool with a buxom bimbette. Next stop—rehab.

Meanwhile, further down the cast list, Sharon Tate's singing husband starts falling down stairs and forgetting who he is. Learning that he has a degener-

ative nerve disease, she puts him in a private hospital, then signs up with a French "art" filmmaker to pay the medical bills. Only after she has thoroughly degraded herself as a foreign nudie star does she discover a lump in her breast. After getting the dire diagnosis, she immediately commits suicide. Blue pills, of course.

Then there's Parkins who has finally landed Mr. Sensitivity, only to lose him to Duke. That sends *her* off on her own downward spiral of pills and self-pity, leaving her bottomed out on her hands and knees in the surf outside her Malibu pad. What's a girl to do?

If she's one of the girls, she'll play her part just the way it was written, saying every line with absolute conviction. If she's Parkins, she'll come off as the poor martyr. If she's Tate, she'll come off as the beautiful dumb blonde. But if she's Duke, she'll get all the howler highlights. While drying out in the sanitarium, Patty sings an astonishing torch duet with Tate's near-catatonic husband, who manages to wheeze out one last verse before falling over the side of his wheelchair. Then, on the Broadway comeback trail, she has an opening night ladies-room fight with fading prima donna Hayward, which ends with her tearing off Hayward's wig and gleefully tossing it in the toilet. Finally, there's her big moment on her knees in a theater back alley. Having come all the way back, only to blow it on booze and pills again, she runs down a litany of the names of all the people she's screwed along the way, finally getting to her own name, which she screams, again and again. "Neely O'Hara!" echoes into the night. It's *so* lonely at the bottom.

In addition to the emotional excesses of this three-tiered soap opera, there are all sorts of kitschy period set pieces that make this an invaluable sixties artifact. There is Parkins's rise to fame as captured in a kicky montage of commercials, posters, and magazine covers. There's an equally pop-artsy sequence full of split screens and freeze frames, depicting dynamo Duke as she huffs and puffs and pill-pops her way to stardom. And there's Tate's crowning creative moment, a fully staged takeoff of a vintage French skin flick, in which a spilled glass of wine provides the perfect climax to a pretentious nude love scene. On top of everything else, there are also sore-thumb cameos by Joey Bishop, George Jessel, and Jacqueline Susann herself. They're completely superfluous, of course, and yet they belong. This movie just wouldn't have been as bad without them.

23

THE GREEN BERETS

1968 ⁙ Warner Brothers

Produced by Michael Wayne. Directed by John Wayne and Ray Kellogg. Screenplay by James Lee Barrett, based on the novel by Robin Moore.

CAST: John Wayne (*Col. Mike Kirby*); David Janssen (*George Beckworth*); Jim Hutton (*Sergeant Petersen*); Aldo Ray (*Sergeant Muldoon*); Raymond St. Jacques (*Doc McGee*); Bruce Cabot (*Colonel Morgan*); Jack Soo (*Captain Cai*); George Takei (*Captain Nim*).

CRITICS ALMOST UNIVERSALLY REVILED this Vietnam tall tale. But at least half the pans were in direct response to the film's superpatriotic stance on American involvement in Southeast Asia. This was the only major movie of the sixties to concern itself with the Vietnam conflict, and it was gung ho for it. Twenty-seven years later, the film seems even more stupid than it did when it was released. Political correctness, however, is only part of the problem.

The movie opens with a high-intensity press conference, in which two Green Berets with bad attitudes explain to the knee-jerk liberal press why we were in Vietnam. The press isn't convinced. Most skeptical of all is big-city reporter David Janssen "I'm from the *Chronicle Herald*," he keeps saying, like it was the *New York Times* or something. "My paper doesn't feel we should be in Vietnam." To prove his paper wrong, the Green Berets, led by Colonel "Duke" Wayne, invite the reporter along with them as they make their way to an army camp somewhere near no man's land.

Between bouts of men-at-war small talk over coffee and cigarettes, Janssen gets a first hand look at what's *really* happening over there. "Are those punji sticks?" he asks, checking out some booby traps on the camp outskirts. "Yep," says a helpful grunt. "A little trick we learned from Charlie. We don't dip 'em in the same thing he does, though." And so it goes. Little by little, Janssen

gets a sobering eyeful of how the filthy dirty Viet Cong fight. When he protests the slapping up of a Viet Cong prisoner, he's told the prisoner butchered an army medic who was returning from delivering a baby. When he accompanies the troops to a local village, he's sickened to see what's left of the massacred and mutilated peasants. Between regular doses of enemy atrocity, he keeps bonding with G.I.'s, only to watch them die before his eyes. Even the camp mutt buys it during an enemy mortar attack. Two hours of this and any knee-jerk liberal would change his lily-livered spots.

Yet if it weren't for *The Green Berets*'s simplistic propaganda, there wouldn't be a hell of a lot going on here. The men are so busy exchanging military lingo, establishing macho camaraderie, and spouting their yellow-peril party line that they don't get around to doing much fighting. The first battle scene doesn't come until an hour or so into the film, and even that is a drag. As the Viet Cong launch an all-out assault under cover of darkness, director Wayne tries to orchestrate it on a grand logistical scale. The trouble is, despite all those coordinates being barked into radios, we have no ideas what's happening or who's winning. It's all explosions, people diving into trenches, and walls of enemy soldiers advancing in the darkness. As a good old-fashioned battle scene, it's a *bad* old-fashioned battle scene. It can't even get the cliches right.

In an effort to convey the complexity of the Vietnam conflict (or maybe just to bail itself out of a dead-end story line) the movie spends its second half on a cloak-and-dagger mission to kidnap an important North Vietnamese general. Since the general is holed up in a fortified sugar plantation, the Green Berets decide they need a little help in the undercover department, so they recruit a beautiful Miss Saigon (Irene Tsu), who's just dying to avenge the murder of her father by the Viet Cong. "Besides being one of our top models, she could be most helpful to our government," says a South Vietnamese colonel, apropos of nothing.

And so off they all go on their Dirty Dozen adventure. While their Mata Hari keeps the general's hands full, the Green Berets sneak up and storm the place. It sort of reminds you of a sorority panty raid, only with fireworks.

On the way back through rugged terrain that resembles the hills around Santa Barbara, the Green Berets lose a few good men. One of the casualties is company jokester Jim Hutton, who gets nailed on a multi-pronged booby trap, setting up the heart-tugging ending involving a little war orphan who had befriended Hutton. This kid's been through hell already. Even the damn dog that died belonged to him! Nevertheless, this neo-Dondi manfully holds back his tears, bravely inquiring, "What will happen to me now?" Just as manfully, Colonel Duke Wayne responds, "Don't worry, son, you're what this is all about." Taking the little urchin's hand, the Green Beret leads him down to the sea, where the sun is majestically setting—in the east!

In any other movie, this bizarro sunset finale would have been an unfortunate gaffe. But in *The Green Berets*, it somehow seems fitting. In a movie as ass-backwards as this, why *shouldn't* the sun set on the wrong horizon? It sort of brings the whole thing full circle.

24

BOOM!

1968 ⁊ Universal

Produced by John Heyman and Norman Priggen. Directed by Joseph Losey. Screenplay by Tennessee Williams, based on his play *The Milk Train Doesn't Stop Here Anymore*.

CAST: Elizabeth Taylor (*Flora Goforth*); Richard Burton (*Chris Flanders*); Noel Coward (*Witch of Capri*); Joanna Shimkus (*Blackie*); Michael Dunn (*Rudy*); Romolo Valli (*doctor*); Fernando Piazza (*Etti*).

FIRST, THEY SCORED an artistic triumph in *Who's Afraid of Virginia Woolf?* Then they soared with a spirited rendition of Shakespeare's *The Taming of the Shrew*. For those two shining moments Elizabeth Taylor and Richard Burton seemed to have found the secret of making good movies together. Then they teamed up on *Boom!*, and divebombed back to earth, with a resounding you-know-what.

This was a project that looked so dubious right from the start that you wonder why anyone would give it a green light. Yes, it was based on a Tennessee Williams play, but we're not exactly talking *A Streetcar Named Desire* here. We're talking about a much shakier vehicle—*The Milk Train Doesn't Stop Here Anymore*—the story of a rich, reclusive widow and her rendezvous with the Angel of Death on her metaphorically beautiful island estate. It was a piece that Williams himself never felt he got right. It had seen two Broadway productions, the first indifferently received, the second an overnight failure. Giving the material another go while adapting it for the screen, Williams still couldn't get it the way he wanted it. No amount of light, fantastic poetry could bring those heavy-handed symbols to life.

But even bad Tennessee Williams is better than the usual Hollywood hackwork, right? Well, frankly, no. Bad Tennessee Williams is usually just bad.

Liz Taylor as Flora Goforth.
Can this shrew be tamed?

When he doesn't get them right, all those mad tragic heroines and high-flying soliloquies tend to be awfully pretentious, and the more abstract his characters get, the more abstruse they sound. When this play's tragic heroine casts her eyes heavenward to bemoan "the insincere sympathy of faraway stars," it's clear, in more ways than one, that she won't be talking about the kindness of strangers.

Just looking at this play on paper, the studio should have immediately deemed it unfilmable. But instead of passing on it, they proceeded with unbridled enthusiasm. As if to further seal their fate, they put the whole project in the hands of Joseph Losey, a director not exactly known for his meat-and-potatoes outlook on life. The result was pure hell: oppressively artsy, stultifyingly stylized—a crushing, crashing, booming bore.

So why *did* Hollywood say yes to this project? Simple: It starred Taylor and Burton, who were in the midst of their renaissance as a viable screen team. Alas, Taylor and Burton turned out to be another of the film's big problems, for the very basic reason that they had been miscast. They were not right for their roles!

Set entirely on a lavish estate overlooking the Mediterranean, the film stars Taylor as Flora Goforth: rich, bitchy, and dying. Except that Taylor looks ro-

bustly glamorous in this film, and nowhere near death. The rather flaccid
Burton looks closer to the Great Beyond, which may seem fitting for someone who is supposed to be the Angel of Death, except this part was originally conceived for a young, beautiful man. Okay, so the difference isn't fatal.
In his human guise as an itinerant poet who sponges off rich older women,
Burton's angel at lest comes off suitably, er, *poetic*. He spouts off spiritual reflections on the human condition, affects a generally brooding stare, and
maintains a rarified air of superiority, even at his most accessible. All right,
so we do find ourselves wondering why the intolerant Mrs. Goforth doesn't
just tell him to get his things and go forth from her island. But then, we also
wonder how he can stand to stay, angel or not. Guess some things were just
meant to be.

Supporting the two stars are a self-consciously odd assortment of characters: a punching bag personal secretary (Joanna Shimkus), a booze-soaked
personal doctor (Romolo Valli), a sadistic midget bodyguard with killer dogs
(Michael Dunn), a gigantic black butler (Fernando Piazza), a pet gorilla,
some resident musicians playing sitars, and a visiting friend known only as
the Witch of Capri—a part written for a woman, but played here by none
other than Noel Coward. And you thought Taylor and Burton were miscast!

Actually, Coward fits right into the part. Playing the witch as an aging gay
recluse from another private island, he briefly alights on Mrs. Goforth's terrace to engage in some arch repartee before flitting off forever. The film is
never again so light or amusing. Once the angle has Mrs. Goforth to himself, *Boom!* settles into endless conversations about life, love, and death. Every
once in awhile, Mrs. Goforth not-so-discreetly coughs blood into a hankie,
reminding us which subject is upper-most in her mind.

For all the impending doom, there really isn't much that's dramatic about
this drama. The closest it gets to emotional is on those occasions when Mrs.
Goforth, fortified by booze and pills, gets feisty and swears at her servants.
"Shit on your mother!" she shouts at one of them, spitting out a line that
became rather infamous after *Boom!* was released, partly because Elizabeth
Taylor had said "shit" in a movie, partly because the phrase itself sounded so
utterly stupid. Now, of course, it just sounds utterly stupid.

With highly charged drama in short supply, the film must rely too heav-
ily on such window dressing as costume and decor. But since they are equally
ostentatious they complement each other very nicely, thank you. Clothed in

Miss Taylor models another amazing ensemble. Noel Coward, as the "Witch of Capri," seems duly amazed.

a white-on-white, mostly full-length wardrobe, adorned by a queen's ransom in jewels, and sporting some outlandish headdresses (one hat looks like an exploding pineapple), Taylor just naturally dominates the screen, even though her surroundings are a gleaming white villa, with ornate wall designs and monolithic sculptures representing her six dead husbands (at least these symbols are *supposed* to be lifeless). Set against the backdrop of azure skies, spectacularly craggy, sheer cliffs, and far below, the deep blue Mediterranean, *Boom!* is indeed a sight to behold. But it's like anything else that's too rich. After a while, it gives you a headache.

All of which *could* serve to explain the movie's title. But, of course, it's not as simple as that. For the real story of how the unfortunate *The Milk Train*

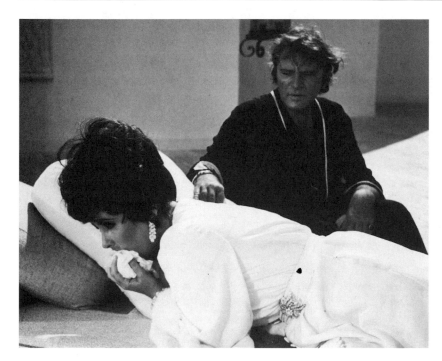

The Death Scene from *Camille*? No, just another of Flora's coughing jags. It all comes out the same in the end.

Doesn't Stop Here Anymore became the even more unfortunate *Boom!*, we must listen to Tennessee Williams's deep purple dialogue. As Burton's pompous poet puts it, "Boom! represents the shock of each moment of still being alive." He should know, after all, he's not only a poet, he's also the Angel of Death. And yet, as this "motion" picture drags on, slowly becoming as ossified as the stone statues on the terrace, the title comes to sum up the collective pretensions of Williams, Losey, Liz, and Dick. "Boom!" the Angel of Death intones, again and again, as he gazes upon the surf hitting the rocks below. "Boom!"

That about says it all.

25

CANDY

1968 ‧ Cinerama

Produced by Robert Haggig. Directed by Christian Marquand. Screenplay by Buck Henry, based on the novel by Terry Southern and Mason Hoffenberg.

CAST: Ewa Aulin (*Candy*); Charles Aznavour (*hunchback*); Marlon Brando (*Grindl*); Richard Burton (*McPhisto*); James Coburn (*Dr. Krankeit*); John Huston (*Dr. Dunlap*); Walter Matthau (*General Smight*); Ringo Starr (*Emmanuel*).

FEW SIXTIES MOVIES were as eagerly awaited—or as instantly forgotten—as this all-star casualty of the sexual revolution. Based on the Terry Southern-Mason Hoffenberg novel (never trust a novel written by two people), *Candy* is yet another failed book-to-film adaptation: It is superficially faithful to its source material, yet somehow misses the point.

Not that there was much of a point to miss. Even allowing for changing times and tastes, the book wasn't really such a big deal. Recounting the amorous adventures of an irresistibly nubile (and improbably naive) young heroine, *Candy* was a fairly clever sex satire that came along at just the right time—on the cutting edge of the sexual revolution. It was cult pulp. It was porno chic. The fact that it was intended as a *parody* of pornography didn't stop horny high school kids (like me) from passing it around in study hall, wolfing it down like forbidden fruit. Hot stuff!

Unfortunately, the filmmakers' interest in the material was just about as mature, but by the time they got around to turning *Candy* into a movie, its sexual escapades were no longer shocking. And even if they were, the finished film would pull so many punches that *Candy*'s porno chic would be reduced to a smirky R-rated tease. Despite the dulled edge (or maybe because of it), the project still attracted a glittering international cast, all dying to play dirty old men. With such names as Marlon Brando and Richard Burton attached,

Ewa Aulin as sweet little Candy.

the movie became practically respectable. However, all respectability went out the window once audiences finally got a look at what all the fuss was about.

A sort of contemporary *Candide* (Get it? Candy-Candide?), the book was a series of carnal encounters that gained a comic momentum as it went along. The movie, however, bumps and grinds from one episode to the next, with so little rhyme or reason (or rhythm) that we're not always sure where we are or why. The only constant here is titular star Ewa Aulin, who squeaks out Candy's native English in a Scandinavian accent that its never satisfyingly explained. Not that that's really a drawback. After all, this *is* a sixties sex farce. If the heroine isn't French, she'd *better* be Scandinavian.

Aulin is in fact a former Miss Teen Sweden—which pretty much sums up her pre-*Candy* showbiz experience. Early on it's clear that, for all her adorable blondness, she doesn't have the presence to carry a major movie. But then she doesn't have to—her hambone costars are more than happy to pick up the slack.

First comes Richard Burton, a poet laureate on a university tour who stops giving readings long enough to give it to Candy. Theatrically lit, with his stage voice booming and his hair blown back by a wind machine, Burton also appears to be sticking it to pompous poets everywhere. "I gobbled up the

Marlon Brando mumbles and mugs as the mystical masher Grindl.

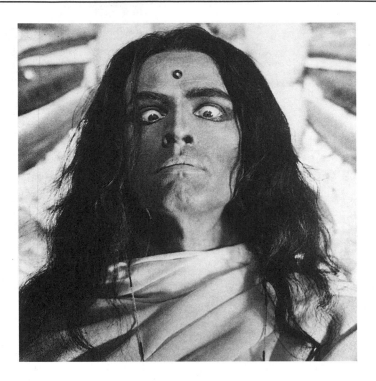

mountains, etched the sky and drank the sea/until I was the universe and the universe was me . . ." quoth Burton. Moments later, he's attempting to gobble up Candy, while wallowing in a sea of whiskey, on the back floor of his limo.

After Burton has his way with our hapless heroine, it's on to Ringo Starr as a Mexican gardener who knows a hot tomato when he sees one. Falling all over himself and her, he works himself up to a climactic "Viva Zapata!" This is screenwriter Buck Henry's idea of a punch line.

In quick succession (but not quick enough), Candy finds herself in a cockpit with Walter Matthau as a gung ho general who meekly misfires, in a hospital room with John Huston as a lecherous chief of staff, in a men's room with Enrico Maria Salerno as a voyeuristic would-be filmmaker, and in the back of a van with Marlon Brando, who babbles mystical mumbo-jumbo as an over-the-top Indian guru. "Now we must find that place where the immutable self resides," proclaims Maharishi Marlon. "You mean my lungs?" inquires the ever-innocent Candy. Close enough, Sweetie. Also giving her a hard time are James Coburn as a leering surgeon who performs a bloody brainectomy in front of a cheering operating theater crowd, Charles Aznavour as a hunchback who wants to make Candy his private Esmeralda, and John Astin in a thankless dual role as Candy's stuffy Daddy and scummy Uncle Jack. (It's important to keep track of which Astin is which, lest you miss how truly tasteless this movie can be—or maybe you've already guessed.)

Under the direction of Christian Marquand, whose main contribution seems to have been to shout "Action!" when the scenes started and "Cut!" before they got X-rated, this cavalcade of caricature actors is allowed to indulge in all sorts of ill-conceived excess. But it's all for naught. As Henry's crass screenplay chews them up and spits them out one by one, they all end up looking far worse than the utterly untalented Aulin, who flounces through the film so obliviously that she merges almost unscathed. At least onscreen. Alas, her future career was quite another story. Having performed so underwhelmingly in such an overwhelming mess, the former Miss Teen Sweden would only get a few more film roles, none of them starring, before returning to her homeland a has-been.

Hollywood, however, wasn't quite finished trying to cash in on the sixties pop culture explosion. More big budget "happenings" were still to come, including the worst of them all—the one that proved that you could give a director LSD, but you couldn't make him groove. Ladies and Gentlemen, We give you . . . *Skidoo!*

26

SKIDOO

1968 ⁴ Paramount

Produced and directed by Otto Preminger. Screenplay by Doran William Cannon, based on a story by Erik Kirkland.

CAST: Jackie Gleason (*Tony Banks*); Carol Channing (*Flo Banks*); Frankie Avalon (*Angie*); Michael Constantine (*Leech*); Frank Gorshin (*man*); John Phillip Law (*Stash*); Peter Lawford (*senator*); Burgess Meredith (*warden*); George Raft (*Garbaldo*); Cesar Romero (*Hechy*); Mickey Rooney (*Blue Chips*); Alexandra Hay (*Darlene*); Groucho Marx (*God*).

OTTO PREMINGER MADE MORE BAD MOVIES than any other so-called serious filmmaker. And as he moved from decade to decade, the movies got worse and worse. By the time he got to the sixties he was scraping bottom. Among the works that almost made it into this book were *The Cardinal* (1963), his overblown portrait of Vatican politics; *In Harm's Way* (1965), his equally overblown all-star war movie; and *Hurry Sundown* (1967), his deeply insulting, Deep South civil rights drama. None of these films, however, could have prepared us for *Skidoo*, which demonstrated the dismal depths Preminger could reach when he tried to be funny.

With its culture clash of hippies and Damon Runyon-type gangsters, *Skidoo* is Preminger's attempt to deal with the shifting social dynamics of the late sixties. Unfortunately, he didn't seem to have the slightest idea of what was happening, or why. Even if he did, he probably wouldn't have known how to make it amusing. For even from Preminger's side of the generation gap, *Skidoo* is an abysmal affair. The reasons have nothing to do with how out-of-touch it is; the failures are more fundamental. They concern such things as plot, performance, dialogue, decor, costume design, lighting, music and . . . oh, why go on? *Skidoo* skids every which way it can.

Kicky Carol Channing surrenders to the Swinging Sixties.

The most stunning thing about it is the comic talent assembled and wasted. Jackie Gleason stars as a former gangster retired in the comfy California suburbs, with Carol Channing as his flighty wife. Among the organized criminals who came barging back into their lives are Mickey Rooney, Cesar Romero, Frankie Avalon, Frank Gorshin, Michael Constantine, George Raft, and Groucho Marx as the godfather, known simply as God. Also trying to be funny here are Peter Lawford as a crooked senator, Burgess Meredith as a corrupt prison warden, Alexandra Hay as Gleason's nymphet daughter, and John Phillip Law as Preminger's idea of a hippie. With a cast like that, you might assume that you'd get a few laughs, if only by accident. You'd be wrong.

The non-fun begins when Gleason gets strong-armed out of retirement to perform one last hit on stool pigeon Rooney. The catch: Rooney is safely tucked away in Alcatraz, living a life of Riley in solitary confinement. To get to this smug little stoolie, Gleason smuggles himself into Alcatraz, where he's received by a rogue's gallery of Groucho's goons, as colorful a group as Preminger could create given the limits of his imagination. But you ain't seen nothin' yet. Wait'll you see what Preminger does with the next generation.

For that, we take you back to the 'burbs, where Channing learns to her horror that her daughter is in love with a hippie. Rather than let the sweet young thing live out on the street, Mom invites the whole hippie tribe to move into her house. As mystical sitar music wafts through the air, the screen fills with long-haired bit players in faded bell-bottoms and tie-dyed T-shirts. Some of them even have their bodies painted with catchy slogans like "Make love not war." There go the property values. And yet, you know, these hippies really aren't so bad. They just have dirty clothes—and crummy dialogue. "If you can't dig 'nothing,' you can't dig anything, dig?" says Law, explaining his career plans. "That's why the establishment cats aren't making it. They're into that nine to five bag." After a few days of this, Channing begins to see the logic. After all, she's a gangster's wife, she *has* to be flexible.

Meanwhile, back in Alcatraz, Gleason is getting nowhere with is rubout attempt. While waiting around for an opening, he befriends an incarcerated college professor (Austin Pendleton) who carries around a generous supply of LSD. Hey, that's what college professors were like in the sixties. Timothy Leary was a college professor, remember? Anyway, to give this movie a reason to continue, Preminger sends Gleason on an accidental acid trip. Reportedly, the director himself actually dropped acid to get a better idea of how to visualize the experience. If he did, it doesn't show. Gleason's "trip" consists mostly of flashing colors and floating talking heads. It couldn't have been less convincing had Preminger just trained his camera on a Peter Max poster and zoomed back and forth.

But those are just the preliminaries. Having expanded his mind, Gleason realizes that killing is wrong. So instead, he decides to break out of prison by slipping LSD into the food supply and freaking the whole place out. The mass acid trip is an awesome display of imbecilic absurdism. Once seen, the images bang around in your brain like bad flashbacks. Among the highlights: Frank Gorshin turns into an angel and floats up to the ceiling; inmates form daisy chains and frolic through the cell block; garbage cans sprout arms and legs and sing a Harry Nilsson nonsense tune; and a football team identified as the Green Bay Packers lines up in the prison yard, stark naked except for their helmets. Hike! Just when things can't possibly get any more asinine, Gleason and Pendleton escape by filling garbage bags with helium and floating up, up, and away in their beautiful balloon. But guess what? The worst is yet to come.

When next seen, our escapees are landing on the deck of Groucho's yacht, where Gleason's daughter is held hostage, Groucho is leching after anything in long hair (Look out, you hippies!), and George Raft is leading the crew in an antiaircraft assault against Gleason's balloon. To the rescue comes a fleet

Jackie Gleason and Austin Pendleton break out of prison in a gas balloon made out of garbage bags. Supply your own symbolism.

of flower people, led by Miss Channing, who's all decked out in a Horatio Hornblower hat, red miniskirt, and go-go boots. As she jumps aboard the yacht singing "Skidoo, skidoo, the world can be a better place for you," we start to feel as if we, too, have been slipped a tab of acid. But before we can get our bearings Groucho gets into the act, making his escape in a psychedelic sailboat, while on the sound track Nilsson sings (yes, *sings*) the movie's end credits. And that means *all* the end credits, right down to the best boy, the key grip, and the dialogue coach. Last but not least, Nilsson warbles the name of Mr. Preminger, who didn't even have the sense to take his name off this travesty before unleashing it on the public.

Amazingly, Preminger's career wasn't over after this. In the seventies he would bounce back to make the merely mediocre *Such Good Friends*, and *Tell Me That You Love Me, Junie Moon*, before nose-diving once again with the unspeakable *Rosebud*. A turbid tale of terrorism, *Rosebud* was to topical drama what *Skidoo* was to topical comedy. The only thing that softened its negative impact was that after *Skidoo*, nothing Preminger could do would catch us by surprise. After all, when you've already hit rock bottom, that's as low as you can go. The rest is anticlimactic.

SIGNS OF THE TIMES
Hell on Wheels

Among the antiheroes of the sixties, none seemed more antiheroic than the Hell's Angels. But on closer examination, the appeal was understandable. The Hell's Angels were free spirits, rugged individuals. They gave the finger to the Establishment and did whatever they pleased. They cruised the great outdoors with the wind in their hair, bugs in their teeth, and their legs wrapped around their horsepower. Were they really so different than cowboys? So what if the cowboys they most closely resembled were Billy the Kid and his gang. Like Billy, the Hell's Angels were romanticized beyond all reality in Hollywood movies, although that romance ended after an Angel "bodyguard" killed a fan at the Rolling Stones' notorious 1969 Altamont concert. A movie genre died that day—but not before giving birth to the careers of several future stars.

The Wild Angels (1966) Cool Peter Fonda and crazy Bruce Dern get in trouble south of the border. Next thing you know, the entire highway patrol is hot on their trail. Between high speed chases, the Angels spend plenty of down time, during which they smoke pot, slobber on their women (Fonda's red hot mama is Nancy Sinatra), and ride their hogs up and down the highway. Through it all nobody gets around to doing much acting—nobody, that is, except for Dern, who literally inhales the scenery during a death scene in which he tries to get one last marijuana buzz before he goes. Peter and Nancy can only watch in wonder.

Hell's Angels on Wheels (1967) Jack Nicholson joins the Angels looking for adventure. What he finds is a nonstop orgy of brawling, balling, and beer drinking. During one interminable pot party, three Angelettes get their bodies painted, and we are there for every brushstroke. But that's just the beginning. Still to come are an endless wedding ceremony, an extended interlude by a lazy river, and a lot of tooling around on the open road. They should have called it *Hell's Angels on Quaaludes*.

The Glory Stompers (1967) Dennis Hopper's dirty Black Souls stomp on the clean-cut Glory Stompers and make off with Glory girl Chris Noel. Next stop: a biker love-in where the guys play bongos, the chicks paint their bodies, and everybody rides his

Motorcycle Mama Chris Noel hitches a ride with Dennis Hopper in the all-too-typical biker flick *The Glory Stompers*.

chopper in a circle while a lame rock band bleats, "There's a party goin' on." Meanwhile, Hopper swaggers around molesting women and ending most of his sentences with "man." The rest he ends with "baby." Can you blame his motorcycle mama for driving a knife into the back of his neck? Like, what took you so long, baby?

Devil's Angels (1967) John Cassavetes mounts a shiny chrome hog to led his gang to a place where they can do their thing without getting hassled by the "heat." "We're just looking for someplace where we can flake-out," he explains. In this case flaking-out means shoplifting at a package store, ransacking Winnebagos, and making a nuisance of themselves at a small-town jamboree. "Adult delinquents," sputters the mayor. "They steal things, they smell bad, they use foul language!" And they're not even mad yet!

Rebel Rousers (1970) Bruce Dern roars into a sleepy town, flanked by Jack Nicholson in prison-stripe pants and Harry Dean Stanton in a porkpie hat. During self-indulgent acting improvisations they fight amongst themselves and terrorize respectable citizens—including Cameron Mitchell and Diane Ladd. Eventually Dern will hold a mock wedding between the leering Nicholson and a petrified Ladd. Nobody has a Bible handy, so Dern reads from the Harley Davidson manual. When you're a biker, you're a biker all the way.

27

PAINT YOUR WAGON

1969 ◂ Paramount

Produced by Alan Jay Lerner. Directed by Joshua Logan. Screenplay by Lerner and Paddy Chayefsky, based on the musical by Lerner and Frederick Loewe.

CAST: Lee Marvin (*Ben Rumson*); Clint Eastwood (*Pardner*); Jean Seberg (*Elizabeth*); Harve Presnell (*Rotten Luck Willie*); Ray Walston (*Mad Jack Duncan*); Alan Dreeben Dexter (*Parson*).

THE SIXTIES WERE THE BEGINNING of the end for the movie musical. With all the sex, drugs, and rock 'n' roll in the air, the atmosphere was no longer conducive to grand, glossy Hollywood versions of big, brassy Broadway hits. Still, at first the studios persevered, doing their best to adapt to the a-changin' times. Eschewing sound stage sets, they took their musicals out on location (well it worked for *The Sound of Music*, didn't it?). And passing up actual singers, they populated their big-budget productions with stars who could barely carry a tune. The prevailing logic seemed to be that if homely new actors like Dustin Hoffman could replace the matinee idols of yesteryear, why couldn't people with non-melodious voices make successful musicals? Thus we got *Camelot* with Richard Harris, Vanessa Redgrave, and Franco Nero; and *Man of La Mancha* with Peter O'Toole, Sophia Loren, and James Coco. But at least those musicals had plenty of theatrically proficient thespians who could sing-speak their lyrics with some degree of lyricism. *Paint Your Wagon*, however, was a horse of a different color. Its leading men were Lee Marvin and Clint Eastwood, tough guys who barely even spoke in their movies, much less sang. The result of this casting calamity truly has to be heard to be believed. Some of it is pretty strange to look at, too.

Loosely adapted from a Lerner and Loewe Broadway musical, *Paint Your Wagon* tells the story of two gold-seekers who build a boom town high up in

Clint Eastwood and Lee Marvin share a mountainful of gold, a dubious taste in clothes, *and* a Mormon wife (Jean Seberg) in this misbegotten musical.

them thar hills. Marvin is Ben, a grizzled old trapper; Eastwood is Pardner, a pioneer farmer. While traveling westward, Pardner falls down a mountainside and accidentally uncovers the mother lode. Coming to his rescue, Ben stakes his name on half the claim. Pretty soon the two men are presiding over an all-male passel of mavericks and misfits—every one of them striking it rich.

Into this fraternity rides Jean Seberg as Elizabeth, the younger of two Mormon wives. Her husband can no longer afford double marital bliss, so he has decided to auction Elizabeth off to the highest bidder. That turns out to be boozy old Ben, who actually cleans up his act and becomes a right nice husband. However, he worries that the rest of the boys won't keep their paws off his wife, so he rides off to rustle up some dance hall girls to fill the local gambling emporium. While he's gone—surprise!—Pardner and Elizabeth fall in love. But instead of shooting Pardner when he gets back, Ben gruffly swallows his pride and agrees to share Elizabeth. So now she's married to both men (it's okay, she's a Mormon), and the three of them settle down in Ben's cozy cabin, where they find themselves doing a lot of "aw shucks" foot-shuffling over who sits where at supper and who sleeps where at night. It doesn't take long before the movie starts moseying around in lazy circles.

Yet if you could somehow overlook all the heavyweights at the helm—Joshua Logan directed, Paddy Chayefsky helped adapt the screenplay, André Previn provided additional music—*Paint Your Wagon* might not seem such a hapless endeavor. Indeed, it goes on for long, drawn out stretches without being particularly painful. But then, just when we're peacefully nodding off, someone breaks into song. That's when this movie becomes a memorable Megaton Bomb.

The worst offender, of course, is Marvin. And though it's possible that his tunes were included as comic relief, that doesn't make them any easier to sit through. During his finest moment (which seems like an hour) he slogs down a muddy street in the pouring rain singing, "I was born under a wandrin' star." He sounds like a bullfrog and looks like one too. At least Eastwood can sort of carry a tune, but unfortunately he is called upon to carry too many. "I still see Elisa whenever I dream of love," he croons, while strumming his guitar by a mountain stream. Later he belts out the unforgettable "I Talk to the Trees" (". . . but they never hear me"), lifting his voice to the treetops and beyond, while a plaintive look struggles to supplant his usual flinty frown. Finally, in a lighter vein, he sings "Gold Fever," a would-be honky-tonk number that he performs at a poker table with a suitably poker face. One can only guess how Seberg would have added to all this caterwauling. At some point, however, somebody decided that her songs would be dubbed by a real singer. The mind boggles at the thought of how bad she must have been.

The film's one legitimate singer is Broadway veteran Harve Presnell, who occasionally pops up out of nowhere to lend his booming baritone to the sagging sound track. Early on, he sings "They Call the Wind Maria," (the only song in the film anyone could hum afterward.) Later he resurfaces to lead a scruffy all-male chorus in a musical celebration of the women on their way into town. This is as close as *Paint Your Wagon* gets to a big production number. A few miners even dance brief little jigs, but let's just say it'll never be confused with *Seven Brides for Seven Brothers*.

As if all this mediocrity warranted the expense, the movie was shot in a custom-built boomtown, erected in a state of instant weather-beaten sham-

Eastwood and friend. At least the horse doesn't sing.

bles high in the Pacific Northwest. The mountain scenery does have a certain rugged appeal, but it comes at a steep price. Between the roaring rapids and that damned Maria blowing through the talking trees, we sometimes have to strain to pick up the dialogue. A blessing in disguise? Maybe, but if so, it doesn't extend to the songs, whose lyrics ring out all *too* loud and clear.

The nonmusical finale finds the town literally falling apart, after the miners have inadvertently eroded its foundations with underground tunnels. We can't help but be impressed by the sheer size of the debacle (Sodom and Gomorrah should have blowed up this good). But we also can't help but note that the town is a lot like the movie itself. Both are big, sprawling jerry-built constructions that completely collapse the moment Maria blows the wrong way. Or maybe it was all that huffing and puffing by Messrs. Marvin and Eastwood. In the end, it doesn't really matter which wind was responsible. *Paint Your Wagon* had blown it long before that last gust.

28

MYRA BRECKINRIDGE

1970 ⁁ Twentieth Century-Fox

Produced by Robert Fryer. Directed by Michael Sarne. Screenplay by Sarne and David Giler, from the novel by Gore Vidal.

CAST: Mae West (*Leticia Van Allen*); John Huston (*Buck Loner*); Raquel Welch (*Myra Breckinridge*); Rex Reed (*Myron*); Farrah Fawcett (*Mary Ann*); Roger Herren (*Rusty*); Jim Backus (*doctor*); John Carradine (*surgeon*).

WHICH IS THE VERY WORST Megaton Bomb of all? It very well might be *Myra Breckinridge*—a movie that set new standards in tacky costumes, oddball casting, sleazeball innuendo, and pseudo-avant garde incoherence. Based on Gore Vidal's satirical novel, it purports to lampoon the changing sexual rules (and roles) of a new generation, while also spoofing Hollywood's attempts to keep up with the changes. Along the way it throws in some radical ideas about rock and roll, higher education, and the American flag. That's a lot to chew on during one ninety-minute movie. But *Myra Breckinridge* chews away. It grinds all its themes into a lumpy mass—and then spits them back up.

Among its other dubious achievements, this movie marked the screen debut of self-styled film critic Rex Reed. In fact, that's him in the title role—more or less. Reed plays Myron Breckinridge, who, in the opening moments, undergoes a sex-change operation performed by ax-wielding John Carradine. After that, Myron becomes Myra, played by Raquel Welch. From there the movie goes downhill, head over high heels.

The "story" finds the newly female Myra journeying to Hollywood to seize her share of a rip-off acting school currently being run by her former cowboy star uncle, Buck Loner (John Huston). But Myra's real goal in life is the seduction and destruction of the macho American male, wherever she encounters him.

Raquel Welch as Myra Breckinridge.

What better place to start than with her own randy uncle? While Myra hangs around coercing Uncle Buck into coughing up half her rightful inheritance, Rex Reed's Myron hangs around with her, as a sort of conscience/alter ego. Myron is invisible to everyone except Myra, and Reed must have wished he was invisible to the audience as well. But he's really no more ridiculous than anyone else in the movie, and decidedly less than some—like for instance, the always game (and in this case gamey) Mr. Huston.

Wearing a twenty-gallon cowboy hat and perched on a stuffed palomino, Huston's Uncle Buck appears to have ridden in from a different, though equally awful, movie. As it turns out, that doesn't make him unique in this one. Done in an artless collage of disconnected scenes, *Myra* jumps around from Uncle Buck's deadbeat acting school, to various beds and boudoirs, to the office and lair of talent agent Leticia Van Allen (Mae West), a man-killing kindred spirit to the liberated Myra. As played by the seventy-year-old Miss West, Leticia is a show all by herself. And whenever she's onscreen, the movie stops dead in its tracks. It all but bumps and grinds to a halt as she auditions some hunky Hollywood hopefuls, who fill up her waiting room like a chorus line. One of these hunks is a young Tom Selleck, who gets singled out for special attention. "You impress me greatly," Leticia says, after rolling him across her casting couch. "I'll keep you in mind as a summer replacement. Next!"

Not to be outdone, Ms. Welch gets her own sacrificial movie virgin, a first-time actress named Farrah Fawcett. As dumb blond acting student Mary Ann, the future Angel finds herself in bed with our horny heroine, fending off tender advances. It's never quite clear whether Myra is lusting as a female or former male, nor does it seem to matter. Like everything else in this movie, the scene has no particular meaning because the filmmakers never bothered to provide one.

To further fragment this narrative, director Michael Sarne (or whoever actually did the final cut) frequently inserts footage from various vintage movies. In the process he manages to sully such icons as Marlene Dietrich, Gary Cooper, Clark Gable, and Marilyn Monroe. Presumably, these silver screen sex symbols were meant to complement and counterpoint the stinging satire unfolding in the main story line. But since there *is* no stinging satire— or any story line for that matter—the old film clips just rattle around, adding to the confusion.

Obviously, no one sensibility could have created such utter chaos. It took many cooks to spoil this mulligan stew. From behind-the-scenes we know that Sarne simply botched his assignment, and that the studio felt the need to perform a major cut-and-paste job to get the movie into some sort of shape. What isn't clear is why they thought their version was any more releasable.

What one takes away from this movie is a handful of random images, most of them ghastly. And most ghastly of all is the ancient Mae West, who was obviously encouraged to parody herself as a much younger movie star. With her hand still on her hip, West struts through scenes mentally undressing those male secretaries and tossing off those double entendres. Considering that she looks like an escapee from the Hollywood Wax Museum, such ver-

Mae West as Leticia Van Allen, who is always surrounded by boys. What does she *do* with them?

bal pelvic thrusting seems absolutely perverse. But in a movie that features Raquel, in a star-spangled cutaway bathing suit, sodomizing a cowboy stud with a strapped-on dildo, nothing Miss West does can come as any shock. By the time she belts out "Baby, give it to me now . . .", backed by a bad rock band and a gaggle of all-black chorus boys, we're ready to accept anything. We'll even believe that Raquel Welch is really Rex Reed. Or is it the other way around?

29

LOST HORIZON

1973 ⁍ Columbia

Produced by Ross Hunter. Directed by Charles Jarrott. Screenplay by Larry Kramer, from the novel by James Hilton.

CAST: Peter Finch (*Richard Conway*); Liv Ullmann (*Catherine*); Sally Kellerman (*Sally Hughes*); George Kennedy (*Sam Cornelius*); Michael York (*George Conway*); Olivia Hussey (*Maria*); Bobby Van (*Harry Lovett*); Charles Boyer (*High Lama*); John Gielgud (*Chang*).

I̲T'S SELDOM A GOOD IDEA to remake a famous movie. If that movie is famous, it was probably done right the first time. Still, Hollywood history is full of tragic mistakes by filmmakers who thought they could build a better mousetrap. Sometimes it's a hotshot director who thinks he has a brand-new vision of the material. More often it's simply a studio that can get remake rights more easily than it can find a surefire original idea. Then the thinking isn't a matter of "Well, it's already been done. Let's do something else," but a simple, pragmatic, "Well, it's already been done, so we know it works." Alas, in art as in nature, lightning rarely strikes in the same place twice. And it's especially difficult to repeat a past success when you tamper too much with the formula.

Producer Ross Hunter didn't just tamper with the *Lost Horizon* formula, he completely changed the chemistry. He updated the characters. He cast the wrong actors. He commissioned a drippy new script. Worst of all, he added songs—*bad* songs. What once had achieved sublimity through a delicately balanced suspension of disbelief became earthbound the second time around. This new *Lost Horizon* has no lightness, no lyricism, no magic. It has only its good intentions—and its bad songs.

As if to keep reminding us of the movie it used to be, the remake stays

Elegant Liv Ullmann leads a silly sylvan sing-along.

very close to the original story line. As before, a group of westerners escape a riot-torn Asian province, only to have their hijacked plane crash-land somewhere in the remotest Himalayas. Just when it looks like they're going to freeze to death, the group is rescued by fur-clad natives and taken through a mountain pass to a magical place where the sun shines, flowers bloom, butterflies are free, and people never grow old. It's Shangri-La!

Now, as we all know, Shangri-La isn't just paradise, it's paradise with a purpose. As High Lama Charles Boyer explains, it's the place where humankind's nobler instincts and achievements will be preserved in the event of the inevitable apocalypse. Thus, anyone who comes to live here can live forever in peace, harmony, and good health—provided they do so with the proper grace and humility. Yeah, it's all pretty pie-in-the-sky, but the original's director, Frank Capra, could make such lofty ideals seem positively idyllic. The remake's director, Charles Jarrott, just makes them seem idiotic.

But for sheer beatific idiocy, nothing beats that song score, by Burt Bacharach and Hal David. In the style of an operetta, the songs are direct extensions of the story line and dialogue—but considering the mealy-mouthed script by Larry Kramer, such fidelity is hardly a virtue. Bacharach's lachrymose melodies are bad enough, but combined with David's simpleminded sentiments they reach a new plane of banality. "The world is a circle without a beginning," goes one lyric. "The chance to live forever is really no illusion," goes another refrain. "Once you get here you may never want to leave," goes yet a third. As nine such numbers spill forth from the sound track, the film itself seems to last as long as a lifetime in Shangri-La. We, however, definitely want to leave.

The actors, on the other hand, are stuck there, and they don't look happy about it. The great John Gielgud dulls his slanted eyes and delivers quasi-mystical aphorisms. Burly George Kennedy frolics through flowers and fountains trying to maintain his balance, if not his dignity. Dour Michael York begins a doomed affair with earth mother Olivia Hussey (we know she's an earth mother because she's visibly pregnant). And nonromantic lead Peter Finch (in the Ronald Colman role) falls for nature girl Liv Ullmann (in the Jane Wyatt role), even though she sings some of the movie's worst songs. To make matters worse (or better?), Ullmann really isn't singing at all. She's lip synching, and all too obviously. Here is Ingmar Bergman's favorite tortured heroine, moving her mouth to someone else's voice while traipsing on a hillside, surrounded by squealing moppets, like some road-company Maria Von Trapp. Truly Bergman was right: God doesn't care—or at least He wasn't listening. But after watching this movie, we can't blame Him a bit.

SIGNS OF THE TIMES
Disaster Movies

America was in a funk during the seventies. It was just one thing after another: Vietnam, Watergate, the energy crisis—disco! How much could one decade take? Hollywood, however, had a remedy for all this enervating real life: disaster movies! What better way to forget your troubles than to watch an all-star cast wallow through soap opera subplots for the first two reels, only to have their personal problems dwarfed by a fire, flood or plane crash? The genre proper took off with *Airport* (1970) which established the formula for all others to follow: Take one stalwart hero, one lovely leading lady, one dastardly heel who is somehow to blame, one lonely spinster or bachelor, one cute little kid, one little doggy or kitty, and one kindly old couple who think they'll never see their grandchildren again, then throw them all into the center of the disaster and see who survives. Part of the perverse pleasure of watching these movies was knowing lots of these stock characters were going to colorfully perish. Another part of the fun was not really caring who lived or died, since everybody was a cipher or cliché, fleshed out only by the fatty tissue supplied by a cast of aging hams. The three *Airport* sequels alone provide a graphic illustration of how to abuse a formula—from the all-star *Airport 1975* (Charlton Heston, Dana Andrews, Myrna Loy, Gloria Swanson) to the non-star *Airport 1979* (Robert Wagner, Susan Blakely, John Davidson, Jimmie "J. J." Walker). But elsewhere in Hollywood, producers like Irwin Allen managed to hit even higher levels of camp before the genre finally went down in flames. From top to bottom:

The Poseidon Adventure (1972) Looking like a toy boat in a studio water tank (you don't suppose?), the S.S. *Poseidon* gets hit by a tidal wave and flips upside down. Within minutes several passengers have splattered on the ballroom ceiling and the best part of the movie is over. After that, the usual survivors slosh their way up through the bowels of the ship, purging their personal problems as they climb. Mad-at-God minister Gene Hackman gets all the heroic speeches, but the medal of valor goes to Shelley Winters, who performs a marathon swim through a flooded corridor with her cheeks puffed out like a blowfish and her dress billowing up over thrashing hammy thighs. Mayday!

The Towering Inferno (1974) Dastardly Richard Chamberlain orders inferior wiring for Paul Newman's brand-new skyscraper. Sure enough, fire breaks out on the night of the gala dedication. Faye Dunaway, William Holden, Fred Astaire, and Jennifer Jones are among the stars trapped up in the penthouse, while below, expendable extras spill from various elevators like so many crispy critters. To the rescue comes fire chief Steve Mc-

Stella Stevens, Ernest Borgnine, Jack Albertson, Shelley Winters, Red Buttons, Eric Shea, Carol Lynley and Pamela Sue Martin in *The Poseidon Adventure*.

Queen, with an assist from security guard O. J. Simpson, who saves two kids *and* a kitty from a smoke-filled suite. But even O. J. can't save that heel Dick Chamberlain, who claws his way over everybody, jumps on a jerry-built tram, and falls a zillion stories to his death. The heroes sometimes die in disaster movies—but the villains *always* do.

Earthquake (1974) A Richter-rattling quake reduces L. A. to rubble—then floods it!—during this Sensurround epic. But first, the standard soap subplots work up their own lather. Especially sudsy is Ava Gardner, as Charlton Heston's lushly alcoholic wife, who knows all about his affair with Genevieve Bujold. "Don't you dare lower your voice to me," Gardner growls, making an instant martyr of cheatin' Chuck. Meanwhile, in another part of the movie, Lorne Greene takes his own bite out of the debris-strewn scenery. "Take off your pantyhose, damn it!" he orders his secretary, commandeering her sensible nylons to rig a pulley system that will carry his stranded employees to safety. The survival instinct brings out the best and worst in everyone—even Hollywood scriptwriters.

When Time Ran Out (1979) In this aptly titled last gasp, a resort island volcano blows its top and an embarrassed all-star cast runs for cover. Among them: Paul Newman, Jacqueline Bisset, William Holden, James Franciscus in the Richard Chamberlain role, and Burgess Meredith, who wins the Shelley Winters award for carrying two kids across a burning bridge. Meanwhile, tidal waves are destroying strategic stretches of beach but leaving others untouched, and flaming chunks of lava are flying through the air like SCUD missiles, consistently finding the most deserving human targets. Hell hath no fury like a volcano with a moral agenda.

30

MAME

1974 ⸱ Warner Brothers

Produced by Robert Fryer and James Cresson. Directed by Gene Saks. Screenplay by Paul Zindel, based on the play by Jerry Herman, Jerome Lawrence, and Robert E. Lee, from the novel by Patrick Dennis.

CAST: Lucille Ball (*Mame*); Robert Preston (*Beauregard*); Beatrice Arthur (*Vera*); Bruce Davison (*older Patrick*); Joyce Van Patten (*Sally Cato*); Don Porter (*Mr. Upson*); Audrey Christie (*Mrs. Upson*); Kirby Furlong (*young Patrick*).

AT LEAST TEN YEARS TOO LATE—and playing to none of her strengths—Lucille Ball made the baffling decision to do a musical movie of the *Auntie Mame* story. The result couldn't have turned out more decrepit if it had been performed in junk store finery by the Home for Retired Vaudevillians. No one comes off looking good here, and no one comes off looking worse than star and centerpiece, Lucy.

With her close-ups filmed through a gauzy soft focus, Miss Ball seems almost embalmed. When she sings she croaks, when she dances she creaks, and unfortunately she does too much of both. Put her together with sidekick Bea Arthur, wearing a Theda Bara wig and makeup, and you've got as garish a pair of *grande dames* as has ever tried to salvage a lost cause.

As we know from the previous versions, Mame is a wealthy Prohibition Era matron who rescues her orphaned nephew from his stuffy Philadelphia upbringing, then raises him in New York City against the colorful backdrop of changing America. Along the way, Mame changes too—or at least her hair color does. Raising a kid through Prohibition, the Great Depression, and World War II will do that to a gal.

Lucy whips the all-male chorus line into a leaping frenzy.

The kid was played by Kirby Furlong, and there's a reason you haven't heard from him since. He isn't cute, he isn't funny, he makes no impression at all. Except when he sings. Then you notice how bad he is. Laboring through one solo, he actually looks as though he has got go to the bathroom; you begin to hate his parents for pushing him into a showbiz career. Fortunately he doesn't have to carry too many scenes. That's Lucy's job, and trouper that she is, she gives her all. But damned if director Gene Saks doesn't keep throwing her into impossible situations.

One nonmusical highlight befalls her during the Depression, which finds a bankrupt Mame working as a clerk in a department store. Down but not deflated, she catches sight of a well-to-do southern gentleman (Robert Preston), who comes in looking for a pair of roller skates. Batting her false eyelashes, Mame volunteers to model the skates, extending those aging gams as if she expected Preston to fall at her feet. The crazy thing is, he practically does. It's the beginning of a boring romance.

The movie's midsection takes place on Preston's Georgia plantation, where bohemian Yankee Mame sticks out like a cow in a china shop. The sight of her in a blond wig and frilly lavender dress is enough to curdle the mint

juleps. Almost as jarring is the sight of her in a jaunty riding outfit as she sets out on an old-fashioned fox hunt. Had a younger, spryer Lucy tackled this sequence it might have been the movie's high point. But of course, that's not even her astride the horse for most of a breakneck ride over hill and dale, only her stunt double.

Somehow, though, Mame overcomes these hurdles, and wins the approval of Preston's extended family. In fact, they're all so tickled that they gather for a grand production number, performing the famous title song from *Mame.* Suddenly, dozens of dancers in riding outfits (red for boys, black for girls) are springing across the great lawn in front of Preston's mansion. As our eyeballs spin, even more dancers spring into view, all singing the praises of their new in-law: "You charm the husk right off of the corn, M-a-a-a-m-e . . ." It's such a heady moment the movie never really recovers. From there on it unfolds in fits and starts, with musical numbers piled on top of each other, and the years flying by in bunches.

Before you know it, Mame's a wealthy widow (so much for second-billed Preston) slowly learning how to live again with the help of her wisecracking sidekick, Bea Arthur. Meanwhile, her nephew (now played by Bruce Davison) is all grown up and engaged to a snooty blue blood. And if you thought Mame's trip down south was a culture clash, wait'll you see her collision with old Connecticut money. Auntie's elaborate scheme to sabotage her nephew's impending nuptials is supposed to make us admire what a righteous dame she is. After all, her prospective in-laws are such boozy, bigoted country-clubbers. But what's really inspiring about the scheme is that it sets the stage for the third—and final—rendering of the *Mame* theme song. Considering all we've been through, it doesn't come an hour too soon.

It's sad to see a legend like Lucy wind down her career in such a lumbering white elephant. Yet you can't feel too sorry for her; she must have known there wasn't much left to add to a character that had already been played by Rosalind Russell and Angela Lansbury. She must have also known that she was way too far over the hill to even try. But she went ahead and did it anyway, and after she was through with the role, nobody would want to go near it again for a long, long time. To date, there have been no further incarnations of old Auntie Mame.

31

AT LONG LAST LOVE

1975 ⋅ Twentieth Century-Fox

Produced, written, and directed by Peter Bogdanovich.

CAST: Burt Reynolds (*Michael Oliver Pritchard III*); Cybill Shepherd (*Brooke Carter*); Madeline Kahn (*Kitty O'Kelly*); Duilio Del Prete (*Johnny Spanish*); Eileen Brennan (*Elizabeth); John Hillerman (*Rodney James*); Mildred Natwick (*Mabel Pritchard*).

Burt Reynolds isn't Fred Astaire. Cybill Shepherd isn't Ginger Rogers. But that didn't stop Peter Bogdanovich from casting them as the leads in this elaborate pastiche of thirties' musicals. Bogdanovich also cast Madeline Kahn, Eileen Brennan, and a young Romeo named Duilio Del Prete. None of them was exactly the song-and-dance-type, either. But in this movie they all sang. They all danced. They all laughed. But we didn't. When people embarrass themselves this publicly, the polite response is to avert one's eyes. Moviegoers did that in droves. The critics were not so kind.

It must have sounded great at the pitch meeting. Here you had a vintage romantic roundelay involving two attractive couples: You had Reynolds as a blasé playboy matched with Kahn as a Broadway star, and Shepherd as a madcap heiress matched with Del Prete as a carefree gambler. Then, halfway through, you had them all change partners and keep dancing, to the tunes of sixteen Cole Porter classics. In addition, you had a filmmaker who had made his considerable reputation directing pastiches of old movie genres (*Paper Moon, What's Up, Doc?*, etc.). And you even had a leading lady who had recorded an album of Porter songs entitled (no kidding) *Cybill Does it to Cole Porter.* Now if only someone had listened to what Cybill actually did

143

Duilio Del Prete, Cybill
Shepherd, Burt Reynolds,
and Madeline Kahn. Is
everybody doing the same
dance?

to Porter on that record, they might have paused to reconsider this project. Unfortunately, no one did. And so away we went.

What's so bad about this movie? It's hard to describe. Words can't adequately evoke the image of Shepherd clubfooting around her lavish apartment while warbling "I Get a Kick Out of You," or of Shepherd, Kahn, and Brennan lurching around the powder room during the dance number "Most Gentlemen Don't Like Love." Nor can the printed page reproduce the tones of Shepherd shouting, "You're the Top" while poking her head through a car sunroof, or of Reynolds flatly crooning, "At words poetic I'm so pathetic . . ." without apparent irony.

Indeed, apparent irony is one of the main things missing in this misconceived musical comedy. Bogdanovich later tried to deflect some of the critical brickbats by explaining that he intended the film to be a parody of those beloved old musicals. But that story just doesn't ring true. Parody usually requires highly skilled performers, people with talents either so refined that they can send up their subjects with the subtlest tic, or so richly abundant that they can take their burlesque right over the top. Bogdanovich's people have neither kind of talent. They can barely carry a tune, much less twirl one in midair. And when it comes to dancing, they can barely get out of their

From left to right:
**Madeline Kahn, Cybill
Shepherd, Eileen Brennan.**

own way, much less each other's. This makes it difficult to appreciate the
slapstick intent of many of the movie's terpsichorean interludes. When Shepherd gets herself tangled in some floor-to-ceiling drapes, we don't know
whether to laugh *with* her or *at* her, so we don't laugh at all.

As if it wasn't bad enough already, Bogdanovich stubbornly insisted that
his performers sing "live" on film, instead of recording their songs first, then
lip synching them later. Considering the voices involved, one might have assumed that Bogdanovich would want to doctor his sound track using any
studio magic available. But no. He had to do it the hard way, and his actors
suffer for his folly—as do we.

So what's to like about this movie? Try the gleamingly expensive Art Deco
sets, or the creamily monochromatic cinematography, or even the costumes—
all crisp dinner jackets and clingy gowns and stylish hats and smart spectator
pumps. But, of course, when you start praising a movie's costumes and cinematography, it's like saying your blind date was a really good dancer—except if she was in this movie, she probably wouldn't be.

In all the important ways, *At Long Last Love* is a major stiff. The fact that
it's all dressed up like *Top Hat* only calls attention to the gaping difference
between them. Adding insult to injury is what Cybill and the others do to

the music of Cole Porter. It's sort of like doing a spoof of Noel Coward by misquoting his repartee. Rule to make movies by: Never spoof anything really classy unless you have the class to pull it off. Bogdanovich didn't, and, indeed, after this, he seemed to lose his enthusiasm for slick pastiches of old movie genres. Unfortunately, nearly twenty years later, he still hasn't found an original style that consistently works for him. As he stumbles through the nineties directing duds like *Texasville* and *Noises Off* we can't help but wonder if he'll ever regain his balance.

32

THE BLUE BIRD

1976 ⁌ Twentieth Century–Fox

Produced by Paul Maslansky. Directed by George Cukor. Screenplay by Hugh Whitemore, Alfred Hayes, and Alexi Kapler, based on the play by Maurice Maeterlinck.

CAST: Elizabeth Taylor (*Light*); Jane Fonda (*Night*); Ava Gardner (*Luxury*); Cicely Tyson (*Cat*); Robert Morely (*Father Time*); Harry Andrews (*Oak*); George Cole (*Dog*); Tod Lookinland (*Tytyl*); Patsy Kensit (*Mytyl*); Nadezhda Pavlova (*The Blue Bird*).

ONCE UPON A TIME, when there was still a Soviet Union, the lands of the East and West would periodically forget their differences and reach out to each other in gestures of goodwill. Whether you called it *glasnost* or *détente* or some other official name, it generally resulted in a historic exchange of great mutual benefit, like a Strategic Arms Treaty, or the sale of tons of wheat, or a major artistic collaboration—like, say, *The Blue Bird*.

Based on a beloved Belgian fairy tale by Maurice Maeterlinck, *The Blue Bird* had twice before been made into a movie. The first try was a 1918 silent film that was quickly silenced by critics; the second was a 1940 Shirley Temple vehicle that turned out to be her first flop. Strange, then, that the material should be selected for the honor of being the first ever Soviet-American coproduction. Maybe a children's story, set in a fantasy land, with no possible political overtones was the only kind of tale that both sides could agree on. But if so, then why not *Alice in Wonderland, Pinocchio*, or some other surefire story? On second thought, what difference would it have made? Judging by how the Great Collaboration butchered *The Blue Bird*, any fairy tale probably would have suffered the same fate.

What went wrong? Everything. Combining some dazzling Hollywood

My outfit's dumber than yours! Cicely Tyson and Jane Fonda vie for the booby prize in *The Blue Bird.*

names with several distinguished Soviet performers—including members of the Kirov Ballet—*The Blue Bird* was so overstuffed with star power that it would have had trouble taking off under the best of circumstances. And these were not the best of circumstances. Filming took place in Leningrad, with a largely Soviet crew and the legendary George Cukor directing traffic with the help of a translator or two. The trouble was that the translators could interpret Cukor's directions in only a very general way. The poor Soviet crew members, already saddled with obsolete equipment and technical know-how ten years behind the times, never seemed to know exactly what Cukor wanted. So he didn't get it.

The result is one of the crummiest looking, crappiest sounding, big-budget musical fantasies ever made. Color tones don't match from one sequence to the next. Singers' lips aren't synched with the lyrics they're supposed to be singing. The Soviet actors' dubbed dialogue sounds it—and looks it, too. Such shockingly cheesy production values make it all the more difficult to see what's *really* wrong with this picture: the lugubrious pace, the forgettable

songs, the regrettable choreography—and the ballyhooed cast of screen dig-
nitaries who get brought out one at a time, like so many guest stars on a Bob
Hope Christmas special.

The sheer mass of the production crushed any hope for whimsy. And
whimsy is what was needed for *The Blue Bird* to soar. About two peasant children (Patsy Kensit and Tod Lookinland) who lament their impoverished lot in
life, the story takes these moppets on magical journey in search of the elusive
Blue Bird of Happiness. Their guide on the trip is the Queen of Light (Elizabeth Taylor in a jewel-encrusted white getup that looks like a leftover from
Boom!). "I am the light that makes men see the radiance in reality," she tells
them. But they follow her anyway. They have no way of knowing that, along
with the magic, they're going to be getting a lot of important life lessons.

Also along for the ride are various animals and inanimate objects that have
suddenly taken human form, which represents the liberation of their souls—
or something like that. Cicely Tyson leads the menagerie as Cat, dressed in
an outfit that might look more fitting as a little girl's Halloween costume.
Somehow, Tyson herself manages to avoid seeming utterly foolish, a fate not
escaped by George Cole as Dog, and various other American and Soviet performers as Bread, Sugar, and Milk.

Already you can see what a weighty bit of wonderment this is going to be.
But the going gets even weightier. The children's enlightening journey takes
them to such places as the Palace of Night and the Land of Memory, where
they wander around abstract theatrical sets and meet equally abstract characters such as Luxury (Ava Gardner), Father Time (Robert Morley), Maternal
Love (Ms. Taylor, in a second role), and Night (Jane Fonda in hooded black
garb that makes her look like Darth Vader's daughter). A couple of Kirov
dancers impersonate Water and Fire, veteran British actor Harry Andrews
sprouts up as an irascible oak tree, and Liz Taylor appears again, in a third
role, as a cackling witch. Last, but not least, is a fluttering flock of white
Russian pigeons all handpainted blue—because nobody could find any *real*
bluebirds in the Soviet Union.

After all this, is it any wonder that the children end up very glad to get
home? And does it come as any surprise that they discover the Blue Bird of
Happiness in their own backyard? It has been there all along! So has Ms. Taylor, in her *fourth*, and final role as the children's mother. And thank God she's

Elizabeth Taylor and Ava Gardner in their *Blue Bird* plumage.

there, for the sight of her in a peasant blouse and bonnet is one of the movie's very few delights.

Not surprisingly, *The Blue Bird* marked the premature end of Soviet-American movie collaborations. But it's probably not fair to blame the film for the ups and downs of superpower relations. World history being what it is, chances are détente would have hit the skids even if the two countries had collaborated on *E.T.* Let's just be grateful they didn't get together on *Star Wars.*

33

A STAR IS BORN

1976 ⋎ Warner Bros.

Produced by Jon Peters. Directed by Frank Pierson. Screenplay by John Gregory Dunne, Joan Didion, and Frank Pierson, based on a story by William Wellman and Robert Carson.

CAST: Barbra Streisand (*Esther Hoffman*); Kris Kristofferson (*John Norman Howard*); Gary Busey (*Bobby Ritchie*); Oliver Clark (*Gary Danziger*); Marta Heflin (*Quentin*); Paul Mazursky (*Brian*).

WHEN A STAR IS AT THE PEAK of her box-office power, there's no limit to what she can do. She can even remake a movie that's twice been a classic and make it a hit all over again. All she needs is a hit theme song, a leading man who hits the right chords, a boyfriend who happens to be the producer, and an ego colossal enough to overshadow them all.

In *A Star Is Born*, the star is Barbra Streisand, and remake or no remake, the movie is Streisand through and through. That's nothing new for a Streisand vehicle. (What would *Yentl* have been without her?) But this time around, that ego at the wheel drives the vehicle right off the track. In the process, she totals it. And yet, the whole spectacle is fascinating to behold, because Streisand really seems to think she's pulling it off. She's starring in a rock and roll version of a Hollywood success story, and she's *getting down*! But of course, she *isn't* really getting down. Streisand is Streisand. She couldn't win a getting-down contest if the competition was Karen Carpenter and Olivia Newton-John.

So it doesn't matter that serious writers Joan Didion and John Gregory Dunne were brought in to update the screenplay; that Kris Kristofferson was cast to provide bona fide rock star cachet; or that no expense was spared in setting up authentic concert sequences. The minute Streisand shows up, she

Barbra Streisand hogs the spotlight as *the* star of *A Star is Born*

sticks out like a sore thumb. But because that thumb is the biggest one on the screen, the rest of the movie stays under it. And the movie slowly dies there, barely even squirming.

Streisand is Esther, a struggling club singer who gets her big break—and meets the love of her life—when superstar John Norman Howard (Kristofferson) staggers into her gig and makes a drunken pass at her. Right away the movie is in big trouble because we can't figure out what he sees in her. She's up there belting out funky blues like, well, Barbra Streisand. The logical thing for him to do would be to pass out. Instead, he follows her home. A love affair is born.

Between candlelit bathtub interludes, John Norman launches Esther's career. He arranges unlimited studio time, helps her pick material, produces her first record with all the best session-men money can buy, and finally drags her out to sing a solo at one of his concerts—where she leaves the crowd screaming for more of her middle-of-the-road pop pap. Now, even in an era when Barry Manilow ruled, the idea that Esther's brand of easy listening could wow an arena rock audience is ludicrous, to say the least. Suddenly,

Streisand's attempts to pass herself off as a rock star stop seeming pathetic. Now they're getting downright insulting.

And it goes downhill from there. When Streisand isn't singing songs from the platinum sound-track album, she and Kristofferson are going through the motions of a soullessly slick love story. The movie's dreary middle is devoted to an idyllic honeymoon on John Norman's desert ranch, where the newly-weds make love, ride horses, wear Indian blankets, and have a beautiful life. Of course it can't last. No sooner does Esther say, "Do you realize how long it's been since you've seen anybody but me?" than, right on cue, a caravan of business associates drives up to their front door. It's the future intruding, and it doesn't include John Norman.

You know the rest. Esther becomes a big star. John Norman becomes a has-been. Esther hits the top of the charts. John Norman hits the bottom of a bottle. You know both he and the movie have sunk pretty low when a groupie stringer for *Rolling Stone* shows up at the ranch offering him a roll in the hay in exchange for an interview. Trying to impress John Norman, she keeps spouting inane anachronisms like "outasite" and "far out." For this they needed Joan Didion and John Gregory Dunne?

Actually, the screenwriters publicly disclaimed responsibility for the fin-ished movie, as did director Frank Pierson, who put the blame on Streisand and her producer-paramour Jon Peters. Surely they're being too modest. Surely they must have contributed their fair share of false notes. They must have had *something* to do with a revision of the old "James Mason-punches-Judy Garland-at-the-Oscars-scene," which starts with Tony Orlando handing Esther her Grammy award and ends with John Norman drunkenly crashing the party and hitting everyone in sight—*except* Esther.

On the other hand, it's hard to imagine that any card-carrying Hollywood Guild member could have conceived the hanky-wringing scenes following John Norman's car crash suicide. In one long wallow, Esther sits alone in their big old house, hears John Norman's voice playing on a cassette, then runs from room to room shouting, "John Norman, where are you?" Uh, Esther, he's dead, remember? Right after that, physically spent from all that running and shouting, she rails at her dear departed husband for telling her everything was going to be all right. "You promised! You lied! You lied!" she sobs, tearing that mischievous cassette tape into a million pieces.

Who really dreamed up those dramatic highlights? Who knows? Even Bar-

Streisand and Kris Kristofferson make a Southwest fashion statement.

bra Streisand movies are a collaborative art. However, there's no mistaking who's responsible for the big finale, an overwrought memorial concert for John Norman Howard, which naturally turns into a showcase for you-know-who. Singing songs supposedly written by her rock-legend husband, Esther majestically segues from tearful ballads to full tilt boogie, vamping and strutting and biting her lip and crossing her eyes and making one last attempt to *get down*! It's extremely embarrassing, watching Streisand make an ass of herself. Seeing this display, we suddenly understand why she avoided live performance for so many years. Unfortunately for her, this one has been preserved for posterity.

34

ORCA

1977 ◄ DeLaurentiis/Paramount

Produced by Luciano Vincenzoni. Directed by Michael Anderson. Screenplay by Vincenzoni and Sergio Donati.

CAST: Richard Harris (*Captain Nolan*); Charlotte Rampling (*Rachel Bedford*); Will Sampson (*Umilak*); Bo Derek (*Annie*); Keenan Wynn (*Novak*); Robert Carradine (*Ken*).

IN THE SIZABLE WAKE of Steven Spielberg's *Jaws*, moviegoers couldn't get enough of big fish stories—or so moviemakers seemed to think. In the summers after Spielberg's great white shark gobbled up the movie business, we were deluged with finny imitators, including three *Jaws* sequels, each more waterlogged than the last. There were also *Tentacles*, in which Henry Fonda, John Huston, and Shelley Winters tangled with a giant squid; *Barracuda*, starring a whole school of killer fish; *Tintorera*, featuring yet another marauding shark; and a couple of nifty spoofs of the whole sea craze, *Piranha* and *Alligator*. Some of these films were funny, some hilariously inept. All were essentially B-movie knockoffs, made for the quick cash-in.

Orca, however, was different. Presented by Dino DeLaurentiis with his usual prerelease fanfare, this killer whale story wasn't just meant to rip off *Jaws*, it was meant to blow it out of the water. At least that's what Dino would have had us believe. Of course, this was the man who thought his *King Kong* remake would put the original to shame. So much for his grip on reality. Still, with *Orca* he would outdo himself. Bloated, full of bilge, and bogged down with a truly bizarre variation of the *Moby-Dick* theme, *Orca* was the big fish movie that got away from its makers. It's not that the production went out of control (though it wasn't cheap or easy), it's that the

**Richard Harris makes like
Captain Ahab.**

movie itself—the story, the themes, and the characters—was completely over the edge. Looking at what's onscreen, it's hard to believe anyone thought *Orca* would float, much less make any money. Only one man could have had such faith—the one and only Dino.

The movie begins with commercial fisherman Richard Harris trying to capture a gigantic male orca and accidentally harpooning the whale's pregnant mate instead. From that moment on, our sympathies are with the whales, which makes it hard to care about any of the people onscreen. What makes it even harder is that most of them are jerks—sour, self-absorbed, and generally unpleasant. But just when you think you'd be safer in the water, the movie slaps on a layer of sentimentality thicker than ambergris, going all out to arouse our compassion for those cuddly carnivores of the deep. From the huge heartbreaking close-up of the surviving male's weeping eye, to a killer whale funeral procession into the setting sun, the film invokes all the clichés of a classic people tearjerker. But the scriptwriters don't stop there. Bringing on Charlotte Rampling as a marine biologist and Will Sampson as a noble Native American, the story piles up a curious confusion of scientific data and tribal folklore, all designed to provide a psychological profile of your typical killer whale. Unless you're a scientist yourself you may not know *what* to believe. But once sea captain Harris asks the local priest, "Can you commit a sin against an animal?" you know you've crossed over into *Jonathan Livingston Seagull* territory. And once the whale has launched his personal vendetta—with all the single-minded wrath of Charles Bronson in *Death Wish*—you know you've totally left the land of reality.

But the film does offer plenty of guilty pleasures, mostly from watching whale attacks that colorfully cut into the human population. First mate Keenan Wynn is an early casualty; he gets plucked right off the boat's bow by a leaping orca—just like a stunt at Sea World! After that, the humans stay on dry land. But this whale is a mammal with a mission—no body of land is going to stop him!

But the writers *do* slow him down, loading on a lot of time-wasting talk designed to spell out their Melvillean pretensions. "The whale is out there waiting. Just waiting," one local fisherman says. And sure enough, every so often the orca pops up in the harbor to give Captain Harris the evil eye— always in extreme close-up. As if poor Richard didn't feel guilty enough, the whole town is blaming him for the orca's reign of terror, urging him to sail out to sea and settle this thing so they can go back to fishing for a living.

But poor Richard just can't bring himself to kill his finny nemesis. He just wishes he could *talk* to the beast. "I'd tell him I didn't mean to kill his wife," Harris says, in all sincerity. "I'd tell him I was sorry." Harris, you see, can relate. He, too, once had a pregnant wife, and she was killed by a drunk driver. Okay, so she wasn't harpooned in her backyard, but hey, grief *is* grief.

However, such male-whale bonding isn't enough. As the orca starts leveling the entire town without ever leaving the sea (amazing what a few gas tanks at water's edge can do), Harris is quickly running out of options. "The monster's message to us is clear," Sampson says. "We must send him the captain or he will never leave us alone."

The last straw comes when the orca destroys the captain's dockside house, tipping the whole building sideways so that its contents—including costar Bo Derek—slide into the drink. Tearing off one of Bo's legs for good measure, the whale lays down a challenge even Harris can't refuse. Enough *is* enough! Anchor's aweigh!

The protracted finale finds Harris, Rampling, Sampson, and two expendable deckhands playing cat and mouse at sea with their favorite whale. First, one crew member gets swept off the deck, then the other disappears. And then there are only three (just like in *Jaws*) huddled around their underwa-

Harris hangs on for dear life while his nemesis, the orca, drags his whole house into the drink.

ter sound equipment, listening to the orca's broadcast from the briny deep. "What's he telling you?" Rampling actually asks. Harris can't quite put it into words.

The voyage finally ends up at the North Pole, where the whale makes a sacrificial meal of Sampson before rocking Harris and Rampling out of the boat. The two stars end up huddled on a chunk of ice, where Harris makes his last heroic stand. Just like Captain Ahab, he doesn't stand a chance. But after all this stubborn old salt has put us through, it's almost a pleasure to see the orca exact his revenge, bouncing poor Richard off the nearest iceberg with a flip of his tail. Giving us one last close-up, the orca swims away, alone but avenged, leaving the waters safe for Namu, Shamu, and Willy.

All things considered, we'd have to call this a happy ending, but it's really no cause for rejoicing. When a movie's this awesomely awful, there are no winners. Everyone and everything looks bad by association—even a natural wonder like a twenty-foot killer whale.

35

SEXTETTE

1978 ⸆ Crown International

Produced by Daniel Bridges and Robert Sullivan. Directed by Ken Hughes. Screenplay by Herbert Baker, based on the play by Mae West.

CAST: Mae West (*Marlo Manners*); Timothy Dalton (*Sir Michael Barrington*); Dom DeLuise (*Dan Turner*); Tony Curtis (*Alexei*); Ringo Starr (*Laslo*); George Hamilton (*Vance*); Alice Cooper (*Waiter*); Keith Moon (*Dress Designer*); Rona Barrett (*herself*); Regis Philbin (*himself*); George Raft (*himself*).

HAVING COME OUT of a quarter-century retirement to parody herself in *Myra Breckinridge*, Mae West decided to end the decade the way she began it—with one last self-lampooning screen role. Needless to say, at seventy-eight, she was considerably more decrepit than she'd been in her previous appearance. But even if she'd been half that age, at her peak in the late 1930s, *Sextette* would still have been a pretty creaky affair. Of course, she wouldn't have made this film in the 1930s. In those days, she had better material.

So what compelled Miss West to totter back in front of the camera to do this dying swan song? Think of it as a double ego stroke by the film's producers. Not only did they flatter her by asking her to star in their move, they also offered to adopt one of her own plays—in this case a flimsy little bedroom farce that had flopped when she tried to star in it, out of town, way back in 1961. A second chance times two! How could a lady refuse? For their sins the producers got just what they bargained for: Mae West *and* her play.

Of course, it's often hard to tell the two apart, for in spite of a sizable all-male case of costars, Mae *is* the play. She's the whole show. And though she goes by the name Marlo Manners in the movie, she's not fooling anybody. As usual, she's playing herself.

Sextette begins on Marlo's wedding day. It's her *sixth* wedding day, but

159

Mae West props herself up in her boudoir doorway. Can rigor mortis be far behind?

who's counting. With great fanfare, bride and groom pull up in front of their London luxury hotel, where hundreds of adoring fans have gathered to scream her name and catch a glimpse of her—even though she looks ancient enough to play the death scene from *She*. Indeed, as she is helped from her limo and slowly ushered into the hotel, we fear she'll trip over an extra and shatter before our eyes. Director Ken Hughes doesn't help matters, letting West mince forward for a few steps, then cutting to a shot of the crowd, then cutting back to West in a totally different place. He does this several times, lending a sense of disorientation to the entire procession. Then, while we're still waiting for things to stabilize, Hughes launches right into the movie's big production number, choreographed to the tune of "Hooray for Hollywood." As West gets shifted from place to place, bellhops and bystanders run up and down the main staircase, pausing every so often to let a crowd of reporters jump in and ask the star a loaded question—to which she wheezes ostensibly risqué rejoinders that sound as old as she looks. Sample question: "How do you like it in London, Miss Manners?" Sample answer: "Ooh, I like it anywhere." Replies like that are bad news for her new husband (Timothy Dalton), who stands by her side for support (in more ways than one), while staring straight ahead in an apparent daze. We just know he's contemplating their first love scene.

Luckily for him, this farce revolves around a classic case of *consummatus interruptus.* No sooner are the newlyweds ensconced in their honeymoon suite than various ex-husbands and lovers start barging in. There is also an international peace conference which requires Marlo's special brand of shuttle diplomacy, and a little matter of Marlo's dictated memoirs, the contents of which could embarrass just about every man in the hotel. As a result, there is so much coming and going that the newlyweds never get near the connubial bed. Dalton, however, doesn't get off scot-free. In one unforgettable interlude, he is called upon to serenade the bride with a painful rendition of the Captain and Tennille's "Love Will Keep Us Together." While Dalton winces his way through the verses, West gently sways to the beat, every so often chiming in with a well-timed "Whatevah." It's the kind of scene that leaves mouths agape.

Almost as astonishing is West's one-woman fashion montage, in which she models a succession of sequined gowns, tossing off a new quip with each costume change. "I'm the girl who works at Paramount all day and Fox all night," she tells dress designer Keith Moon. And the scary thing is she seems to be warming up!

Following the lead of its leading lady, the movie falls forward on shaky pinions, receiving a little boost as each ex-husband makes a token appearance. First comes Tony Curtis as Soviet diplomat "sexy Alexei," who invites Marlo up to his suite, then squanders the evening by endlessly quoting "the great Soviet poet Shakespeare." Duly inspired, West does a wobbly solo of "After I'm Gone," keeping one hand clamped on the doorknob, either to prolong her exit or to prop herself up.

After a brief fling with the U.S. Men's Olympic Team, it's onto the next ex-husband, Ringo Starr, a Czech film director who recruits Marlo for a scene rehearsal, then spends their time together yelling, "Cut! Cut! Cut!" Ringo is

Miss West does a duet with an unrecognizable Alice Cooper. What a time to forget his glam makeup!

such a bore that West can't be bothered singing another song. In fact, she seems to be dozing. But she perks up considerably when George Hamilton shows up as yet *another* ex-husband, who also happens to be a big-time gangster. "Is that a gun in your pocket, or are you just glad to see me?" she purrs. By this point, we'd have been disappointed if she *didn't* say it.

But it isn't over. Having gotten her second wind, West bounces back for two more numbers, singing "Baby Face" to a roomful of heads of state who are almost as old as she is, then vamping on the sidelines while a startlingly clean-cut Alice Cooper leads a chorus of maids and bellboys through a pseudo-disco production number involving Marlo's luggage. With the movie's so-called story line now hopelessly scattered in the wind, West and Dalton escape to his yacht, where they prepare to finally consummate their marriage. "You've done more for your country than Paul Revere," Dalton tells her, putting off climbing into bed. "Well . . ." Miss West replies, "I'm looking forward to saying the same thing he said. 'Umm, the British are *coming*!' "

Thankfully, we're spared *that* spectacle. For the next sight we see a lonnggg cannon discharging as Dalton's lonnggg yacht sails out to sea. Full steam ahead! Good old Mae, she always did like to leave a little to our imagination, even if she left little doubt as to what we were supposed to be imagining. In this case, of course, a little bit goes a lonnggg way. The mind's eye reels at what might be going on down in the hold of that yacht. Whatevah!

36

Sgt. Pepper's Lonely Hearts Club Band

1978 ⁴ Universal

Produced by Robert Stigwood. Directed by Michael Schultz. Screenplay by Henry Edwards.

CAST: Peter Frampton (*Billy Shears*); Barry Gibb (*Mark Henderson*); Robin Gibb (*Dave Henderson*); Maurice Gibb (*Bob Henderson*); Donald Pleasence (*B.D. Brockhurst*); Sandy Farina (*Strawberry Fields*); Dianne Steinberg (*Lucy*).

BASED ON THE BEATLES' ALBUM that changed rock and roll, *Sgt. Pepper* was producer Robert Stigwood's ambitious follow up to his twin blockbusters, *Saturday Night Fever* and *Grease*. After the multimedia success of these two movies, Stigwood must have felt that he (and only he) had his finger on the pop pulse of the seventies. He must have assumed that anything he did would turn to gold and platinum. *Sgt. Pepper* is resounding proof that he was wrong. It brought Stigwood down to earth with such a crash that he never really got up again.

After suffering through this piece of blatant commercial claptrap, it's satisfying to contemplate how utterly it failed. It's also mystifying how anyone, even an arrogant mogul with illusions of infallibility, could have thought he could fob this off on the moviegoing public. Stigwood had no actors, no characters, no "book"—no ideas, really. His movie was little more than an extended revue featuring a far too ample repertoire of Beatles compositions— all bungled, butchered and bad mouthed by a bunch of Fab Four wannabes.

The main culprits are Peter Frampton and the Bee Gees, who portray descendants of the original Sgt. Pepper's band. As they act out the movie's barely discernible story line (giving barely discernible performances), they sing one Beatles classic after another, maintaining such slavish fidelity to the original arrangements that they only call attention to what's lacking in their

From left to right, Peter Frampton and the Bee Gees.

renditions. Hey, these guys are all pop stars in their own right; were they really so awed by the songs that they couldn't try one their own way?

Somewhat better are such guest performers as Alice Cooper, Aerosmith, and Earth, Wind and Fire, who at least put their own spins on old Beatles favorites. Also chirping in are various members of the supporting cast, who try interpreting Lennon and McCartney in what can only be called suicidal career moves. Not surprisingly, the whole lot is put to shame by none other than George Burns, who handles the mid-tempo "Fixing a Hole" like the old vaudevillian he is. His brief, doddering soft-shoe offers more showmanship than Frampton and the Bee Gees can muster in the whole movie.

Indeed, whenever they're not performing music, Frampton and the Brothers Gibb have little to do, and even less to say. True to its revue form, the move shuffles its characters from one scene to the next, relying on the songs to tell the whole story. Thus we watch as the boys move from Heartland, U.S.A. to big bad Hollywood, where they fall into the clutches of an evil mogul (Donald Pleasence), then escape back to their hometown just in time

to rescue their neighbors from a ruthless real estate developer. It's a good old-fashioned melodrama—as told through songs written years apart, with nothing in common except their composers.

So much for the way the movie sounds. The way it *looks* is even more of a mess. All ice cream colors and marmalade skies, the visual scheme is a riot of ostentatious artificiality: There *is* no visual scheme. We sit, undazzled, as the performers trip through one pre-MTV production number after another, trying to seem involved—or at least alive—while the scenery does all the acting. It's all too obvious that the filmmakers were trying to ape the pop-absurdist style of *Help!*, but they only manage to make us wish we were watching a *real* Beatles movie. Any Beatles movie! Even *Magical Mystery Tour*.

*Sgt. Pepper'*s final insult is a reprise of the title tune featuring a motley crew of stars who showed up to sing in the chorus. Faces in the crowd include

Tina Turner, Peter Allen, Gwen Verdon, Chita Rivera, Carol Channing, Connie Stevens, Keith Carradine, Frankie Valli, Helen Reddy, José Feliciano, Bonnie Raitt, Johnny Winter, John Mayall, Etta James, Donovan, Wolfman Jack, Monti Rock III, Seals and Crofts, Sha Na Na, Peter Noone of Herman's Hermits, and Mark Lindsay of Paul Revere and the Raiders. Those who still had careers look vaguely sheepish, standing there. Those who were washed-up look like they actually want to be heard. The former *should* be concerned, the latter shouldn't bother. *Sgt. Pepper* is the sort of abomination that takes people down with it—maybe just a peg, or maybe into a bottomless pit. Just ask Robert Stigwood. Or Peter Frampton.

SIGNS OF THE TIMES
Rock Operatics

Sgt. Pepper, the album, revolutionized rock. Suddenly, the music parents loved to hate had become respectable. Even *Time* magazine had declared it art! Now, in the Beatles' hands, maybe it was. But when other, less talented bands tried their hands at ambitious "art-rock" song cycles what we usually got were bloated, bombastic "concept albums." And yet, the more operatic rock music got, the more the mainstream embraced it. And the more the mainstream embraced it, the more rock embraced the mainstream. Under these happily homogenized circumstances, it wasn't long before Hollywood started looking to rock as the last, best hope for reviving the moribund musical tradition. Instead, rock musicals provided the final nail in the coffin. How could it have been otherwise? If corporate-minded record companies didn't know what to do with dinosaur rock, what chance did corporate-owned studios have? You saw what they did to *Sgt. Pepper*. Now look what they did to *Tommy*'s songs, Ma.

Jesus Christ Superstar (1973) Andrew Lloyd Webber's rockin' take on Our Saviour's final days plays on the screen like an amateur theater production. Sourpuss Jesus (Ted Neely) screeches his preachments at the top of his lungs. Glowering Judas (Carl Anderson) unwittingly impersonates Elvis in a spangly white jumpsuit. Black-clad Pharisees skulk along the sidelines like a race of Rasputins. And on top of all that nobody can sing. Of course, if you had to wrap your tongue around Tim Rice's banal lyrics and Lloyd Webber's Vegas-style orchestrations, *you'd* have trouble singing, too.

Michael Jackson (before plastic surgery) as the Scarecrow in *The Wiz*.

Tommy (1975) Between character assassinations of classical composers (*Mahler*, *Lisztomania*), Ken Russell attacked the Who's famous rock opera about that deaf, dumb, and blind kid who sure plays a mean pinball. The result is a sensory overload that only Tommy could love. See Roger Daltrey act! Hear Jack Nicholson sing! Feel Ann-Margret roll around in chocolate sauce! Add Elton John as the Pinball Wizard and Tina Turner as the Acid Queen and, well, *Tommy* will never be the same. But hey, it could have been worse—it could have been the Broadway show.

The Wiz (1978) Sidney Lumet tackles the funky Broadway update of *The Wizard of Oz*— and wrestles it right to the ground. The scene of the crime is New York, here rather garishly reimagined as a musical fantasy land. Easing on down those glitzy streets are Diana Ross as a Harlem schoolteacher named Dorothy and Michael Jackson as the Scarecrow. Maybe it all would have been more convincing if they'd simply switched roles.

The Wall (1982) Director Alan Parker interprets Pink Floyd's dark side in this lugubrious account of a rock star's mental breakdown. Real-life rocker Bob Geldof shaves off his eyebrows and demolishes his hotel room, while unhappy childhood flashbacks and hallucinatory animated sequences hit us over the head at random intervals. It's just like MTV, only bigger. And slower. Much . . . much . . . slower.

37

1941

1979 ⁴ Universal/Columbia

Produced by Buzz Feitshans. Directed by Steven Spielberg. Screenplay by Robert Zemeckis and Bob Gale, from a story by Zemeckis, Gale, and John Milius.

CAST: Dan Aykroyd (*Sergeant Tree*); Ned Beatty (*Ward Douglas*); John Belushi (*Wild Bill Kelso*); Tim Matheson (*Birkhead*); Toshiro Mifune (*Commander Mitamura*); Robert Stack (*General Stillwell*); Treat Williams (*Sitarski*); Nancy Allen (*Donna*).

ANYBODY CAN MAKE A BAD MOVIE, even a whiz kid like Steven Spielberg. Of course, back in the late seventies, he hadn't actually made one yet. After *Jaws* and *Close Encounters of the Third Kind*, it was easier to assume that he could make any kind of movie he wanted and make it good. So Hollywood let him try. Gave him carte blanche. Told him to shoot the works, no matter how big the budget got. Now, in this day and age, we know that's how studios get into trouble. But this was the seventies, a more innocent time, a time before *Heaven's Gate* and *One From the Heart*. It was the era of the director as God, of filmmakers who could fulfill their most flamboyant visions just by saying "Roll 'em." Well, in *1941*, Spielberg rolled 'em, all right. Rolled 'em and emptied their pockets.

Where did the money go? That's no big mystery. In *1941*, it's all up there on the screen. The trouble is it's being burned up. Thrown away. Flushed right down the toilet. It's being *wasted*. Never before had so much serious cash been so frivolously spent. Nor would it again until at least 1980, when *The Blues Brothers* came out. In that sense, *1941* was ahead of its time—an eighties movie made in the seventies.

What makes it all the worse is that the film had a potentially good idea. Set just after Pearl Harbor, the story is an ambitious attempt to parlay a cou-

John Belushi makes one of
many crash landings in
1941.

ple of historical anecdotes into the stuff of vivid revisionist history. First, let's consider the anecdotes: Back in the early days of World War II, some southern Californians spotted what looked like a Japanese submarine just off the coast. Word spread like wildfire, and pretty soon everybody was running down to the beach with binoculars in their hands. Along about the same time, someone mistook a private plane for an enemy bomber, touching off a small chain reaction of civilians peppering the sky with shotguns and deer rifles. Now, imagine if these isolated pockets of paranoia had somehow got connected and snowballed into mass hysteria. Spielberg did just that. He imagined a stupendous pull-out-the-stops spectacular, half Fourth of July, half *War of the Worlds*. The action had to be big and the laughs bigger. We're talking huge-scale slapstick here, and as Spielberg labored to pull it off, no submarine, city block, or lady's skirt was left unturned.

The movie begins with promise, cleverly spoofing the opening scene from Spielberg's own *Jaws*: Just like in *Jaws*, a pretty blonde, swimming alone in the ocean, is suddenly yanked below the surface, then violently pops up again. Only this time she's not in the mouth of a shark; she's on the periscope of a (Japanese!) submarine. It's actually full of bumbling sailors who are way off course and lost, but no matter. Once they make their presence known all hell breaks loose. Citizens panic. Armed forces mobilize. The Japanese totally freak. And weapons and vehicles of all shapes and sizes take on lives of their own.

Call it the comedy of destruction carried to absurd extremes. It starts small and simple, with plates breaking and soup splashing, then quickly escalates to colossal proportions. The slapstick set pieces are so enormous that you can see them building a mile down the road. Of course, if there's a warehouse full of paint, a tank will have to plow through it, exploding every paint can on impact. Of course, if a plane has to make a crash landing, it will do so down Hollywood Boulevard. Of course if there's a house on a hill overlooking the Pacific, it will get blasted off its foundation and tumble into the ocean. And of course, if there's a ferris wheel at a seaside amusement park, the Japanese will take a pot shot and send it rolling, like a giant lit-up wagon wheel, off the end of a long pier.

But those are just the biggest bangs. Almost from the start, Spielberg stuffs his movie with bombs, brawls, bumps on the head, guns going off, mouths going off, and clothes coming off. For sheer, sustained volume, this is the all-time champ. Yet all that sound and fury signifies nothing, because as slapstick it's a total misfire. Maybe it's because he's working on such a large scale, or maybe it's because he's not Charlie Chaplin, but Spielberg's physical humor lacks the timing, the touch, the kinetic pop. It's just stuff crashing together and blowing up. It's just not funny.

All this might not have seemed so oppressive if the people in the foreground weren't such gross caricatures. But, of course, they're larger than life too, and just as loud. All the actors seem to think they have to overdo it, just to be heard and seen above the din—and above each other. John Belushi belches and bellows as a maverick fighter pilot. Dan Aykroyd babbles and blathers as a shell-shocked commander. Treat Williams rants and raves as a hotheaded sergeant. Tim Matheson leers and leches as a horny soldier. Nancy Allen plays it dumb and dumber as a general's secretary who only gets off in the cockpit of a B-17. And then there is Ned Beatty as a zealously patriotic private citizen, Murray Hamilton and Eddie Reese as two drunken rubes with loaded rifles, and Slim Pickens as a hick junk peddler who spends most of his screen time sitting on the john because the Japanese want a compass he swallowed. Talk about bathroom humor. This movie's got it—along with juvenile insults, macho epithets, and sexual innuendoes broad enough to drive a truck through. They don't do that, of course. Why use a truck when you can use a plane?

Spielberg puts forth a yeoman's effort to yank all these people and subplots together. But the best he can do is send everybody racing out of a burning

Dan Aykroyd and John Candy (*center*) chow down. Can anything follow but a food fight?

Los Angeles to converge at that house on the hill—just in time to watch it groan, collapse, and crash into the sea. You have to hand it to him, though. After sitting through this high-decibel debacle, you really *do* feel as if you were there. Your ears ring for days.

As if *1941* wasn't bad enough in itself, it also helped inspire a noisy new era of oversize action comedies that ended with a bang because they couldn't think up a third act: from *The Blues Brothers*, which trashed every car in Chicago for its big finale, to *Howard the Duck*, which went literally out of this world for its cataclysmic climax. Call them wall-of-sound comedies: They try to blast you out of your seat so that maybe you won't notice how puny they truly are.

38

CAN'T STOP THE MUSIC

1980 ⌃ Associated Film Distribution

Produced by Allan Carr, Jacques Morali, and Henri Belolo. Directed by Nancy Walker. Screenplay by Bronte Woodward and Carr.

CAST: Valerie Perrine (*Samantha*); Bruce Jenner (*Ron*); Steve Guttenberg (*Jack*); Paul Sand (*Steve*); Tammy Grimes (*Sydney*); June Havoc (*Helen*); Barbara Rush (*Norma*); and the Village People (*as themselves*).

AFTER *SATURDAY NIGHT FEVER* became a huge hit—both as a movie *and* a multiplatinum soundtrack album—Hollywood couldn't wait to duplicate the formula, churning out several more similar-but-different disco-era musicals. The first to glitz up the screen was *Thank God It's Friday*, and that was utterly forgettable. The next was *Can't Stop the Music*, and that was too outlandish to be forgotten. There are moments in this movie that lodge themselves in your memory bank, never to be purged, and yet you find yourself wanting to see them a second time because you can't quite believe what you think you just saw.

Unfortunately, between those memorable moments this is a truly inept amateur hour. Loosely conceived along the lines of an old let's-put-on-a-show musical, the movie is populated by actors who can't sing, singers who can't act, singers who can't sing, and actors who can't act. Put them all under the supervision of self-styled impresario Allan Carr (whose main claim to fame was lucking out as the producer of *Grease*) and first-time director Nancy Walker (whose main claim to fame was playing Rosie the Bounty paper towel picker-upper) and you've got a movie that had no business being any good. And it didn't do any good business either.

When Steve Guttenberg quits his record store job and boogies down Broadway on roller skates, we know we're in for a bumpy ride—and the

Valerie Perrine makes like a maraschino; the Village People drink it all in.

opening credits aren't even over yet! Soon enough, however, our worst fears are confirmed. Guttenberg is, indeed, the movie's protagonist, an aspiring composer-producer who gets a shot at overnight success—if he can assemble a singing group overnight. Fortunately, relief arrives in the voluptuous form of Valerie Perrine. She's Guttenberg's strictly platonic roommate (wouldn't *you* be?), and she's also a retired supermodel with a record mogul ex-boyfriend *and* a knack for meeting people who'd be just perfect for a singing group. Since all these people live in Greenwich Village, you might even call them Village people. A group is born.

And what a group they are! There's one who dresses like a cowboy, one who dresses like an Indian, one who dresses like a soldier, one who dresses like a construction worker, one who dresses like a cop (and really *is* a cop), and one who dresses like a leather biker, although he's really a New Jersey Turnpike toll collector. However, he can sing "Danny Boy" like Dennis Day. At least *someone* in the group can sing.

Of course, since all these guys are at least implicitly gay, it sort of leaves a hole in the traditional boy-girl romance department. For balance (and box office) the picture needed a handsome, red-blooded all-American leading man, someone for Perrine to wrap her ample self around during the quiet moments. Who better than Olympic decathlon champ Bruce Jenner, in his first (and last) screen role, as a button-down tax attorney who flops around

The Village People *front and center*) spearhead a bevy of boys.

in this milieu like a cold fish out of water. "Your friends are a little far out for me," he carps to Perrine. But, of course, even the Bee Gees would be a little far out for him.

The script makes lame attempts to turn this bunch of loose screws into a screwball comedy, but all that nontalent keeps getting in the way. Director Walker herds the cast from apartments to offices to studios to nightclubs, where they mill around chirping their lackluster one-liners at an unvarying pitch. When we're lucky, the dialogue gets lost in the din of the disco scenes. At least when we can't hear what anyone's saying we don't waste time trying to make sense of nonsensical chitchat.

All of this—even Jenner's clodhopping performance—is quite forgettably bad. What makes this movie a memorable Megaton Bomb is its handful of high-camp production numbers, which combine to give new meaning to the movie's title. You can't stop the music when it's over the top. The only question is which of these production numbers goes furthest beyond the pale. Is it the S & M fantasy sequence, featuring the construction worker Village Person and a bevy of ice beauties in blazing red dresses, who bite and scratch and pierce the poor boy with their stiletto heels? Is it the "YMCA" center-piece, starring scores of studs stripped down to their gym shorts (and beyond) as they box, wrestle, play racquetball, pump iron, take showers, and dive side-ways into the pool, à la Esther Williams? Or is it the grand finale "Libera-tion," in which the boys from the Village sing "We won't let small minds stand in our way," while prancing around in blinding white versions of their regular costumes? Faced with such a cavalcade of kitsch, who could choose?

At moments like these, *Can't Stop the Music* rises above its general tacki-ness to become truly glittering trash. Indeed, it's almost worth wading through the rest of this mess just to get a look at the musical "highlights." Not that too many moviegoers did. By the time the film was released, in summer 1980, the disco era had already begun to fade. No one was breath-lessly waiting for a suddenly out-of-vogue musical. Nevertheless, Allan Carr launched its $20 million baby with a big promotional splash—and it promptly sank. Several promising careers got sucked down with it. After such a high-fatality disaster, any other producer would have hung his head in shame and quit the business. Instead, Allan Carr stuck around to put to-gether such future failures as *Grease II* and *Where the Boys Are '84.*

Can't stop the music, indeed.

39

XANADU

1980 ‹ Universal

Produced by Lawrence Gordon. Directed by Robert Greenwald. Screenplay by Richard Christian Danus, Marc Reid Rubel, and Michael Kane.

CAST: Olivia Newton-John (*Kira*); Gene Kelly (*Danny McGuire*); Michael Beck (*Sonny Malone*); James Sloyan (*Simpson*); Dimitra Arliss (*Helen*); Katie Hanley (*Sandra*); Sandahl Bergman (*a muse*).

THE SAME SUMMER THAT SAW *Can't Stop the Music* also saw this misbegotten mishmash, obviously produced by people who only think of movies as "packages." The main elements of this one are Gene Kelly, Olivia Newton-John, the rock band Electric Light Orchestra, and a fleeting fad known as roller disco. Put them all together in a loose remake of *Down to Earth*—in which Rita Hayworth played the Greek muse Terpsichore, who descended to earth to save a Broadway show—and you've got an even more dismal affair than can be imagined sight unseen.

Still, just looking at those elements on paper, you know they can't add up to anything good. That's what makes it so surprising that this project ever got off the ground. Any idiot could have looked at the movie's game plan and known it couldn't work. Apparently, however, the producers didn't have any idiots to advise them, and so they made all the decisions themselves. Let's look at the mistakes they made.

Mistake No. 1: Inexplicably convinced that Michael Beck was an actor, the producers cast him in the central role, as a struggling young artist who thinks he can find fulfillment by opening up a dance club.

Mistake No. 2: Foolishly thinking that Olivia Newton-John was the reason *Grease* was a hit, the producers put her in the retooled Rita Hayworth

"Singing in the Rain"? Not quite. Gene Kelly (*right*) grins and bears it, alongside Michael Beck and Olivia Newton-John.

role, as a roller-skating muse who descends from a wall mural to inspire our young hero.

Mistake No. 3: Suspecting that these two kids would need some professional help, the producers lured Gene Kelly out of semiretirement to play a former big band clarinetist who fulfills his dream of running a nightclub by becoming Beck's business partner.

Mistake No. 4: Obviously trying to appeal to young and old alike, the producers dreamed up a nightclub that was half forties swing, half eighties disco. In a production number intended to provide an embarrassment of riches— but instead is just an embarrassment—the two halves of the nightclub come together in a battle of bands and chorus lines. As we cut between forties glamour and eighties glitz, the sets merge, the singers converge, and all hell breaks loose. After a couple of minutes of this chaos, we begin to feel the physical need for a nice quiet Chopin nocturne.

Of course, entrusting the score to the Electric Light Orchestra was no way to make a musical soar. Dinosaurs even in their own time, these synthetic pseudo-classical rockers specialized in flatulently overproduced compositions that were hard enough to hum along with, much less dance to. Nevertheless, the people in this movie dance to them—or at least they try. When they aren't dancing, they're roller skating. Even Gene Kelly gets into the act.

It's far too painful to discuss the sight of Kelly—so classy, yet so past his prime—as he stiffly goes through the motions of these primitive production numbers. To see him skating around in circles, bombarded by colored lights, clapping his hands and shouting, "Go!" is to fall into a deep depression. But that's nothing compared to the despair you'll feel as he goes on a wardrobe shopping spree, modeling zoot suits, jump suits, cowboy hats, and Hawaiian shirts in a gaudy montage guaranteed to disrupt your equilibrium.

But at least Kelly had some dignity to lose. Beck and Newton-John were dubious to begin with, and their very presence drags dreary musical interludes down even lower. The effect can be positively desultory, as it is during their dance in an empty recording studio against a superimposed Manhattan skyline. Arms linked, the two stars do long lackadaisical sweeps around and around the room. This is no doubt supposed to be dreamy and lyrical, but it's more like watching two people swim laps. When it's finally over they sigh and smile. "That was great," she says. "*You* were great," he says. Did we miss something?

But wait, there's more. In a relative highlight, animated versions of Beck and Newton-John frolic through a cartoon wonderland, gliding through verdant woods, over a glistening lake and across a moonlit sky. It's like a cheap imitation of Disney, circa *Cinderella*. Even so, it's a letdown when "reality" intrudes, popping these cartoon figures back into human form.

There's just no getting around it, the movie's two stars just aren't star material. Beck is all wrong for a would-be musical fantasy. Sometimes angry, sometimes just glum, he acts (make that carries on) as if he's in a gritty street drama. If he really were, of course, he'd be in way over his head. Meanwhile, Newton-John is as close to nonexistent as a pretty girl can be. Her acting is one-dimensional, her singing hardly better, and try as she might, she simply can't dance. She visibly loses her footing during one big production number. Very embarrassing for a modern-day Terpsichore.

But even Gene Kelly and Rita Hayworth at their peak couldn't have saved this movie. It's so utterly brainless it almost seems deliberate—as if the producers thought they *had* to stoop this low to hit their target audience. The

Olivia and her chorines vamp their way through a vintage forties number.

Olivia and her chorines vamp their way through a vintage forties number.

tip-off comes during a scene in which Newton-John tries to convince Beck that she is, indeed, a muse. Together they look up *muse* in the dictionary, so all the stupid kids who were supposed to go see this movie would know what the hell a muse was.

Maybe it's the filmmakers who didn't know what a muse was. Considering the absence of inspiration here, it's a distinct possibility. But regardless of how they did it, they managed to carve a permanent place for themselves in the history of Megaton Bombs. *Xanadu* represents the absolute nadir of the American movie musical. If there's a worse one yet to come, let's hope we're all dead and gone before it gets here.

40

HEAVEN'S GATE

1980 ⁴ United Artists

Produced by Joann Carelli. Written and directed by Michael Cimino.

CAST: Kris Kristofferson (*Marshal James Averill*); Christopher Walken (*Nate Champion*); John Hurt (*Billy Irvine*); Isabelle Huppert (*Ella Watson*); Sam Waterston (*Frank Canton*); Jeff Bridges (*John Bridges*); Brad Dourif (*Eggleston*); Joseph Cotten (*the Reverend Doctor*).

MANY A FAILED BLOCKBUSTER has put its studio in the red (see *Cleopatra*), but few have literally destroyed a movie company the way *Heaven's Gate* did United Artists. Costing upwards of $50 million—and making back one or two—the movie sent the studio into a tailspin from which it never recovered. But it was more than just the lost money that made this such a colossal folly. It was the blind faith of executives, the blind ambition of director Michael Cimino, the wretched excess of every aspect of production, and the reckless abandon on every level of filmmaking—from the narrative flow to the character motivation to the chaotic crowd scenes. Making it all seem sadder are the occasional bursts of brilliance that suggest that, somewhere in this undigested—and undigestible—material, there was a good movie struggling to take shape.

You know a film is in trouble when it lists four editors in the opening credits. But then you learn that Cimino shot some five hundred hours of footage and you marvel that four editors were enough to get the job done—not that they did so very satisfactorily. At its original running time of 220 minutes, *Heaven's Gate* remained a shapeless, sluggish slog through a murky time and place inhabited by people we never feel we know.

The movie gets off to a grand romantic start, yet gorgeous as it is, it proves to be a harbinger of all that will keep going wrong. The scene is Harvard

Kris Kristofferson is looking a little glassy-eyed. Is Michael Cimino telling him he wants to do one more take?

1870, where a class of idealistic young men is graduating with great fanfare. They march across the hallowed grounds and assemble in a great hall. They listen to blowhard speeches and give a few themselves. They waltz with beautiful women to Strauss's "Blue Danube." They brawl and bond and sing of their alma mater, drunk with the promise of the future. The whole ritual takes nearly half an hour, and if Cimino had just cut the number of reaction takes during commencement alone, he could have shrunk the sequence by half.

Don't worry, there are over three hours to go. And Cimino needs every minute of that time to tell the story of how immigrant farmers fight for their slice of the American Dream, even though wealthy ranchers would rather shoot them than share it. Based on the Johnson County War of 1892, the movie doesn't lack for epic potential, but for all his passion and political correctness, Cimino has a great deal of trouble dramatizing his history lesson. While his innocent, huddled masses remain faceless and nameless in the background, the director fills the foreground with halfhearted revisions of old-fashioned Hollywood stereotypes. The most blatant is Sam Waterston as the county's wealthiest rancher, who couldn't be more villainous if he called himself Snidely Whiplash. He dresses in black. He has a mean little mustache. He even sneers on cue. He does everything but tell the settlers they must pay the rent.

But at least we know where Waterston stands. Far more fashionably ambiguous is the movie's hero, Kris Kristofferson, a strong, silent, vaguely disillusioned lawman who *sort of* tries to help the settlers when the ranchers put a bounty on their heads. One reason Kristofferson doesn't get much accomplished is that he spends so much time in a traditional romantic triangle involving feisty frontier madam Isabelle Huppert and ruthless gun-for-hire Christopher Walken. These three do a lot of hemming and hawing about who's gonna end up with Isabelle, yet they never seem to get anywhere. What's worse, though, is that we don't know where they've *been*. Who *are* these people? What's their history? Even after that elaborate prologue, we don't know what Kristofferson's story is. We don't know how he became a U.S. Marshal, how he became so jaded, how he befriended a bad guy like Walken or how his effete Harvard classmate John Hurt wound up a wealthy rancher in the same county. We don't know *anything*. A couple of simple reminiscences might have helped. A voice-over narration would have worked wonders. But Cimino gives us none of that. Instead he keeps digressing with sweeping scenes that are really only good for atmosphere and local color.

But oh, what local color. We see immigrants arriving on trains, city streets teeming with citizens, buckboards dwarfed by mighty mountain peaks. We see homesteaders eking out a living from the soil and holding cockfights in back rooms. We see whores and their customers bustling in the bordello. We see a lovely, lyrical mass roller-skating sequence. We see crowds gathering, arguing, dispersing, and going about their business. We see so much that, after a while, we don't see it anymore. It's too much—and not enough. The movie does *so* much digressing that it's nearly intermission before the plot moves forward with any sense of purpose.

In the movie's second half, things start building toward a climactic shoot-out between the poor settlers and the rich ranchers. But if you're thinking a grand finale will redeem all that has (or hasn't) gone before, think again, Cimino keeps the mounting tensions slackened with still more atmospheric meandering, and as he brings the settlers together to argue about a battle plan, he seems to go out of his way to ensure that chaos will prevail. For authenticity—and, of course, atmosphere—the director lets the immigrants do all their bickering in their native tongues. Thus, there is a lot of very loud, completely unintelligible hubbub, with only occasional subtitles to convey such key dialogue as "Shut up!" and "Come on!" and "There's no time to lose!" Once again, Cimino loads on so much local color that we don't even know what we're looking at.

Casper, Wyoming, as
painstakingly recreated . . .
for a precious few scenes.

While we're still trying to figure it out, the settlers apparently reach some sort of decision. Then everyone rides off to an open field, where the ranchers have circled their horses and battened down for battle. As the settlers ride around and around, the final shoot-out *finally* erupts. Unfortunately, it's all obscured in smoke and dust so thick that we can't tell who's shooting who, and even if we could, Cimino's artily abrupt editing only adds to the confusion. People shoot, get shot, fall off their horses, and die—not necessarily in that order. C. B. De Mille, where are you when we need you!

Still, it only seems fitting that Cimino should leave us with such a non-climax. After all, the whole film is full of scenes that never get going because the director was paying too much attention to the little things—the little things that added millions to his budget. Like, for instance, his nationwide search for just the right vintage steam engine, which would end up onscreen for maybe ten seconds. Or like his obsessive decision to tear down a whole town and then rebuild it, simply because he wanted Main Street to be six feet wider. Or like his infamous fifty-three takes of a shot in which Kristofferson cracks a bullwhip at some cowering townspeople. Sure, Kristofferson finally delivered the picture-perfect whip crack. But what was his motivation?

After its historically disastrous premiere in front of the New York media, *Heaven's Gate* was unceremoniously pulled from release—at Cimino's re-

John Hurt and Kris Kristofferson (*front*) pose with their Harvard graduating class.

quest—before the rest of the world could see it. Then, following four more months of feverish reediting, the film came back out at a leaner, cleaner one hundred forty minutes. To no one's great surprise, it was different, but it wasn't better. Along with the clutter, Cimino had removed much of the scope and spectacle. The remaining story line was too sketchy, too shallow—too small—to support any epic ambitions. What that last-ditch reedit confirmed was that Cimino had never seen the forest for the trees. And it wasn't until he finally cleared away those trees that he discovered that there wasn't any forest at all. There never had been.

41

MOMMIE DEAREST

1981 ◄ Paramount

Produced by Frank Yablans. Directed by Frank Perry. Screenplay by Yablans, Perry, Tracy Hotchner, and Robert Getchell, based on the book by Christina Crawford.

CAST: Faye Dunaway (*Joan Crawford*); Diana Scarwid (*Christina Crawford*); Steve Forrest (*Greg Savitt*); Howard Da Silva (*Louis B. Mayer*); Mara Hobel (*young Christina*); Rutanaya Alda (*Carol Ann*).

THAT THIS MOVIE WAS DESTINED to be a camp classic was obvious the moment it hit the screen. The only question was how much of it was intentional. Based on the tell-all book by Christina Crawford about her nightmare life with adoptive mother Joan, the movie is over the top, all right. Certainly, Mommie Joan couldn't have been the monster the movie depicts. Or could she? Nah. Impossible. Nobody could be *that* bad. Surely this is another Hollywood exaggeration, pumped up larger than life to sell more tickets. But regardless of it's intention, this movie is camp like you wouldn't believe. The reason it's not as much fun as most camp classics is that the element of truth keeps getting in the way. Reality keeps rearing its ugly head, perched atop padded shoulders.

But however the movie hits you, you've got to hand it to Faye Dunaway. She *is* Joan Crawford—or at least Christina's Joan Crawford. Her face masked by a startling makeup job—all thick black eyebrows and huge red lips, with a dark wig on top—she gives a wholly unhinged performance full of mercurial mood swings. One minute rabid, the next in glacial repose, the next as giddy as a schoolgirl, she makes life sheer hell for the other people in the movie—and for the people watching it. But as overpowering as Dunaway is, she's helpless to alter the character's fatal flaw: She's a caricature. She's a caricature of a woman who was a caricature of herself.

Faye Dunaway as Joan,
Mara Hobel as Christina.

And so we watch in growing disbelief as this double caricature rages across the screen, spreading her reign of terror. All that keeps us from eventually going numb is the increasing viciousness of her behavior. At first, Joan is depicted as manageably neurotic: obsessive about her image, possessive about her men, a freak for order and cleanliness. "I'm not mad at you," she explains to her maid, barely containing her fury. "I'm mad at the dirt." But as soon as she decides to become a mommie, the beast inside is released, and Christina, her brother, the maid—and the audience—are trapped inside the house with it.

Indeed, most of *Mommie Dearest* takes place behind the closed doors of the Crawford mansion, giving the movie a claustrophobic field of vision, unrelentingly focused on Mommie Joan's crimes against the people closest to her. However, since this is Christina's version of the story, most of the crimes we witness are committed against poor little her.

Like a series of absurd revue sketches, the movie settles into a schematic pattern of Christina actions and Mommie Joan reactions, which quickly escalate into an all-out war: Christina raises her voice, Mommie locks her in the pool house, where she can't be heard. Christina mimics her mother in front of a mirror; Mommie chops off her hair. Christina can't get her bathroom floor suitably sterilized; Mommie clobbers her with a can of Bon Ami. Christina hangs her dresses on wire hangers instead of wooden ones; Mommie beats her with a wire hanger, screaming, "No wire hangers!!!" The last straw comes when Christina has the gall to stumble in on Mommie and her latest beau in the boudoir. For this unpardonable sin, Mommie packs the incorrigible little brat off to boarding school, where she spends the rest of her miserable childhood.

When next we see Christina, she has survived to become a teenager (played by Diana Scarwid), but the terror continues. After getting caught with a boy in a riding stable hayloft, Christina is promptly suspended from school. When she gets home, a humiliated Mommie practically chokes her to death—then enrolls her in a convent!

To be sure, Christina isn't the only target of Crawford's wrath. For balance, we also get to see the movie queen harass, harangue, and finally drive away her lawyer boyfriend (Steve Forrest). Then we witness her fit of fury after being fired from MGM by Louis B. Mayer (Howard Da Silva). All tanked up in the middle of the night, she chops down every flower in her beautiful garden, then starts in on the trees. "Christina! she bellows, "Bring me the ax!" Finally there's her moment of triumph when her third husband dies and leaves her at the head of Pepsi-Cola's board of directors. "Don't fuck with me, fellas!" she warns as they wither from the blast, "This ain't my first time at the rodeo."

At moments like these it's possible to enjoy the outsized proportions of this grotesque portrait. But *Mommie Dearest* is more often horrific than hilarious, and its cumulative effect leaves you feeling as battered as poor little Christina. The movie is repugnant on so many levels: as a cartoon depiction of child abuse; as the bile spewed out by a psychologically poisoned victim; as a char-

**The resemblance couldn't
be more frightening.**

acter assassination of a public figure who, however rotten she might have been, isn't around to defend herself.

Still, the question remains: Did the creative people behind this adaptation intend to camp it up this bad, or couldn't they help themselves? The inclination is to believe it was intentional. After all, the director was Frank Perry, who followed up this travesty with the ludicrous *Monsignor*, in which Christopher Reeve plays an amoral priest blackmailing bishops and sleeping with nuns on his way to the top of the Vatican. A one-two punch like that doesn't leave much doubt where a director is coming from. On the other hand, you've got Frank Yablans, who produced both these movies and apparently really did think he was delivering hard-hitting dramas. He even stuck his hand into the script for *Mommie Dearest*, and took a screenwriting credit for himself. The idea that somebody could actually regurgitate such swill and call it art—and believe it—is perhaps the sorriest, scariest thing about *Mommie Dearest*.

SIGNS OF THE TIMES
Slasher Movies

When *Halloween* opened in 1978, it was hailed a a masterstroke of B-movie ingenuity. No less an expert than Roger Ebert compared it to no less than *Psycho*. High praise, that. But in Hollywood what really mattered was that *Halloween* was a hit. And so, in the years that followed, a truly blood-curdling number of imitators skulked into movie theaters, all clearly patterned after *Halloween*'s method of murdering horny teens. None of the hacks who churned out the schlock could match the surgeon's skill of *Halloween* director John Carpenter. In fact, they were more like butchers. But no matter. They knew the basics. They knew enough to pick a red-letter day to commemorate the bloodbath (*Black Christmas, New Year's Evil, April Fool's Day*). And when they ran out of special days, they settled for special occasions (*Graduation Day, Rush Week*), or just special locations (*Sorority House Massacre, Cheerleader Camp*). In the end, though, any old time and place would do—as long as the victims were young, promiscuous, preferably stupid, and most important, plentiful.

The *Halloween* sequels. Shrugging off multiple mortal injuries, madman Michael Myers returns in *Halloween II* (1981) to terrorize Jamie Lee Curtis. To the rescue comes Michael's private shrink Donald Pleasence, who torches Michael and ends the horror forever. Ah, but not so fast. Michael will return twice more to make mincemeat of countless victims, only to be killed again and again by the increasingly obsessed Dr. Pleasence. How can this be happening? "He isn't human," rants the wild-eyed Pleasence. "We are talking about evil on two legs." Oh. That explains everything.

Friday the 13th (1980) The most enduring slasher of all is hockey-masked Jason Vorhees, who keeps coming back to avenge his own death in movie after movie. The trouble is, he's never satisfied, as can be seen in *Friday the 13th*, parts 2 (1981) through 10 (1996). Of course, it's frequently hard to tell one *Friday* from another, since Jason maintains the same slice-and-dice motif throughout his reign of terror. Only the murder weapons change, from knives to axes to shovels to boat hooks. If it slices or dices, Jason has used it. He may be a single-minded murder machine, but at least he knows how to accessorize.

Prom Night (1981) Jamie Lee Curtis goes back to high school, just to be terrorized at her senior prom. And she's not the only one. The class bitch gets it in the girls' room, two heavy petters go down in the parking lot, and the school punk literally loses his head, which rolls across the dance floor. Even the adults are in danger, including Leslie

Halloween's **Michael Myers and** *Friday the 13th*'s **Jason set the tone for terror in the eighties.**

Nielsen as Jamie's dad—the principal—who foolishly hits the dance floor in front of the whole school. "Principal by day, disco king by night," Jamie chirps. When a psycho killer's loose, everyone gets weird.

Slumber Party Massacre (1982) A serial killer escapes from—where else—the insane asylum. Next stop, an all-girl slumber party. Revving up a three-foot power drill, this killjoy barges right in. "You know you want it," he drools, dangling his drill bit over one cowering coed. As if to punish him for such obvious symbolism, the heroine grabs a big, sharp knife and cuts off his . . . hand! Not how Loreena Bobbitt would have done it—but you get the idea.

Silent Night, Deadly Night (1984) Cute little Billy sees a killer dressed as Santa butcher his whole family. Then he spends the rest of his childhood in an orphanage, being whipped by nuns. Is it any wonder that, one foggy Christmas Eve, he dons a Santa suit and goes on a killing spree? Four sequels later, the slay ride continues. Run, Rudolph, run!

42

ONE FROM THE HEART

1982 ⁴ Columbia

Produced by Gary Frederickson, Armyan Bernstein, and Fred Roos. Directed by Francis Coppola. Screenplay by Bernstein and Coppola.

CAST: Frederic Forrest (*Hank*); Teri Garr (*Frannie*); Raul Julia (*Ray*); Nastassia Kinski (*Leila*); Lainie Kazan (*Maggie*); Harry Dean Stanton (*Moe*).

THE GODFATHER. Apocalypse Now. The Conversation. If Francis Coppola never made another decent movie, those films alone would win him a permanent place among Hollywood's great filmmakers. And yet, it was the standard set by those master-works that made *One From the Heart* seem so disappointing when it finally had its long-awaited premiere. Of course it didn't help that Coppola had spent years on the project. Or that he'd devoted so much prerelease hype to ballyhoo his ahead-of-its-time movie technology. Or that he had begun to refer to himself as a "film composer." Or that he pretentiously unveiled his $30 million baby at a reserved-seat engagement at Radio City Music Hall. But the bottom line is that, all expectations aside, *One From the Heart* is one awesomely empty experience. It's the best-looking movie you ever saw about absolutely nothing.

Billed as "a new kind of old-fashioned romance," the movie takes place in a faux Las Vegas completely reinvented inside Coppola's Zoetrope Studios. Never once did the director's cameras venture out of doors, not even for teeming street scenes or moody midnight interludes in moonlit desert junkyards. But this, of course, was what Coppola meant by a "a new kind of old-fashioned romance." With its bold production design and candy-colored neon lighting, the movie is a throwback to the days when Hollywood made almost all of its movies within the confines of the soundstage. Now if

Nastassia Kinski walks the tightrope, without a net. Behind the camera, Francis Coppola was doing something similar, with his reputation. *Ker-splat!*

Coppola had only harkened back to the days of good storytelling, inspired dialogue, interesting characters, and appealing actors, he might actually have had some sort of framework for all his window dressing. As it is, he has a puny, pointless, annoying, so-called love story that seems even less substantial on paper in stark black and white.

These are the romantic tribulations of Frannie (Teri Garr) and Hank (Frederic Forrest), a very average couple who have been together long enough to be tired of being together. "You used to shave your legs all the time. Now

Will Frederic Forrest and Teri Garr live happily ever after? Who the hell cares?

you don't shave 'em for weeks," comments Hank. "What about yourself?" protests hirsute Frannie "You used to have a pretty good build. Now you're starting to look like an egg." And so the witty repartee goes, throughout a futile attempt to celebrate their fifth anniversary of living together. When they finally argue themselves into a dead end, Frannie announces, "I'm walking out on you, ass face!" And out she goes.

For the next never-ending hour and a half, our irresistible couple wanders around separately, without a clue, while complaining to their respective friends (Lainie Kazan and Harry Dean Stanton) and having brief flings with romanticized strangers. Frannie meets a Latin waiter (Raul Julia) who is also a nightclub singer. Hank meets a Vegas showgirl (Nastassia Kinski) who is also a tightrope walker. Make of this what you will. What Frannie and Hank learn from it all is that they really do belong together—if only because they're both such boring, ordinary, unattractive losers.

Given the total absence of substance here, Coppola might have been forgiven for piling on the style. Yet instead of gilding this fragile lily, he has so encrusted it with rhinestones that it just sits there, twinkling like a tacky casino sideshow. The movie is all lighting and production design; every scene is an eye-catching showcase of spotlights, silhouettes, scrim effects, lilting camera movements, and backdrops that suddenly shift to reveal a new perspective, sometimes a whole new set. It's all quite stylized, all quite theatrical. And it all just serves to distance us even further from these boring characters and their mundane lives. As the actors mope, meander, and indulge in private method-actor moments—while Tom Wait's bluesy song score drones on incessantly, commenting on the movie's two or three plot developments—they begin to look like they're rehearsing a movie that has yet to be made. There are times when they truly seem lost, wandering around those multi-million-dollar sets.

This is the production in which Coppola first tried directing from the cozy solitude of his high-tech trailer. Removing himself from the set, he sat behind control panels viewing the proceedings on TV monitors and phoning in his direction. The idea was to observe from an objective distance, to view instant "rushes" via video technology, to get an immediate feel for how a scene was playing onscreen. The lesson learned here was that a scene has to play in real life before it can play on a screen. Sitting in his trailer, distracted by all his gadgetry, Coppola either didn't notice or didn't care that his scenes had no charm, no chemistry, no life—no point.

One From the Heart was anything but.

43

INCHON

1982 ◂ MGM/United Artists

Produced by Mitsuharu Ishii. Directed by Terence Young. Screenplay by Robin Moore and Laird Koenig, from the story by Moore and Paul Savage.

CAST: Laurence Olivier (*Gen. Douglas MacArthur*); Jacqueline Bisset (*Barbara Hallsworth*); Ben Gazzara (*Maj. Frank Hallsworth*); Toshiro Mifune (*Saito-San*); Richard Roundtree (*Sgt. August Henderson*); Dorothy James (*Jean MacArthur*).

IN THE GLORIOUS HISTORY of war movies, there is one sub-genre that stands out from all the rest—for all the wrong reasons. Let's call it the all-star, big-budget, great battle collection. These are the war movies that feature famous actors playing famous generals who sit around war rooms moving their armies like chess pieces, while slightly less famous actors, playing captains and sergeants, hit the beaches and trenches. With the exception of *The Longest Day* (1962), these films are almost never exciting. They're too top-heavy with stars, too preoccupied with strategy, too bogged down with big-scale scenes of armed forces on the move. Sometimes, when they're really bad, they try to heat up the history lesson with a few *From Here to Eternity*-style personal stories—like the Charlton Heston-Edward Albert father-son conflict in *Midway* (1976), or the various earthbound affairs of RAF pilots in *The Battle of Britain* (1969). It's heartfelt, human scale subplots like those that make war-monger movie fans scream, "Tora! Tora! Tora!"

Yes, a whole chapter could be devoted to analyzing the botched big battle movies of cinematic commanders in chief. But let's just single out the biggest Waterloo of them all: the one that combined the most boring battle plans, the most ridiculous romantic subplot, the most grotesque impersonation of a great general by a great actor, and one of the three or four biggest budgets in motion picture history. Ladies and gentlemen: *Inchon*.

Olivier, mugging shamelessly as General MacArthur. Caesar is not amused.

A vanity production of the highest order, *Inchon* was the inspiration of the Reverend Sun Myung Moon, the Korean founder and leader of the Unification Church. Apparently Reverend Moon wasn't satisfied being the millionaire messiah of millions of so-called Moonies; he had to be a millionaire mogul as well. So Reverend Moon teamed with Japanese tycoon Mitsuharu Ishii, and together they went into the movie business. Briefly, they considered doing the life story of Jesus Christ, but finally settled on something more uplifting: General Douglas MacArthur's Korean War landing at Inchon. Not only was this a military coup that turned the tide against the North Korean army, it was also considered by some (namely Reverend Moon) to have been an act of divine intervention. Douglas MacArthur, Messenger of God! What a concept.

To fill MacArthur's shoes the producers had to get the best actor money could buy. And for the right seven figures, they got him. Insured by the promise of lifetime financial security for his family, Sir Laurence Olivier signed on to lead the *Inchon* invasion. Unfortunately, this wasn't the Olivier anyone envisioned. Nor did he play a MacArthur anyone recognized. Wearing what looks like dance hall makeup, Olivier presents the camera with a truly bizarre countenance, especially in close-up. His nose is altered with putty. His dyed black hair, augmented by a toupee, is plastered to his head. His eyes are lined with mascara. He's possibly wearing rouge. He's *definitely* wearing lipstick. He looks like a drag queen in an open casket, and all because someone told him that MacArthur himself wasn't above a little facial touch-up before important public appearances. That's Olivier for you; he always had to look the part before he could play it.

But this is a total performance. Taking his cue from his makeup, Olivier mugs, smirks, purses his lips, and bats his eyelashes. Once, confronted by a bust of Julius Caesar, he even does a Laurel and Hardy double take. And to complete the package, he makes sure that MacArthur sounds as weird as he looks. Whether delivering a spiel to his chiefs of staff or unloading his heavy burdens over breakfast with his wife, Olivier's MacArthur imbues his every line with not-so-subtle snideness. The actor is clearly sending up the divine Doug, not to mention the divine Reverend Moon. And he seems to have had the full complicity of the screenwriters, who even give him the opportunity to exit a room with the immortal line, "I shall return."

But then, this movie was so preposterously conceived that Olivier's absurd portrayal seems an appropriate response. Indeed, if the rest of the cast had followed his example, they could have hit an all-time high of hilarious camp. Unfortunately, everyone else plays it more or less straight, which makes them seem more sorry, if not more silly, than their fearless leader. Ben Gazzara and Jacqueline Bisset have no fun as a world-weary major and his estranged wife; Richard Roundtree has no role as a sergeant who spends most of his screen time sitting in a jeep; and Dorothy James has no *room* as Mrs. Douglas MacArthur. She, after all, has to play her scenes opposite Olivier. Supplement them with Toshiro Mifune as a stoically pacifist Korean and various stone-faced actors as MacArthur's coterie of military minds, and you've got the most desolate supporting cast that ever visibly suffered through a high-paying job.

As audience members, we can sympathize. *Inchon* is a two-hour-and-twenty-minute haul through military history, and the way it has been assembled, it seems a lot longer. The film falls into place, section by bulky section: first, a lengthy strategy session in which Olivier holds court, then an in-your-face taste of Communist torture techniques, then a scene of domestic disharmony between Gazzara and Bisset (for diversity, Gazzara also has—what else?—a Korean mistress), then a repeat of the whole cycle as events inexorably build toward the climactic invasion. As if *Inchon* weren't already the worst big-budget, great battle movie ever made, it's not-so-great battle footage further seals its fate. All tanks and trucks and battleships—and thousands of Moonie extras—the scenes are as lumbering as any in the genre. However, they have the added attraction of being utterly inept. Big guns go off, seemingly shooting at nothing. Bodies fly through the air, hurled by explosions that haven't gone off yet. Sergeant Roundtree gets blasted off a bridge in his jeep, only to later resurface, still in his jeep, to rescue Jackie Bisset, who was out marketing in her polka-dot halter top when the shooting started. Even in the heat of battle, *Inchon* never loses its human touch.

When it's all over and the smoke has cleared, the good guys have won the battle, if not the war. Yes, they've incurred some heavy losses, but since we couldn't care less about anybody onscreen, we can walk away without a heavy heart. After this long siege we feel lucky just to be alive, and perfectly happy to join in with General MacArthur as he steps up in front of a huge throng to deliver his victory address—in the form of The Lord's Prayer. "Thy Kingdom come, Thy will be done," Olivier intones, for the first time not smirking. And it did and it was, at least in the gospel according to Reverend Moon. No matter that he'd lost all but two of the $50 million he'd sunk into this movie. Forty-eight million is a small price to pay for divine inspiration.

44

DUNE

1984 ⁴ Universal

Produced by Raffaella DeLaurentiis. Written and directed by David Lynch. Based on the novels of Frank Herbert.

CAST: Kyle MacLachlan (*Paul Atreides*); Francesca Annis (*Lady Jessica*); Jürgen Prochnow (*Duke Leto Atreides*); José Ferrer (*Emperor*); Kenneth McMillan (*Baron Harkonnen*); Richard Jordan (*Duncan Idaho*); Linda Hunt (*Shadow Mapes*); Dean Stockwell (*Dr. Wellington Yueh*); Max Von Sydow (*Dr. Kynes*); Paul Smith (*The Beast Rabban*); Sting (*Feyd Rautha*).

WITH ITS MESSIANIC HERO, mystical forces, interplanetary warfare, and giant sandworm monsters, Frank Herbert's supercult novel *Dune* was just sitting there, daring some producer to make it into a movie. And in the aftermath of *Star Wars* what producer could resist? Well, many *sane* producers could and *did* resist, knowing that, however it might tickle the imagination, a movie version of *Dune* was destined to be a dinosaur: too big, too dark, too unwieldy, too expensive. It took Dino DeLaurentiis—he of *King Kong* and *Orca*—to overlook all the potential pitfalls and throw a large fortune into the project. But then nobody, not even Dino, ever said he was sane. As he declared in an interview at the time: "To make *Dune* you must be crazy. And I believe I am crazy enough and have the courage enough."

What he had was money enough—some $50 million, as a matter of fact. Throwing some of it at a big international cast, and some more of it at such special effects wizards as John Dykstra (*Star Wars* and Carlo Rambaldi (*E.T.*), he dumped the rest on Mexico's Chubusco Studios, where he commandeered all eight soundstages on which he built seventy-five sets. There, he re-created the legendary world of Dune—with the help of a thousandfold crew, and some twenty thousand Mexican extras.

Rock star Sting emotes as the evil Feyd Rautha.

To direct this undertaking, DeLaurentiis hired David Lynch, at that time best known for *Eraserhead* and *The Elephant Man*. With his eye and ear for the strange and wonderful, Lynch may have *seemed* like a good choice for the job. However, this job proved to be too massive for him. It might have proved too massive for any director. To do the story justice, it probably would have taken a *Star Wars*-type trilogy, or perhaps even a TV miniseries. Stuffed into a mere two hours and twenty minutes, *Dune* was a stillborn epic. It had all the narrative flow of a clogged-up drain.

Briefly, *Dune* is the story of three planets at war over a life-giving spice that grows only on a fourth planet—the planet called Dune. The evil emperor of Kaitain (José Ferrer) has allied himself with the grotesque leader of the Harkonnëns (Kenneth McMillan) to plunder Dune's natural resource and enslave its people, the Fremens. What no one realizes is that the young prince of the third planet, Caladan (Kyle McLachlan), is in fact the long-awaited Messiah, and that once he arrives on Dune he will discover his true destiny,

Francesca Annis holds her
own with the overwhelming
art direction. But what
chance did Linda Hunt
have?

Francesca Annis holds her own with the overwhelming art direction. But what chance did Linda Hunt have?

develop his mystical powers, and lead Dune's underground citizens to revolt and victory. "Long live the fighters!" is the Fremen battle cry. Whenever we hear that, we know who we're supposed to be rooting for.

But it's okay to be confused. Confusion is the natural response to a narrative text that involves four planets, a complex conspiracy, a lot of elaborate folklore, and a whole slew of characters who are not what they at first seem. Lynch tries to help by cramming in some densely detailed exposition before the action starts. But all he manages to do is boggle our minds. Only confirmed *Dune* cultists can be sure what the hell is going on here; the rest of us have to play a game of catch-up-with-the-story. The problem is that the movie is such a mess we have no way of knowing when or *if* we've caught up.

Indeed, Lynch needs so much time just to set up his convoluted scenario that he winds up having to do a *Cliff Notes* version of the rest of the story. The result is less a movie than an illustrated companion piece to the book. Lynch eventually does get all the plot points in, but there is little room left for anything else. Meanwhile, as we travel from planet to planet, so many characters climb aboard that the movie's impressive cast is largely reduced to cameo appearances. Max Von Sydow turns up just long enough to get killed off. Sean Young can be seen in the background as Kyle MacLachlan's warrior lover. Sting has a few brief scenes as the evil Feyd Rautha. But even the actors who get a lot of screen time don't make much of an impression. They don't so much portray their characters as represent them.

With so much saga and so little time, Lynch can't afford the luxury of any set pieces. Consequently, there aren't too many scenes you'd single out as your favorite. Too much of the movie takes place in caves and chambers and tunnels. Even though it encompasses four different worlds, it has no scope. Even though its battle scenes employ all those thousands of extras, it has no spectacle. Even its vast desert scenes seem hemmed in by the edges of the screen. Sure, *Dune* has its share of inspired visuals: polished jade floors, throne rooms gilded in gold, boil-covered Harkonnën villains, and of course, those subway-size sandworms. But under such generally gloomy conditions, all those ornate touches only add to the confusion. When you're slogging through a movie trying not to get lost, you don't have a lot of time to stop and admire the scenery.

Needless to say, *Dune* wasn't "high concept" enough to attract a mainstream audience. Nor was it true enough to the novel to please *Dune* cultists. Nor was it very satisfying for David Lynch fans, who were not accustomed to seeing the director compromise his own eccentric vision in the spirit of collaboration. In short, it was a movie nobody could embrace. And nobody did. *Dune* was a total box-office bust, dying away so quickly and quietly that today almost no one thinks of it anymore. It's among the most invisible of all the failed blockbusters: a true black hole.

45

SANTA CLAUS—THE MOVIE

1985 ◄ TriStar

Produced by Ilya Salkind and Pierre Spengler. Directed by Jeannot Szwarc. Screenplay by David Newman, from a story by David Newman and Leslie Newman.

CAST: David Huddleston (*Santa Claus*); Dudley Moore (*Patch*); John Lithgow (*B.Z.*); Judy Cornwell (*Mrs. Claus*); Christian Fitzpatrick (*Joe*); Carrie Kei Heim (*Cornelia*); Burgess Meredith (*Ancient elf*).

ALEXANDER AND ILYA SALKIND—the producers who gave us *Superman*—just didn't know when to quit. First they pressed their luck with three Man of Steel sequels until, by *Superman IV*, we were praying for kryptonite. Then they gave us *Supergirl*, in which heroine Helen Slater was flagrantly upstaged by supervillainess Faye Dunaway, in a nostril-flaring performance that suggested she was still possessed by the spirit of *Mommie Dearest*. Okay, we could live with all that. But when the Salkinds mustered all their resources to give us *Santa Claus*, they were really asking for it. They were toying with an icon far more near and dear to kids of all ages (if not all creeds), and they were just plain wrecking it for everybody. For their sins, they lost a bundle at the box office and belatedly learned a hard lesson about what you can (and can't) do when making bad movies: You can bastardize the Bible. You can remake Hollywood classics. You can tug on Superman's cape. But you can never, ever mess around with Santa.

The Salkinds start treading on thin ice right away, serving up a revisionist version of the old St. Nicholas legend. Santa (David Huddleston) and Mrs. Claus (Judy Cornwell) first appear as a kindly old couple who make toys for their north country neighbors and deliver them every yuletide. Then one snowy Christmas Eve, they get lost in the woods and drift off into a deep,

Dudley Moore poses with his fellow elves. Isn't he just too precious?

Dudley Moore poses with his fellow elves. Isn't he just too precious?

frosty sleep. When they awaken, who knows how much later, they see a heavenly light in the sky and are suddenly surrounded by—my goodness—elves! Leading the elves is Burgess Meredith, who proclaims, "The prophecy is fulfilled." What he means is that Santa and the missus will live happily every after in their magical North Pole workshop, where they will supervise the production of many presents, which Santa will load into his sleigh drawn by eight tiny reindeer and ... oh, you know the rest.

But just when we're peacefully dozing off with visions of sugarplums dancing in our heads, we become aware of an annoying presence disrupting our long winter's nap. It's Dudley Moore as a mischievous elf named Patch, and he's starting to hog the spotlight. Suddenly it's clear what the Salkinds are up to—Santa is, in fact, a figurehead in his *own* movie. The real entertainment value here is supposed to come from Dudley, who's doing yet another variation of his usual lovable scamp.

Always slacking off to work on some half-baked invention, Patch is the workshop maverick. He's irresponsible, unreliable, and has an irritating conversational habit of replacing the prefix *self* with *elf*, as in "elf-confidence," "elf-control," "elf-assurance," etc. Spiced with Dudley's familiar English accent, the words take on a quasi-cockney flavor that is ever so damned endearing. Or so the scriptwriters must have thought, because every other sentence out of Patch's mouth seems to contain another elf-satisfied pun.

What with Dudley working double shifts, life at Santa's workshop gets to be sort of a drag. But as soon as we leave the North Pole, the movie *really* goes south, in more ways than one. While delivering presents in New York City, Santa gets involved with a poor little street kid (Christian Fitzpatrick) who doesn't believe in Christmas, and a poor little rich girl (Carrie Kei Heim) who needs somebody to love. Put them together and you've got a poor little plot development. What makes it even poorer is that the filmmakers don't even try to warm our hearts with this kiddie connection; they just throw the kids together and let them bore us to tears while they teach each other the true meaning of Christmas. It couldn't be more obligatory.

Things are getting just as bad back at the North Pole, where problem elf Patch has allowed a lapse in quality control. Suddenly, toys are being sent back for the first time, and everybody blames poor Patch. Wallowing in elf-pity, Patch runs away to New York, where he meets up with a greedy toy tycoon (played with great, gleeful gusto by John Lithgow). The tycoon is under congressional investigation for making unsafe toys, so when Patch shows up offering to make magical playthings—free of charge!—the tycoon practically drools at the possibilities. Little does Patch realize that he has hooked up with a modern day Scrooge. And little do the Salkinds realize that no one in the audience cares.

It gets worse. When Patch invents a lollipop that makes kids levitate, the Scrooge tycoon drools some more and starts dreaming of ruling the world. Now Patch knows he's in trouble, but who's he gonna call? Santa is way back at the North Pole, moping because his toys have been rejected. "Maybe Christmas isn't such a good idea anymore," he mumbles to Mrs. Claus. Meanwhile, back in New York, the Scrooge tycoon has declared Santa Claus obsolete, and is making plans for a sequel to Christmas. "We'll call it Christmas II," he chortles. Nothing can stop him now! Not even Patch's magic lollipop, which, as it turns out, explodes at room temperature.

Want more? Here it comes. When Santa gets word that his little street-kid pal has been kidnapped by the tycoon, he flies to the rescue in his magic sleigh, accompanied by music that sounds a lot like the *Superman* theme. Three weeks into January, Santa's back in town. And this time, he's an action hero!

The grand finale finds Santa and the street kid swooping down to save Patch, who doesn't know he's flying around in a car full of candy canes about to go up in flames. (Don't ask.) Meanwhile, in a last-ditch effort to escape the police, Lithgow wolfs down a heaping helping of magic candy (along

David Huddleston does a hearty Ho-ho-ho, as jolly old St. Nick.

with most of the scenery), and ends up launching himself into outer space. While he floats around in orbit, Santa and friends fly back to the North Pole, where they will all live together, happily ever after, making toys the old-fashioned way—with magic. Christmas has been saved!

But only in the movie. In real life, this tinselly pile of celluloid junk pretty much snuffed the spirit out of holiday moviegoers. With avarice as their main inspiration, the Salkinds had unloaded one of the crassest commercializations ever committed in the name of Christmas. In the process, they did more damage to the image of Santa Claus than all those *Silent Night Deadly Night* slasher Santa movies. So let's all pray that the Salkinds never decide to do a movie about the Easter bunny. If they did, it would probably turn out a lot like our next Megaton Bomb. . . .

46

HOWARD THE DUCK

1986 ⨭ Universal

Produced by Gloria Katz. Directed by Willard Huyck. Screenplay by Huyck and Katz, based on the Marvel Comics character.

CAST: Lea Thompson (*Beverly*); Jeffrey Jones (*Dr. Jennings*); Tim Robbins (*Phil*); Ed Gale, Chip Zien, Tim Rose, Steve Sleap, Peter Baird, Mary Wells, Lisa Sturz, Jordan Prentice (*Howard T. Duck*).

THIS BIG-BUDGET BOMB is the movie equivalent of a loaded cigar: It starts out as a dubious joke, then blows up in your face. That the filmmakers designed it that way makes it twice as obnoxious. That the film failed so cataclysmically serves them all right.

This is another of those movies churned out by a major name who had earned the privilege of doing whatever he wanted—with his studio's blessing. As the man behind *Star Wars* and the Indiana Jones movies, George Lucas could have proposed another remake of *The Blue Bird* and Universal would have asked "How much can we pay you?" Instead, he proposed a big-screen adaptation of a not-so-popular Marvel Comics character, and asked his old friends Willard Huyck and Gloria Katz to write and direct it. Since Huyck and Katz had previously written Lucas's *American Graffiti*, Universal was even more ecstatic. "We'll pay you all a lot of money," the studio said. And it did. It's been paying ever since.

Right from the start we can sense we're in for trouble. When we first meet the three-foot Howard T. Duck, he's sitting in his Marshington, D.C., apartment, flipping through a copy of *Playduck* magazine, while other ducks on television are hawking Crazy Webby's Appliance world and remedies for feather fungus. What planet is this anyway? Another one, obviously. But not for long. All of a sudden the room shakes, lights flash, the volume shoots up,

Howard T. Duck. It seemed like a good idea at the time.

and Howard is being zapped through space, kicking and screaming. The next thing he knows, he's crawling out of a trash can in a back alley in Cleveland, Ohio. After he accidentally rescues punkette rocker Lea Thompson from some would-be muggers, she gratefully takes him home with her. It's the beginning of a beautiful, if somewhat bizarre, friendship.

Readily adjusting to a three-foot duck from another planet, punkette Lea dedicates herself to helping him find his way home. And so it's off to the local scientific institution, where she enlists the aid of lab geek Tim Robbins. After that, it's off for a series of comic encounters on the street, in the park, in a rock club. Predictably, everyone else he meets finds Howard an *odd* duck, to say the least. Only punkette Lea can see the real person inside.

But of course there's a real person inside—a very little person, to be exact. And since Howard reminds us of nothing so much as one of those cartoon characters who prowl Main Street in Disney World, it's almost impossible to

Lea Thompson looks incredulously at her "leading man." Well, what would *you* do?

lose ourselves in the illusion. Every so often, we pull back and ask ourselves, "Why am I watching this little person in a duck costume waddle around Cleveland, Ohio?"

But even if we could accept Howard at face value, he's forever ruining it the moment he opens his beak. Apparently trying to make their Howard as hip as the one in the comics, Huyck and Katz have supplied him with a steady stream of fowl puns and wisequacks. "That's it, no more Mr. Nice Duck," he says when someone ruffles his tailfeathers. He even gets Lea doing it. "Book him, Ducko," she chirps to her pal after they turn the tables on a bumbling cop. It all gets old in a hurry.

It gets even harder to take during those intimate moments when Howard is lounging around punkette Lea's apartment, making lame duck passes at her. She, of course, thinks it's cute. In fact, she plays along. "You think I might find happiness in the animal kingdom, Duckie?" she coos, crawling into bed and stroking his down. She's just calling his bluff, thank God, but it still gives you the willies.

Fortunately, this romantic interlude is soon interrupted by Jeffrey Jones and his team of scientists, who barge in to explain that they're the people responsible for beaming Howard down to earth. They'd been working on this laser spectroscope, see, and, well, the darn thing went off. Offering to send

Howard back home, they set up another experiment. Wouldn't you know it? The darn thing misfires again! "What if we brought down something else this time?" a nerd assistant asks. Little does he know they have—and it has taken over the body of Dr. Jeffrey Jones.

Before you can say Mr. Hyde, Dr. Jones is calling himself The Dark Overlord and going through some gross changes—from mutant freak to fire-breathing demon to hideous dragon with scorpion claws. While he's going through this metamorphosis, so too is the movie, flying increasingly out of control in a senseless series of chase scenes, crashes, and explosions. The denouement finds Howard battling the Dark Overlord in a hail of laser blasts and lightning bolts. At about this time we begin to wonder: Did Lucas and company really plan it this way, or were they, too, taken over by the Dark Overlord?

Upon further reflection, however, we realize that the filmmakers were trying to repeat the success formula of the hugely popular *Ghostbusters* (1984), which began with Bill Murray tossing off smart remarks while flushing out gremlins at the public library, and ended with the busters on a high-rise rooftop blowing away live gargoyles and Godzilla-sized marshmallow men. But *Ghostbusters* never lost its sense of humor (or balance) as it escalated into special effects overdrive. In contrast, *Howard the Duck* just gets more deafening and dumbfounding, until it finally flies apart. There's nothing else it *can* do.

But wait! It isn't over yet. After the smoke clears and the Dark Overlord is defeated, our plucky duckie is still alive and quacking. However, he is now stranded on earth, all too obviously leaving the barn door open for the usual sequel. To celebrate having saved the world for another *Howard the Duck* movie, our hero joins punkette Lea onstage for a blistering rendition of the *Howard the Duck* theme song. During a hot guitar solo, Howard does—what else—a *duckwalk* all the way across the stage. Sort of figures, doesn't it?

If there were any poor saps out there in movieland who had somehow retained a fondness for our fine feathered friend, that duckwalk was the last straw. Had the Dark Overlord come back during the end credits to cook Howard's goose a deep-fried golden brown, audiences across America would no doubt have erupted in cheers. As it was, they wobbled out of cineplexes a little bit woozy and the worse for wear.

There would be no *Howard the Duck II*.

47

ISHTAR

1987 ⁴ Columbia

Produced by Warren Beatty. Written and directed by Elaine May.

CAST: Warren Beatty (*Lyle*); Dustin Hoffman (*Chuck*); Isabelle Adjani (*Shirra*); Charles Grodin (*Jim Harrison*); Jack Weston (*Marty Freed*); Tess Harper (*Willa*); Carol Kane (*Carol*).

EVERYTHING IS RELATIVE—even the badness of movies. If *Ishtar* had been a cheap quickie filmed on the back lot and starring Judd Nelson and Judge Reinhold, you'd think it was pretty lame and never give it another thought. But that isn't what *Ishtar* was. Nobody's ever been quite sure what writer-director Elaine May had in mind with this outsized shaggy dog comedy. Whatever it was, she spared no extravagance trying to realize her vision. She cast not one, but two difficult stars. She packed off her production to exotic Morocco. She spent month after month in the desert, waiting for sand dunes to swirl into just the right shapes. And when she was all finished, she had spent over $40 million and set the release of her movie back half a year. As for her career—well, she set that back a lot farther.

Some revisionist critics will tell you that *Ishtar* really isn't all that bad—that the public's mind was poisoned by all the prerelease stories of runaway budgets and production delays, and that if you judge the movie solely by what's on the screen, and not by how much it cost or how long it took to make, then it's really a passably enjoyable little film. Well, maybe that theory works if you live in Antarctica and the only other movie you ever saw was Mike Nichols's *The Fortune*. But in this hemisphere, we bring certain expectations to a movie, and they don't have anything to do with inflated budgets and overextended schedules. So let's not talk about time and money; let's just talk about talent.

Hoffman and Beatty, stranded in the desert. Only the camel will emerge unscathed.

Dustin Hoffman is a brilliant actor. He can also be very funny (see *Tootsie*). Warren Beatty is a bona fide movie star. He can also be very funny (see *Shampoo*). Elaine May is a brilliant writer. She has also directed some very funny movies (see *The Heartbreak Kid*). Put them all together in a modern day Hope-Crosby road picture and, gee, you sort of think it might be funny. But gee, it isn't.

Looking at it on paper, it seems like it should be. Hoffman and Beatty play songwriters so bad that they can't even get booked at open-mike nights. The best their cut-rate agent, Jack Weston, can do is offer them one of two out-of-town gigs: either Honduras or Ishtar, next door to Morocco. The boys pick Ishtar because it sounds safer. No sooner do they land than they're getting involved in a holy war that could threaten the oil-based economy of the entire Middle East. The players include a beautiful terrorist (Isabelle Adjani), a double-dealing CIA man (Charles Grodin), a blind camel, some silent assassins, some bumbling gunrunners, and some pushy desert vultures who don't have the courtesy to wait until our heroes die of exposure before gathering for dinner. But see, that's the thing about expectations: You hear what this movie's about; you hear who's in it; you see a coming attractions trailer featuring the movie's three or four funny moments; then you go see the movie and—ka-boom! Or rather, ka-thud.

A movie's got big trouble when it starts out with two boring guys crying in their beer in New York, then moves them to an exotic land where beautiful women try to seduce them, bad guys try to shoot them, vultures try to eat them—and you find yourself wishing they'd never left home! But see, at least while the movie was still in New York, you still had hope. Hoffman and Beatty showed signs of becoming a good team, and besides, they were such inept songwriters that they were just bound to make hilarious heroes, right? You listened to Beatty's song lyrics ("Hot fudge love, cherry ripple kisses/Lip smackin', back slappin', perfectly delicious") then imagined what he'd do with a femme fatale in his arms. Or you watched Hoffman warble "I'm leaving some love in my will," then pictured what would happen when he wound up holding the fate of the western world in his hands.

But there are those expectations again. *Ishtar*'s audience (what there was of it) had every right to anticipate that something would develop here. And yet, it never does. The scenes don't build on each other; they just pile up. The jokes don't have any zing; they seem rehearsed to death. The director doesn't make the most of her situations; she lets them trickle away. Like sand through her fingers. She keeps her beautiful femme fatale covered up in a burnoose. She lets a blind camel step on Grodin's foot and eliminate the movie's funniest performer. She stages half her action in a stereotypical marketplace that could easily be a back lot, and the other half in a Moroccan desert that might as well be a stretch of sand on the road to Palm Springs. As for what she gets from Hoffman and Beatty—well, let's just say she doesn't get Hope and Crosby.

Not that anyone could have made much of this material. But Hope and Crosby, or Bill Murray and Steve Martin—or even Charles Grodin and Jack Weston as the leads instead of the second bananas—could have salvaged some scenes on personal shtick alone. Hoffman and Beatty, on the other hand, aren't comedians by trade. They can't wing it in a scene when it's not working. They can't get a laugh just by being themselves. They couldn't improvise a pratfall on an icy sidewalk. Of course, May didn't ask them to. All she asked

Hoffman and Beatty, as Chuck and Lyle, doing their nightclub act. And you should hear how they sound!

them to do was find the comedy in their characters. But Hoffman and Beatty don't do that. They make sure we know they're smarter than their characters. They're acting conspicuously stupid and they're not having much fun. And it shows.

But maybe we should have expected it to turn out this way. Maybe we should have known that when a perfectionist like Beatty is teamed with the painstaking Hoffman under the direction of pathologically indecisive May, the result will be a movie as shapeless, lifeless, and mirthless as *Ishtar*. We *should* have known that, but moviegoers' minds don't work that way. Moviegoers remember all the reports that Hoffman's *Tootsie* was in trouble and say, "Look how well *that* turned out." Moviegoers remember that Beatty's *Reds* went over budget and over schedule and then went on to win all sorts of awards. Moviegoers are essentially optimistic. If they weren't, they wouldn't still be moviegoers. But *Ishtar* is the sort of enervating flop that turns even sunny optimists into sour cynics. For what it does to the spirit of moviegoing—and moviemaking—it deserves its permanent place on *any* list of Megaton Bombs.

48

THE BONFIRE OF THE VANITIES

1990 ⌃ Warner Brothers

Produced and directed by Brian De Palma. Screenplay by Michael Cristofer, based on the novel by Tom Wolfe.

CAST: Tom Hanks (*Sherman McCoy*); Bruce Willis (*Peter Fallow*); Melanie Griffith (*Maria Ruskin*); Kim Cattrall (*Judy McCoy*); Saul Rubinek (*Jed Kramer*); Morgan Freeman (*Judge White*); F. Murray Abraham (*D. A. Weiss*).

"THIS IS THE BEST MOVIE we've ever made," said Warner Bros. chief Mark Canton, after viewing an early cut of *The Bonfire of the Vanities*. He really thought it was a work of art, that it might even win a few Oscars. The rest of the world didn't agree with him. Can five billion people be wrong?

Actually, only a few million people bothered to see this movie. Everyone else was warned away by excessively bad word of mouth. The buzz was so bad, in fact, that it made *Bonfire* sound even worse than it is. The reality, however, is awful enough.

The film is based on Tom Wolfe's best-selling novel of greed, intolerance, and the power of the press in 1980s New York. The hero is Sherman McCoy, an old-money Yalie who lives on Park Avenue and works on Wall Street, where, as a self-proclaimed Master of the Universe, he makes multimillion-dollar deals for his rich and powerful brokerage firm. Sherman is on top of the world until the night he and his mistress take a wrong turn into the South Bronx and encounter two youths, who might be muggers, on an exit ramp. In a panic, Sherman's mistress takes the wheel and accidentally runs down one of the youths, leaving him in a coma. Now hit-and-run drivers, Sherman and his lover set off a chain of events that will turn Sherman McCoy from Master of the Universe to Scapegoat of the City. The whole

Tom Hanks, Melanie
Griffith, and Bruce Willis
loom larger than life in the
Vanities poster art.

town comes after Sherman, from callous cops to ambitious D.A.s to ambu-
lance-chasing lawyers to self-promoting neighborhood activists to a feeding
frenzy of reporters to a media-manipulated angry public. They all have different agendas, but they all have one thing in common: They want Sherman's
blood. It isn't a pretty sight, but it is perversely fascinating.

At least it is in the book. Wolfe's *Bonfire* is a savagely satirical version of a
big city full of predators and scavengers. Like many great books, it is too
teeming with ideas and incidents to translate very successfully into a two-
hour movie. But director Brian De Palma and screenwriter Michael Cristofer
don't even come close. In skimming the novel's surface and picking up only
the major plot points—invariably out of context—they've reinterpreted
Wolfe's story in big, bold, exaggerated strokes. And yet, without Wolfe's context—without his wealth of sociological detail—this really isn't the same
story. *Bonfire* becomes a movie about people screwing other people in a senseless series of coincidental assaults. In trying to simplify matters for the mass

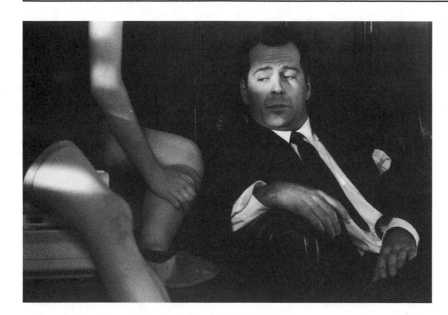

Willis, as pie-eyed Peter Farrow, slouches through another broadly played encounter.

audience, De Palma and Cristofer have missed the nuance, the subtlety, the irony, the essence. In short, they've missed the point.

Perhaps already knowing they were doomed to artistic failure, the filmmakers made their other creative decisions based solely on what they thought might help their film sell tickets. Nowhere is that strategy more obvious—or more obviously wrongheaded—than in the movie's casting. First, they hired Tom Hanks for the all-important role of Sherman. Hanks, of course, is no one's idea of a typical blue-blood WASP, although his sad sack comic style does make him a good victim, if not a good Yale man. The rest of the cast however, isn't even half right. There's Melanie Griffith as mistress Maria, whose southern-belle accent comes and goes; Kim Cattrall, who gives a one-note nonperformance as Sherman's "social X-ray" wife; and Bruce Willis as muckraking tabloid reporter Peter Fallow, who was a drunken Englishman in the book, but here is just Bruce Willis pretty much playing himself. Put him together with all the other miscast main players—most notoriously Morgan Freeman, who plays a black judge who was a Jewish judge in the book—and you've got a motley crew inhabiting a New York that only Hollywood could have dreamed up.

Freeman, of course, was cast as the judge simply because the filmmakers felt they needed a positive African-American character to balance their negative portrait of the predominantly black South Bronx. But they forgot (or perhaps they never noticed) that nobody was supposed to come off looking good in Tom Wolfe's scheme of things. It didn't matter if they were black, white, brown, or pinstriped—they were all greedy, grasping, and equally guilty. Having a big-budget movie full of utterly unsympathetic characters just won't do, however. So Wolfe's embittered Jewish judge becomes a black man you can believe in. Except that you can't believe in him. The character doesn't make sense as a black man. When a courtroom spectator jumps up and accuses the judge of racism for letting a white man go free, it becomes resoundingly obvious that the filmmakers' commercial compromises have compromised the very logic of their movie.

As if they still weren't sure they'd pandered low enough to pull in the hicks from the sticks, De Palma and company came up with a handful of scenes obviously designed as crowd pleasers. The first is the movie's opening salvo: a long, showy sequence following Peter Fallow's drunken progress as he makes his way to his own testimonial—staggering from a parking garage to the reception hall while waving a bottle, shoving his hand in a platter full of salmon, and then slobbering all over a babe in an elevator. Having thus established his level of wit and sophistication, De Palma repeatedly reverts to it whenever he feels the need to appeal to the audience's lowest common denominator. There's something here for every emotional need: a fed-up Sherman shoots up his wife's dinner party with a pump-action shotgun just to give *us* a chance to blow off steam; the ambitious D.A. (F. Murray Abraham) launches a rabid tirade of racial slurs just to give us a *really* bad guy to root against; Sherman's dad (Donald Moffat) shows up at his son's darkest hour to tell him a sappy story and give us something to care about; and, finally, judge Morgan Freeman rises up at Sherman's trial to give us a rousing speech that contradicts everything *Bonfire* is supposed to be about.

"I'll tell you what justice is," says da judge. "Justice is the law. And the law is man's feeble attempt to set down the principles of decency. Decency! And decency is not a deal. It isn't an angle, or a contract, or a hustle. Decency is what your grandmother taught you. It's in your bones. Now you go home. Go home and be decent people. Be decent."

Lovely speech, isn't it? And it really says it all about how *Bonfire* mixes its signals and messes up its message. There hasn't been a literary theme this garbled since Ayn Rand adapted *The Fountainhead* for the big screen. But at

Hanks as "Master of the Universe" Sherman McCoy. All things considered, he'd rather be in Philadelphia.

least that film had Patricia Neal whipping Gary Cooper with a riding crop. This one doesn't have a single scene that funny—or that heartfelt. A movie of miscalculated calculations, *The Bonfire of the Vanities* is one of the rare ones: It has absolutely no artistic value and absolutely no entertainment value. It's a noisy nonexperience.

49

HUDSON HAWK

1991 ∢ Columbia

Produced by Joel Silver. Directed by Michael Lehmann. Screenplay by Steven E. deSouza and Daniel Waters, from a story by Bruce Willis and Robert Kraft.

CAST: Bruce Willis (*Hudson Hawk*); Danny Aiello (*Tommy Five Tone*); Andie MacDowell (*Anna Baragli*); James Coburn (*George Kaplan*); Richard E. Grant (*Darwin Mayflower*); Sandra Bernhard (*Minerva Mayflower*).

TOO MUCH STARDOM TOO SOON can be bad for an actor. All it takes is one big blockbuster hit to bloat his sense of self-worth. After that, his price goes up to eight figures, he starts assuming he can get away with anything, and, considering his box-office clout, his studio will let him try. Then, so full of himself that he can't see past his own nose, he goes out and falls flat on his face.

That explanation is as good as any for the abomination known as *Hudson Hawk*. Coming off his smash hit *Die Hard* (which probably would have been as big a hit with any number of actors in the lead role), Bruce Willis was, indeed, the next action hero. And since action heroes are the most desired commodity in modern movie-making, all of Hollywood was at his feet. Of course, they hadn't seen *The Bonfire of the Vanities* yet. But even if they had, it probably wouldn't have mattered. *Bonfire* wasn't an action movie. It wasn't a *real* Bruce Willis movie. He would never have to answer for that one. Taking full advantage of this state of grace, Willis teamed with action mogul Joel Silver (*Die Hard, Lethal Weapon*) to make his version of a personal statement: a big, ballsy comic adventure that would embody Bruce Willis's style, his sensibility, and his sense of humor.

Yes sir, no two ways about it, this was Bruce Willis's baby. It had a screenplay worked on by various reputable writers. It had a director, Michael

Bruce Willis and Andie MacDowell romp to the rescue. At least *somebody* was having fun.

Lehmann, who had previously done the cult hit *Heathers*. But forget all that. Bruce was "the Man" here. He improvised his dialogue. He overruled his director. He out-shouted his costars. He made it up as he went along. And Silver encouraged him every step of the way. The result is an off-the-cuff, seat-of-your-pants, rough-and-tumble romp that doesn't always know where it is going even after it gets there. But wherever it is, at any given moment, we find ourselves wanting to be somewhere else, because it turns out that Willis's personal style and sensibility aren't very funny at all. In fact, they're downright obnoxious.

Willis, of course, is Hudson Hawk, also known as the World's Greatest Cat Burglar. Hawk is just out of Sing-Sing and planning to go straight when some mobsters try to blackmail him into doing an auction house art heist. "Slurp my butt!" he tells them, in a typical burst of Hawksian humor. However, the mob insists. Soon Hawk is off on his latest escapade, accompanied by old partner Tommy Five Tone (Danny Aiello). While infiltrating the auction house, the buddies time their burglary to the tune of "Swinging on a Star." Yes, they actually perform a smirky musical number while sauntering down hallways, tripping surveillance cameras, and pilfering the goods, with oh-so-much panache. It's such an astonishing interlude that the inclination is to block it out as a one-time aberration—like, say, an embolism. But this movie won't let us forget it. We keep getting more where that came from.

Hawks's successful heist sets off a chaotic chain of events that finds him conscripted by the CIA, who want him to help them steal the key component to Leonardo DaVinci's legendary alchemy machine. This puts Hawk in direct competition with a brother-sister team of evil entrepreneurs (Sandra Bernhard and Richard E. Grant), as well as with an undercover Vatican nun (Andie MacDowell), who gives sensuous back massages and long lingering kisses—in the line of duty. The movie is full of cloak-and-dagger double-crosses. But it's never really clear who's doing what to whom, why they're doing it, or why we should care. This is what happens when people make up movies as they go along. They wind up with movies that make no sense.

Not that Willis and company care about making sense. They're much more concerned with cooking up on-the-spot comic set pieces—you know, those improvised bits that, according to Willis, truly reflect his rare sense of humor. So then, let's take a look at Bruce's idea of a joke.

Is your preference crude wit? *Hudson Hawk* has got it. When his buddy Tommy blurts out something smart about art, Hawk shouts him down with a snappy, "Okay, Mr. PBS!"

Or maybe you like sharply pointed barbs. *Hudson Hawk* has them, too. Confronted by two look-alike CIA goons, Hawk unflappably inquires, "What do they call you guys—Igg and Ook?"

Or maybe you get your kicks from good old jock-itch humor. Hudson Hawk knows how to scratch with the best of them. "I always did want to sing like Frankie Valli," he quips after taking a hard shot in the family jewels.

Brilliant, isn't it? And Hawk just keeps lobbing those zingers, acting out everyone else in the movie. "I wish I could come up with glib repartée like you do," says CIA man James Coburn at one point. "But I can't, so I'll just paralyze you." That's pretty much the technique the filmmakers have used in throwing together the rest of this mess.

When *Hudson Hawk* isn't firing off dazzling one-liners, it is bludgeoning you with physical humor. There are the kinky Bernhard and Grant, who shamelessly mug and shout at the top of their lungs and practically swallow each other's tongues. There is a slapstick struggle in an ambulance, which results in one thug getting a face full of hypodermic needles while Hawk flies out the back on a hospital gurney. And when all else fails, there are bone-crushing punches, deafening explosions, slam-bang chases, and still more shots to the crotch. After a couple of hours of this, we feel so shell-shocked

Willis and Danny Aiello tap their way through one of two renditions of "Swinging on a Star." It's not as funny as they think.

that nothing really registers anymore. By the time sexy nun MacDowell gets nailed by a tranquilizer dart and starts squealing like a dolphin—over and over and over—we can't even feel compassion for an actress who is doing serious damage to her career.

Adding insult to debilitating injury, Willis and Aiello team up once again to break into the bad guys' stronghold while performing another smirky duet ("Side by Side"—six minutes). Among other things, this stupefying dose of overkill forces us to admit that the previous musical interlude was no aberration. It also leaves us with the distinct impression that Willis and Silver really thought they were doing a Hope-and-Crosby road movie for a new generation. What they've actually done, however, isn't even an *Ishtar* for the nineties.

Yes indeed, *Hudson Hawk* is that bad. It's not just the incoherent plot or the juvenile jokes, the senseless cartoon violence or the budget-busting demolition derbies. It's not just the way some of our favorite performers wind up looking like fools. It's also the way Willis and Silver serve up these insults with such smug self-satisfaction. It's as if their movie was some sort of private Planet Hollywood party to which we'd been magnanimously invited. The trouble is, *they're* all drunk and *we're* still sober.

After *Hudson Hawk* some people started to wonder if Bruce Willis should have gotten more of the blame for *The Bonfire of the Vanities*. Since then he's done such rickety action vehicles as *The Last Boy Scout*, and proven himself as blameworthy as anyone. But Willis still has a career in Hollywood, even if some of his *Hudson Hawk* collaborators don't. We can only take solace in knowing that he couldn't sink any lower than this.

Here's to the future.

50

CHRISTOPHER COLUMBUS: THE DISCOVERY

1992 ⁀ Warner Brothers

Produced by Ilya Salkind. Directed by John Glen. Screenplay by John Briley, Cary Bates, and Mario Puzo.

CAST: George Corraface (*Christopher Columbus*); Marlon Brando (*Torquemada*); Tom Selleck (*King Ferdinand*); Rachel Ward (*Queen Isabella*); Robert Davi (*Martin Pinzon*); Catherine Zeta Jones (*Beatriz*); Mathieu Carriere (*King John*).

To CELEBRATE the five hundredth anniversary of the "discovery" of America, two major movies about Christopher Columbus were produced and released. One, Ridley Scott's *1492*, was a big, dark disappointment. The other *Christopher Columbus: The Discovery*, was a colossal joke. During the quincentennial year, Native American activists had vehemently protested the accepted image of Columbus as some kind of hero. After *Christopher Columbus* came out, the protests hardly seemed necessary. Who could take old Chris seriously anymore?

Produced by Alexander and Ilya Salkind, the men who gave us *Superman* and *Santa Claus*, *Christopher Columbus* begins with a ludicrous concept, then goes wrong every way it can. In the Salkinds' eyes, the story of Columbus is not a serious historical drama, nor even a high seas adventure like *Mutiny on the Bounty*. Nope, *Christopher Columbus* is pure escapist hokum, more like a Saturday matinee swashbuckler than a portrait of an explorer who gave us a national holiday.

True to the Salkinds' vision, George Corraface makes a disarmingly dashing Columbus. He looks like a young Al Pacino and fights like a young Errol Flynn. See him battle one-against-four, brandishing swords and knives. See him swing on ropes from the mast of the Santa Maria. See him slug it out with an onboard saboteur, finally subduing the villain with a vintage 1990s

Marlon Brando stonefaces his way through another top-billed cameo. Rachel Ward still manages to get upstaged.

head butt. And at least Corraface looks comfortable in his role. He's an un-known—what's he got to lose? Meanwhile, the movie's more famous stars never do quite fit in. And the more famous they are, the more out of place they seem.

Tom Selleck costars as King Ferdinand, and a comical king he is. Looking stiff and stern, and saying things like "I defer to my queen," he cuts quite a figure in his shoulder-length wig and brocaded robes. He reminds you of the captain of the football team doing a walk-on in the senior play. You can al-most hear him thinking, "Gee, I hope the guys aren't laughing."

Opposite Selleck, Rachel Ward makes a perfectly lovely Queen Isabella. But it's as if she'd been directed to be strictly a figurehead in all her scenes. Every once in awhile she casts a coy smile in Columbus's direction. If she'd added a little body language you might even think she was coming on to old Chris. But since she barely moves at all, she just looks like Rachel Ward doing an impression of the Mona Lisa.

Most embarrassing of all, however, is massive Marlon Brando, who here makes another of his top-billed, glorified cameo appearances. It's a lot like the one he did for the Salkinds' *Superman*, only with a lot less effort ex-pended. As the zealous court adviser known as the Grand Inquisitor, Brando is on screen for all of five minutes. Because of his girth you can't miss him, but because of his inertia, all he does is take up space. His performance consists of reading his lines without moving his lips. Every so often, apparently feeling persecuted, he casts his eyes heavenward and mumbles, "Lord, why have you forsaken me?"

After nearly an hour of such dreary preliminaries, it's a relief when Columbus finally sets sail, even if his voyage *is* the silliest part of this movie. Our time at sea mainly consists of beautiful sunset tableaux, but as the weeks wear on the crew gets increasingly ornery, breaking up the tedium with fistfights and sabotage attempts. Eventually the tension builds to the brink of mutiny and Columbus faces his first test as a leader. Taking full responsibility for getting three whole ships lost at sea, Columbus boldly vows to let his men behead him if land isn't sighted in three days. In a true measure of this movie's melodramatic soul, his neck is literally on the chopping block and the ax is falling when somebody shouts, "Land ho!"

America itself is a wondrous place, where the sea is turquoise and the sand is like sugar, where the native men have the fear of white gods and the native women have breasts the size of pineapples. But we knew that about America. In an attempt to tell us something we *don't* know, the movie presents Columbus's colonization as an allegory of grand imperialist ideals gone terribly awry. Predictably, however, the parabale falls apart in a graphic orgy of sex and slaughter.

Pushing right along to its muddled conclusion, the movie shows Columbus returning home to a hero's welcome, while behind him the New World burns in all-out anarchy. But if all this is supposed to be ironic, it doesn't come across that way. As a deified Columbus stands on a seaside cliff, stretching his arms out to embrace the distant horizon, we have no idea what in the world we're supposed to be thinking. How can we, when the filmmakers have even less of a clue?

The screenwriters for this gobbledygook just happen to include John Briley, who once won an Oscar for *Gandhi*, and Mario Puzo, who once wrote a book called *The Godfather*. But when you're working for the Salkinds such laurels matter little. When you're working for the Salkinds, you check your brains at the door and give the men what they want: a brainless movie.

The movies have come a long way since Sam Goldwyn made *The Adventures of Marco Polo*. But you couldn't prove it by the Salkinds' *Christopher Columbus*. In most respects, these two movies are equally, inherently silly, but

Tom Selleck as King Ferdinand, Rachel Ward as Queen Isabella. Is there hope for the New World?

at least *Marco Polo*, the product of a less ambivalent age, has the courage of its preposterous convictions. *Christopher Columbus*, on the other hand, doesn't even know what its convictions are. It's but one more example of what we've known all along: Movies are getting worse all the time. Even Megaton Bombs.

P A R T   I I

So Many Bad Movies, So Little Space

HOLLYWOOD DOES NOT DIE by Megaton Bombs alone. Year after year it has managed to make awful movies with no need for blockbuster budgets or overblown ambitions. In fact, as the decades pass, the studios have only gotten more adept at making really bad movies during the course of business as usual. They've gotten so they can do it without half trying.

The process is simple, really. All you have to do is stick with that high concept until it no longer works. Reheat that winning formula until it blows up in your face. Ride with that bankable star until he picks the wrong vehicle. Or trust that *wunderkind* director until he goes over the top with that invariably artsy second film.

The new, noncreative Hollywood is getting better and better at boiling down the process to these precious few equations. But for all their so-called progress, the studios are still making the same mistakes they've always made. They're still stumbling over the infinite variables that trip up even the best of intentions, and they probably always will. After all, you've got to have a hundred things go just right to end up with even a halfway decent movie. But mishandle even a couple of key ingredients and you've got a high concept that collapses. You've got a formula that blows up in your face. You've got an *awful* movie. Nothing monumental, mind you, just an ordinary, everyday, utterly *awful* movie.

What makes an ordinary awful movie different than a Megaton Bomb? It's a matter of scale, scope, historical experience, and even cultural impact. It's the difference between, say, *Valley of the Dolls* and *The Lonely Lady*. The former set the standard for glitzy, sudsy schlock based on trashy best-sellers. The latter simply ran it into the ground.

But an ordinary awful movie doesn't have to be a cheaper, cruder version of a big bad idea. It can also be a garbled message (*Zabriskie Point*) or a star-powered ego trip (*Ocean's Eleven*) or a rotten remake of an all-time great (*King Kong*) or merely the fourth sequel to a movie that didn't need any (*Rocky V*). In short, it can be awful in so many ways that you'd need a book the size of Leslie Halliwell's to fit them all in. Who has room for that many bad movies? Who wants to *read* about that many bad movies?

Instead, let's just take a random, selective, very subjective sampling: Thirty-three awful movies that somehow lack the scope or significance to be Megaton Bombs, but which are nevertheless really, really bad. Together, they don't begin to span the sprawling spectrum of badness. But what unites them is that each is the very worst of its kind . . . even if it happens to be one of a kind.

The Worst Remake of a Classic
King Kong (1976)

It was bad enough that Dino DeLaurentiis even dared to dis the memory of the best monster movie ever made. It was worse that he hyped it so shamelessly that P. T. Barnum might have blushed. And even worse was that his ballyhooed technical marvel turned out to be just another man in an ape suit (albeit one who was replaced in some scenes by a giant, hairy hydraulic hand). But when all was said and done, it was beauty that killed this beast. Unintentionally camping it up in the Fay Wray role, Jessica Lange ranges from hysterical ("You goddamn chauvinist pig ape!") to flirtatious ("I'm a Libra, What sign are you?"). It's enough to make a great ape go all gooey inside. Audiences, however, weren't so easily charmed. How did Lange's career survive this movie? How did Dino's?

The Worst Love Story for the Ages
Love Story (1970)

What can you say about a twenty-five-year-old girl who died? That she loved Mozart, Bach, the Beatles . . . and Ryan O'Neal. Sadly, this movie's about her love for O'Neal, who'd be the worst actor in the movie if it weren't for costar Ali MacGraw. Staring at each other all dewy-eyed, the two handle lame dialogue with all the style and grace of the leads in a junior high school play. For their diligence they both get to deliver the immortal line, "Love means never having to say you're sorry." But only Ali gets to die, lying in her sickbed looking even lovelier than she did the first time they met. Her mysterious ailment would forever after be known by film buffs as Ali MacGraw's disease. There is still no known cure.

"You goddam chauvinist pig ape!" Jessica Lange is Silly Putty in the hands of the mighty *King Kong*.

The Worst Movie Ever Made by a World-Class Director
Zabriskie Point (1970)

After helping to invent the European "art film," Italian master Michelangelo Antonioni (*L'Avventura*, *Red Desert*) decided to make a movie in America. Unfortunately, it was also supposed to be *about* America. In it, a pseudo-hippie couple wanders around the desert, talking utter nonsense about life (or whatever), until the guy gets shot by police and the girl gets revenge by blowing up a custom-built house owned by capitalist pig Rod Taylor. This is what Antonioni thought the sixties were all about? Maybe something got lost in the translation.

The Worst Remake of a Megaton Bomb
One Million Years B.C. (1966)

The booby prize here could easily go to Ursula Andress in the remake of *She* (1965). But instead, let's give it to Raquel Welch in the remake of Victor Mature's infamous caveman epic. Playing the fairest Cro-Magnon of all, Raquel

Raquel Welch makes like
Carole Landis in *One Million
Years B.C.*

sports blond hair, white go-go lipstick, and loads of liquid eyeliner to complement her skimpy animal-skin bikini. She's the perfect sixties cover girl, one million years ahead of her time. Best of all, she has no dialogue—unless you count "Tumak!" and assorted other grunts. Liberated from the burden of reading lines, Raquel actually holds her own with the other cave-people actors. Only the stop-motion dinosaurs are more animated.

The Worst Elvis Presley Movie Ever Made
Change of Habit (1969)

Poor Elvis spent most of his career remaking the same movie. (Quick: What's the difference between *Blue Hawaii* and *Paradise Hawaiian Style?*) By the time he was ready to change that two-fisted, fun-lovin', singing daredevil image, he was no longer convincing as anything else. He bit the dust as a cowboy (*Charro*) and stiffed as a medicine show ramrod (*The Trouble With Girls*). Then came this final indignity, in which he plays a dedicated ghetto doctor opposite Mary Tyler Moore—as an undercover nun! Together, they take on sanitized versions of junkies, prostitutes, unwed mothers, Latino gang members, black militants, and neighborhood Mafiosi. Along the way, Elvis sings one simpy song, has one wimpy scuffle, and barely gets to touch his spoken-for leading lady. Is it any wonder that this was The King's last movie?

The Worst Madonna Movie (So Far)
Body of Evidence (1993)

As a femme fatale in this *Basic Instinct* rip-off, Madonna looks embalmed and acts even deader. That's poor form for someone who's supposed to have killed her rich, older lover with, as the prosecutor puts it, "increasingly strenuous sex." But poor form is contagious in this trashy travesty, which couples rampantly ridiculous dialogue with equally silly sex scenes—including one in which Madonna hogties lawyer and lover Willem Dafoe, then showers him with champagne and hot candle wax. "It's not a crime to be a great lay," Dafoe tells the D.A. Yet the body of evidence hardly suggests that this bad girl is a great *anything*. Given a role she should have been able to play in her sleep, Madonna...plays it in her sleep.

The Worst Ronald Reagan Movie of Them All
That Hagen Girl (1947)

It's easy to make fun of *Bedtime for Bonzo*, but our former president was actually more embarrassed by this nonsensical sudser, costarring Shirley Temple as an adopted small-town teen who thinks war hero Ronnie may be her real dad. The trouble begins when the rest of the town starts suspecting it too. Idle gossip takes its toll on Ronnie's romance with Lois Maxwell, and pretty much wrecks Shirley's high school social life. Why she even loses the lead in her school play! Rising above the rumors, Ronnie and Shirley carry on a terribly cutesy friendship—which doesn't stop Shirley from trying to drown herself. Guess who sloshes to her rescue? Things get even soggier in this very strange affair, which reaches an even stranger conclusion when Ronnie and

Shirley board a train to someplace kinder and gentler. It looks like they'll live happily ever after, but as what? Father and daughter? Husband and wife? Just good friends? The movie never tells. And really, who wants to know?

The Very Worst Rat Pack Movie
Ocean's Eleven (1960)

Frank Sinatra, Dean Martin, Peter Lawford, Joey Bishop, and Sammy Davis, Jr.—assemble them all in one place and you had the notorious Rat Pack. Every so often, they got together to make a movie for fun. The results weren't so much motion pictures as slow-motion parties, in which the boys sat around nightclubs and penthouses patting girls' fannies, putting away tumblers of whisky, and tossing off hipster phrases like "Koo-koo" and "Cool it." Director? What director? These cats were calling the shots—and having a koo koo time doing it, baby! In this epic of all Rat Pack movies, the boys plan a simultaneous heist of five Las Vegas casinos. Of course the movie is 99 percent planning (in nightclubs and penthouses) and only 1 percent heist. But hey, at least they get a lot of drinking done.

The Worst Excuse for a Comedy Starring Sylvester Stallone
Rhinestone (1984)

After several broad swipes at comedy, Sly has finally faced the fact that he's not cut out for the genre. Of course, everyone else knew that after his first effort, *Rhinestone*, which, sad to say, was also his musical debut. As a New York cabbie trying to learn the art of country singing, Sly heads down to Dolly Parton's farm, where he suffers some stock sight gags while trying to fit in. See Sly climb into the saddle! See Sly force down funny lookin' vittles! See Sly hitch up his jeans and walk like a cowboy! See Sly throw back his head, swallow his pride, and—sing! The resulting caterwaul is enough to make the cows kick down the corral. Moviegoers did something similar to the exit doors.

The Worst Burt Reynolds Good Ol' Boy Movie
Cannonball Run (1981)

Burt used to bitch that posing in the buff for *Cosmopolitan* cost him any chance of being taken seriously as an actor. Right, Burt, it couldn't have been all those Down South, back road car chase movies you did throughout the

Sly and Dolly give new meaning to the term "musical comedy" in this numbing number from *Rhinestone.*

seventies. With all due disrespect to *Stroker Ace* and *Smokey and the Bandit II*, the pits of this crew was *Cannonball Run*, in which a smirky "all-star" cast (Dean Martin, Dom DeLuise, Jimmy the Greek, et al.) shticks its way through a cross-country race that takes forever to get started, then goes nowhere at a crawl. Burt followed this with *Cannonball Run II* (1984), which actually isn't much worse. But that's only because it couldn't *get* much worse.

The Worst John Travolta Career Move
Perfect (1985)

From *Moment by Moment* to *Staying Alive*, Travolta has bounced back from bad career decisions that would have buried most actors. But his most re-markable comeback was from *Perfect*, a movie so obnoxiously overhyped that its dismal failure made it the laughing stock of 1985. Playing a hotshot *Rolling Stone* reporter, Travolta takes on the ostensibly oversexed world of L.A. health clubs. "They're the single's bars of the eighties!" he claims. He's looking for the decline of western civilization. Instead he finds Jamie Lee Curtis leading a hot aerobics class. The Pulitzer Prize can wait. Travolta feels the burn in endless workout sequences, then feels the heat when Jamie discovers he's there to dig up dirt. Poor Jamie gets so mad she calls John a sphincter muscle. That's an-other way of saying he's an asshole for the eighties.

Travolta dances again, in the unfortunately titled *Perfect.*

The Worst Tom Cruise Teen Hunk Heartthrob Movie
Cocktail (1988)

As if *Top Gun* wasn't vapid enough, Tom Cruise kept his head way up in the clouds for this hard-hitting, happy-hour drama in which he learns about life and love behind the bar of a swinging singles joint. Eventually the cocky cocktail shaker will learn that filling beer mugs is an empty existence, but not before he dazzles teenage moviegoers with his hip-swiveling, eye-twinkling, wineglass-twirling display of good old-fashioned . . . juggling! Okay, so it's not the same as flying a fighter jet upside down, but if you lose your concentration it can still get pretty scary. Kamikazes, anyone?

The Worst Movie Produced by, Directed By, and Starring Jack Webb
The D.I. (1957)

If you only know Jack Webb as *Dragnet's* Sgt. Joe Friday, you haven't seen him in the role he was born to play. As the ultimate hard-ass drill instructor, he doesn't just harangue the troops, he also trades put-downs with the other sergeants, plays straight man to a buffoonish buck private, worries about a lost-lamb recruit, and (are you ready?) romances a pretty war widow. Their

Tom Cruise shows off his dubious talent in the half-sloshed *Cocktail.*

first kiss has all the tenderness of a rifle inspection. Come to think of it, so does their second. Webb, the director, has filmed this labor of love with some of the artsiest camera angles you'll ever see in a gung-ho, grunts-in-training movie. But you've still got to give him points for *cinema vérité:* After this workout you really do feel like you've spent ten weeks in boot camp.

The Worst Movie Starring Joan Crawford as a Caricature of Herself
Torch Song (1953)

As a past-her-prime prima donna, Joan bitches, bullies, and bites off heads while rehearsing a Broadway show. Then she falls in love with blind pianist Michael Wilding and suddenly this bitter pill of a backstage drama becomes

Joan Crawford leads with her jaw in this dance duet from *Torch Song.* Her partner: Director Charles Walters.

. . . less bitter. But it's still a pill. Taking it upon herself to alleviate the boredom, Joan does several fishnets-and-leotards song-and-dance numbers, including the unforgettable "Two Faced Woman—which she performs in blackface! But wait, there's more!. At the end of the number she throws a big tantrum, tears off her wig, and reveals a bright orange mop that causes a Technicolor riot with her face full of greasepaint. Not even Faye Dunaway could have topped this.

The Worst Movie Bob Hope Ever Made
Without Bing Crosby
How to Commit Marriage (1969)

After a whole decade of stale, square sitcom movies, the star of *I'll Take Sweden* tried to get hip by taking this comic look at the free-lovin' sixties. The result was enough to make audiences nostalgic for *Call Me Bwana*. The not-so-high concept sticks Bob and wife Jane Wyman with their hippie daugh-

Bob Hope and Jackie Gleason let it all hang out in *How to Commit Marriage.*

ter's out-of-wedlock baby—just when they were ready to get a divorce! Presumably the laughs derive from this unhappy couple's attempts to play house while still sneaking off to their respective lovers. For added hilarity, Bob has head-on collisions with long-haired rock musicians, hippie commune members, and sixties fashions. The sight of him in a Nehru jacket elicits this zinger from Jane: "Who are you supposed to be? Sabu's mother?" Unfortunately, that barb would have been better aimed at Professor Irwin Corey, who plays a guru named Babu Ziba but dresses more like Ali Baba. At least costar Jackie Gleason has the good sense to dress his age. Not that it makes much difference. He already looks pretty dopey just by *being* in this movie.

The Worst Movie Bing Crosby Ever Made Without Bob Hope
High Time (1960)

Bing's first mistake was producing this corn-starched comedy. His worst mistake was starring in it. Looking ten years too old, Der Bingle plays a middle-aged millionaire who decides to enroll in college as a freshman. He just wants to be treated like one of the kids, and waddya know, that's exactly how they

Marlon Brando and Jean Simmons in the costume drama *Desirée.*

treat him. Fitting right in with Fabian and Tuesday Weld, he helps smuggle girls into the dorm, performs complicated hand-clapping cheers at the big basketball game, and endures a fraternity initiation that puts him in Scarlett O'Hara drag for a formal dance. Of course he's the belle of the ball. In fact, this Scarlett impression is the only acting he does in the movie. The rest of the time he just stands around in his jaunty hat, smoking his long-stemmed pipe—as if his mere presence were enough to support this ten-ton turkey. If only he knew how much he was dragging it down.

The Worst Marlon Brando Period Piece
Desirée (1954)

Brando broods as Napoleon Bonaparte—but this is not Marlon's usual brand of brooding. This is more like he's pouting because he has to dress like a fop and wear a pretty curl in the middle of his forehead. That hairdo is the crowning touch to this overstuffed, overdressed, overlong costume drama in which Marlon conquers Europe while hanging around the place—where he actually plays second fiddle to Jean Simmons's Desirée. Maybe *that's* why he's in such a sour mood.

The Worst Rocky Movie (by a Split Decision)
Rocky V (1990)

Sure, Rocky movies are all alike. But there can only be one last gasp, and *Rocky V* is it. This is the one that finds the Italian Stallion broke, brain damaged, and back in the old neighborhood. Since the WBA won't let him in the ring anymore, he has to fight his climactic bout, against turncoat protégé Tommy Morrison, in the street outside a corner bar. After this, there truly *was* no place left to go—except, of course, the gutter.

The Worst Tarzan Movie
Tarzan the Ape Man (1981)

Big, dumb-looking Miles O'Keeffe is the worst big-screen Tarzan since surfer dude Denny Miller put on leopard print trunks and lip-synched Johnny Weissmuller's yodel. As if he wasn't handicapped enough, he's stuck with an orangutan sidekick instead of the usual cute chimp. No matter, they both play second banana to Bo Derek as an unabashedly bimboesque Jane. Stumbling through the jungle, losing her clothes as she goes, Bo perpetrates a tropical tease that ends with her getting stripped and smeared with mud by ugga-bugga natives. Bo barely changes her expression throughout her ordeal, but Richard Harris more than compensates by chewing up acres of rain forest scenery as Jane's hammier-than-thou missionary daddy. Weissmuller would have tossed this guy to the crocodiles faster than you can say, "Hungawa!"

The Worst Pirate Movie by at Least 20,000 Leagues
Pirates (1986)

A mangy-looking Walter Matthau shivers his rotting timbers in Roman Polanski's perversion of the pirate genre, which goes out of its way not to be swashbuckling. Polanski marshals his extras for some blasé battle scenes, and keeps a few rubber sharks around for atmosphere. But he saves his real creativity for a series of gross-out sight gags which come at you in waves, just like nausea: from the rats in the soup to the doo-doo on the deck to a vine-

Bo Derek takes to the trees with Miles O'Keeffe in *Tarzan, the Ape Man*.

gar purge in the captain's chamber pot. Getting into the swim of things, Matthau hits a heroic high point when he bites the swollen big toe of a gout-ridden enemy. This was either Polanski's idea of revisionist genre satire or a giant joke on his producers. Either way, the question is—Why?

The Worst Rendition of State Fair
State Fair (1962)

Inexplicably, Hollywood has produced three versions of this cornball Rodgers and Hammerstein musical. The first two had their fans. The third one, however, was charmless. Never mind that stage and screen veteran José Ferrer directed this ode to 4-H family values as if he had a clothespin on his nose. The real problem is the casting. Farmboy Pat Boone falls for fairground dancer Ann-Margret and sweet thing Pamela Tiffin falls for hipster deejay Bobby Darin—and it's a toss-up which couple is the more unlikely. Pat and Ann-Margret, however, are definitely more hilarious. When she cautions him that she's "been around," he looks at her like she's against his religion. "Does that mean you're a bad girl?" he gulps. And because he's Pat Boone we believe him. For added comic relief, there's also Pat and Pam's pop, Tom Ewell, who spends most of his time in the pigpen singing "Sweet Hog of Mine" to his prize boar Blue Boy. "Now I've seen everything," says a passerby. We sort of feel the same way.

The Worst Deluxe Soap Opera Directed by Douglas Sirk
Magnificent Obsession (1954)

In some circles, Douglas Sirk is admired for the elegant way he handled gloppy melodramas. But he had his hands full with this epically overwrought weeper, which stars Jane Wyman as a rich, blind widow and Rock Hudson as a reckless playboy who indirectly caused her blindness *and* her widowhood. Wracked by guilt, Rock finds God, becomes a doctor, falls in love with Jane, searches the world for her after she disappears, and finally saves her life with a delicate brain operation—his first! All this comes accompanied by heavenly choirs and radiant beams of light, a combination that worked such box-office miracles that the stars were immediately reteamed in Sirk's *All That Heaven Allows* (1955), in which Jane plays another rich widow and Rock plays a nature-boy gardener who wears pressed flannel shirts, sings a song called "Flirty Eyes," and eventually falls off a cliff while running after Jane's car. It's okay to cry.

The Worst Overgrown Grab-Bag of All-Star Cameos
The Story of Mankind (1957)

Before he started making disaster movies, Irwin Allen made a shambles of world history with this star-studded folly. The "story" is that mankind is on trial for having invented the atom bomb. Enter Ronald Colman as the Spirit of Man, who must debate the Devil—Vincent Price!—over the future of the human race. To make his case, Colman cites historical highlights across the ages—which Allen dramatizes in a series of vignettes that range from simpleminded slapstick (Harpo Marx getting showered with apples as Sir Isaac

Rock Hudson and Jane Wyman, bathed in celestial light, in a publicity pose for *Magnificent Obsession*.

Newton) to empty-headed epic (an ancient-Egypt segment featuring borrowed footage from *Land of the Pharaohs*). The intentionally comic casting includes Groucho Marx as a cigar-wielding Peter Minuit, fast-talking the Indians out of Manhattan. The unintentional comic casting includes Dennis Hopper as Napoleon, Peter Lorre as Nero, and Hedy Lamarr as a drop-dead gorgeous Joan of Arc. Sort of makes you wonder why mankind was spared.

The Worst High-Toned Drama Starring Hollywood Stars Made Up to Look Like Asians
Dragon Seed (1944)

In the good old Golden Age, Hollywood thought nothing of putting Caucasian stars in eye-slanting makeup and calling them Oriental. This was insulting enough in Mr. Moto movies, but somehow even worse in so-called serious films. Even Katharine Hepburn can't help looking silly in this meant-to-be-uplifting epic about Chinese peasants under Japanese occupation. But even sillier than how she looks is how she sounds, spewing that stilted, stylized dialogue that Hollywood hacks always dream up to evoke distant times and places. It ranges from the convoluted, as in "Come see your second brother, mother of my children," to the downright condescending, as in the words of some peas-

Katharine Hepburn goes
Hollywood Oriental in
Dragon Seed.

ants who witness a bombing raid by Japanese "skyships." Says one, inspecting a crater, "If one of us had stood near here, he would no longer live." Rarely has a celebration of human dignity seemed more insulting.

The Worst High-Camp Melodrama Starring Hollywood Stars Made Up to Look Like Asians
The Shanghai Gesture (1941)

Welcome to Josef von Sternberg's idea of Shanghai, where spoiled, rich Poppy (Gene Tierney) is literally gambling her life away at Mother Gin Sling's palace of iniquity. Poppy's scandalized father (Walter Huston) is a stuffy English diplomat, but Poppy herself is Eurasian! Guess who the mother she never knew turns out to be? Tierney's exotic Poppy is more sloe-eyed than slant-eyed, but Ona Munson's Mother Gin Sling is a regular dragon lady—complete with Siamese cat eye shadow, goddess Kali hairdos, and dagger-like fingernails. Add Victor Mature as Dr. Omar, a "Persian" in a fez who calls Poppy "my Little Lotus," then throw in various rickshaw coolies and slave girls in cages, and you've got a veritable sideshow of Oriental stereotypes.

The Worst Sequel to an Oscar-Winning Movie
The Sting II (1983)

In this foredoomed follow-up to the Best Picture of 1973, Jackie Gleason and Mac Davis take over the roles made famous by Paul Newman and Robert Redford. They also get a hand-me-down script which blandly rehashes the original hustle. The result resembles a bad TV series based on a hit movie. Now granted, Newman and Redford are a tough act to follow. So what was the point of going through the motions? Didn't anyone learn anything from *Butch and Sundance: The Early Years*? This one's even worse than that because it's so obvious that everyone involved quit on the movie before they even got started. Which, of course, is not the same as quitting while you're ahead.

The Worst Sequel to a Brainless Box-Office Smash
Grease II (1982)

Can a movie starring Michelle Pfeiffer possibly be a come down from a movie starring Olivia Newton-John? Only in a different universe—which is apparently where Robert Stigwood and Allan Carr were when they produced *Grease II*. At least the first *Grease* movie had colorfully kitschy songs from the Broadway show. All this sorry sequel has is Pfeiffer as the new leader of the Pink Ladies. Pretty as she is in pink, Michelle's no singer or dancer. Neither is fifties relic Tab Hunter as a biology teacher who leads his class in a production number about reproduction. To watch them all stumbling around their desks is to be thankful it isn't a song about dissecting frogs.

The Worst Potboiler Based on a Harold Robbins Best-Seller
The Lonely Lady (1981)

From *The Carpetbaggers* to *The Betsy*, producers have always loved Harold Robbins's brand of bestselling trash. But by the time they got to *The Lonely*

Pia Zadora wallows through
The Lonely Lady.

Lady, they were scraping the bottom of the Robbins barrel. And who should be wallowing there but Pia Zadora? As a wide-eyed innocent who actually dreams of becoming a screenwriter (only in Hollywood), Pia endures a brutal rape, an impotent husband, a Eurotrash lesbian encounter, and assorted other humiliations on the rocky road to success. Through it all she drinks herself into stupors and cries herself to sleep. However, she has the last laugh. Accepting the award for Best Screenplay, Pia tells off the black-tie crowd. "I don't suppose I'm the only one who's had to fuck her way to the top," she declares. But of course you aren't, Pia. This is Harold Robbins, remember?

The Worst Movie Starring Animals Who Talk Like People
Jonathan Livingston Seagull (1973)

Fly with us now back to the hippy-dippy seventies, when a studio could make a full-length movie about seagulls who speak in EST-inspired aphorisms, with voice-overs by people like Hal Holbrook and Richard Crenna, and expect to be taken seriously. Based on the novel that sold five million copies (now you know why Hollywood took it seriously), this is the story of a seagull named Jonathan (voice by James Franciscus), who gets fed up with foraging at the dump and sets off around the world in search of better fish. Instead he dies, goes to heaven, learns the meaning of life, then returns to earth to enlighten his old flock, who hail him as "the Son of the Great Gull."

All this comes with a sound track of Neil Diamond songs, which play right along with the greeting card sentiments, and add a few of their own. They sound just as silly set to music.

The Worst Hard-Core Porn Flick Passing Itself Off As an Art Film
Caligula (1980)

In this never-ending orgy of sex and violence, Caligula, Tiberius, and various other Romans rape, maim, sodomize, and murder to their heartless content. Five minutes into the bloodbath you've already seen enough—and there are still 145 minutes to go. *Penthouse* publisher Bob Guccione produced this pile of excrement, then hired Peter O'Toole, Malcolm McDowell, and John Gielgud who give it an aura of class. Unfortunately the plan backfired, and it's the actors who got burned. By selling themselves to this would-be De Mille of the decadent seventies, these distinguished Old Vic thespians came off as nothing more than common whores. But hey—that's showbiz!

P A R T I I I

The Baddest of
the B's

THEY WERE THE SECOND FEATURE at Saturday matinees. The third attractions on drive-in triple bills. The movies you could later find at 4:00 A.M. on local TV channels. Nominally they were "B" movies, but in terms of artistic merit they ranged anywhere from "C" to "Z." In the early days, major studios churned out their own program filler, using their second string stars and directors. But since there wasn't enough profit potential in these productions, the studios increasingly left it to smaller companies, the so-called Poverty Row studios, to handle the demand. In turn, Poverty Row eventually gave way to independent producers, who showed up in town with new ideas, different approaches—and usually a lot less money. Somehow, though, they got their pictures made. And the more Hollywood came to rely on them, the further from the mainstream they nudged the art of B movies. After all, they could afford to. With Bs there were no big budgets invested, no reputations at stake, not even any box-office take. Box-office take was strictly for A movies. The number of tickets was credited to (or blamed on) the main attraction, as though no one was (officially) watching the second feature. But while no one was watching, some pretty strange people put some pretty strange stuff on celluloid—most of it closer to Z than C. And that is our story here: the men who made the baddest of the Bs.

Some of these men were mini-moguls in their own right—men like Samuel Arkoff and James Nicholson, with their American International Pictures, Roger Corman with his New World Pictures, and Albert Zugsmith with his Albert Zugsmith Pictures. Just as often, however, the bad B filmmakers were free agents flying by the seat of their pants, like self-styled producer-director-cinematographer-star Ray Dennis Steckler, who gave us *Incredibly Strange Creatures Who Stopped Living and Became Mixed-Up Zombies*. Or the infamous Hal P. Warren, a Texas fertilizer salesman who sank his savings into the abysmal *Manos, The Hands of Fate*. Or the one and only Ed Wood, Jr., whose *Night of the Ghouls* went unreleased for twenty-three years because he couldn't afford to pay the processing bill.

Shoestring budgets as threadbare as Wood's are rare even in Grade Z movies. But they *do* happen, and invariably they make for some interesting "technical difficulties." We're not just talking bad makeup and bogus monsters. We're talking movies with missing soundtracks (*The Creeping Terror*), movies with actors who do their own sound effects (*Monster à Go Go*), and movies that were never completed until someone spliced in new footage that would forever stick out like a sore thumb (*They Saved Hitler's Brain*). These movies are bad in a way that goes beyond style and content. Indeed, they are beyond *bad.* Yet what blasts most of them into a whole new dimension are the wild and wooly imaginations of directors determined to get their visions on film—no matter what it *doesn't* cost. The baddest of the Bs, then, are a rare, precious mix of jerry-built production values and jazzed-up creative juices. But that's not to say that even with a budget, a B movie can't still bounce way off the wall, as the hepcat campy *Girls Town* or the ultra-trashy *Faster Pussycat! Kill! Kill!* voluptuously demonstrate. In the end, the truest measure of the baddest Bs isn't how cheap they are. It's how absurd they are. How outrageous they are. How utterly, incredibly *out there* they are.

They don't make movies like that anymore, and not just because double features and drive-ins are a thing of the past. It's also because independent filmmaking has changed. Today's off-Hollywood directors are likely to be serious artists who have cut their teeth at New York University or the Sundance Institute instead of Roger Corman's Acme movie machine. These days, the hackwork is largely left to made-for-cable and straight-to-video movies, even the worst of which provide the filmmaker with a professional-size budget—in return for a "vision" that stays within acceptable genre parameters. And that pretty much kills it right there. What good is a B movie if it is conventionally inspired and comfortably subsidized? More to the point—how *bad* can it be?

Nope, for honest-to-goodness Grade Z atrocities, there is simply no substitute for the pre-1980s Age of B Movies: a forty-year epoch which attained its zenith in the post-atomic, commie-paranoid, teenage-rebellious, sexually-revolutionary fifties and sixties. That is where you'll find the big hairy apes, brain-transplanting scientists, prehistoric women, radioactive mutants, rubber-suited aliens, reefer-smoking punks, juvenile-delinquent daughters, and hot rodders to hell. They'll make your eyes pop, they'll make your jaws drop, they'll make you lose your bearings, they'll make you laugh out loud. That's what makes them the baddest of the Bs.

"I don't want to grow anymore! I don't want to grow anymore!" Glenn Langan just can't help himself in *The Amazing Colossal Man.*

The Amazing Colossal Man (1957) Among 1950s nuclear nightmares, mutant humans were almost as "big" as mutant bugs. And none came bigger than *The Amazing Colossal Man.* This is the whopper about an army major (Glenn Langan) who gets flash-fried during a test blast, then wakes up with new skin, a shiny bald head, and an alarming physical growth trend. "His cells are growing at an accelerated, or speeded-up rate," says a doctor, spelling things out in typical fifties sci-fi simple-speak. While we're still pondering that line of dialogue, the major is shooting up ten feet per day. And the bigger he gets, the more bitter he becomes. "You know what they wrote about me in the high school yearbook?" he asks his fiancée (Cathy Downs), laughing ironically. "The man most likely to reach the top!" But even worse than his increasingly bad attitude is the fact that, as he grows, he gets increasingly hard to see. Thanks to Bert I. Gordon's bargain-basement special effects, the Colossal Man actually starts to blend into the "backdrops." He's getting bigger *and* he's disappearing! Just when it seems all is lost, the doctors devise a growth reversal formula which has worked wonders on the bunny-sized elephants and camels in the lab. Alas, it is already too late for the Colossal Man, who has gone berserk and is terrorizing Las Vegas, ripping up fake palm trees and trashing that big neon cowboy atop the Pioneer Club. In the grand finale, the doctors ram his foot with a giant hypo full of growth reversal formula, which only sends him farther over the top. Impaling one slow-moving scientist with the super-syringe, he picks up his fiancée and heads for Boulder Dam, where the army opens fire and sends him plunging into the waters below. Aieee! Miraculously, the big guy will return in *War of the Colossal Beast* (1958), now so disfigured that we aren't supposed to notice he's being played by another actor. As if it would have made the slightest bit of difference!

A*P*E (1976) "Not to be confused with *King Kong*," said the ads. Not to worry, nobody was fooled—even though this chintzy Korean knockoff does act a lot like the King. Escaping from a top secret lab, he stomps around the soundstage countryside until he finds and befriends a pretty blond starlet (Joanna DeVarona). You know how it goes from there. Why, the girl even sits in his naugahyde paw and makes cutesy-pie small talk, just like Jessica Lange. "Be gentle with me, big fella," she pleads, squirming insider her dress. Big ape that he is, he falls for her. He also wrestles a "giant" rubber snake (à la Kong), fights a "giant" shark that looks like it was borrowed from the nearest fresh fish market, and swats a couple of toy helicopters out of the air. Not bad for a stuntman in a moth-eaten monkey suit. But finally, his most memorable act is something all his own. Pursued by the standard small army, this increasingly angry, not-so-great ape goes bananas and—gives the soldiers the finger! Seeing it through their eyes, we can hardly believe our own. Some sort of movie history has been made.

The Astounding She-Monster (1958) She emerges from the vicinity of a UFO sighting. She has a skintight silver space suit and practically vertical eyebrows, and whenever she appears the screen gets blurry and wavy. In a movie as dim as this one, that qualifies her as astounding. Apparently, she has come to Earth to destroy all earthlings, but unfortunately, she has landed in the lonely California mountains, where the minuscule budget limits her to a single, isolated cabin—in which a nice guy scientist (Robert Clarke) and a mink-stoled socialite (Shirley Kilpatrick) are being held captive by desperate kidnappers. One by one, the kidnappers venture outside to see what that noise is out there. This leads to endless wandering in the woods, which is only slightly less pointless than the action inside the cabin, where nerves are fraying and tempers growing short. "You got a drink in this dump?" says the brassy kid-nappers' moll, slouching across the movie's only set to wrap her mouth around a whiskey bottle. Just when you think *she* might be the She-Monster the real thing comes crashing through the window. Has the action finally picked up? Not really. Still to come is a long, meandering escape down a dark mountain road, followed by a mad dash back to the cabin so the She-Monster can come *back* through the window and—again—chase the survivors outside for *another* long trek through the woods . . . after which the scientist and the socialite circle *back* to the cabin, enabling the She-Monster to make one last astounding entrance. *Finally*, the scientist throws a beaker of acid at her, penetrating her "thin coat of protective metal," and ending the longest sixty-minute movie ever made. Whew!

The Astro Zombies (1967) Shades of Dr. Frankenstein! John Carradine is a mad scientist manufacturing quasi-humans in his basement laboratory. He even has a hunchback assistant, whose name, incredibly enough, is not Igor. But these two are not your ordinary grave-robbers. The doctor and his assistant abduct only living humans to get the brains they need for—astro zombies!! Carradine literally never leaves the lab while performing what seem to be chemistry-set experiments and saying things like, "We must dip the patient in the thermal freeze vault, before cellular deterioration takes place." Meanwhile, in the rest of the movie, enemy agents and CIA men are engaged in klutzy cloak-and-dagger competition to find the mad scientist and harness his terrible technology. The CIA men are a boring enough bunch, but the enemy agents are led by exotic Tura Satana, who sports Mata Hari makeup, futuristic dragon lady dresses, and long-stem cigarette holders while bossing around thick-headed thugs with even thicker accents. "Dr. DeMarco has created a subservient zombie," she snarls. "That's something my government *must* have!" To show she means business (as if we had any doubt), Satana occasionally pumps an underling full of lead without so much as batting a fake eyelash. Not even cadaverous Carradine can steal this bad girl's thunder. In fact, her only real competition is one poor astro zombie who loses his power pack during a murder mission, and then must make a mad scramble back to the lab, while holding a flashlight against his forehead—to feed his "photo cell." You don't see sights like this every day, even in Grade Z schlock.

Okay, so the Astro-Zombies
didn't look *quite* this good.
But you really *do* see
corpse stealers and berserk
human transplants!

The Atomic Brain (1964) In this demented brain-transplant movie, rich old shrew Mrs. March (Marjorie Eaton) requires a pretty new body to replace her decrepit old one. While her resident mad doctor tests his atomic brain transplant machine on graveyard corpses, the old crone hires three nubile candidates, who show up at her gloomy mansion thinking they've been hired as maids. When Mrs. March conducts a personal interview by prodding their towel-clad bodies with her cane, the girls sense that something is amiss. But when they start bumping into the mad doctor's failed experiments—such as the hulking dog-man and the zonked-out zombie girl—they *know* they're in trouble. Sure enough, one girl soon receives the brain of Mrs. March's cat, which reduces her to chasing mice, climbing trees, and clawing out the eyes of the second girl. That leaves the third girl, Mynah (Erika Peters), who finds herself modeling Mrs. March's future wardrobe while the ancient bag admires the curves that will soon be hers. "Rounded," observes the narrator, "in all the places men love." See, that's what it's been about all along. "I've never know what it's like to be loved for myself," the rich old lady soliloquizes, feeling sorry for herself.

Alas, she'll never find out. As this moldy old danse macabre wobbles to its conclusion, all hell breaks loose and Mrs. March's world falls apart: The cat girl tumbles off the roof; the dog man chomps away on the zonked-out zombie; the mad doctor gets nuked in his transplant machine; and Mrs. March's brain ends up in her cat. She doesn't stop chasing Mynah, though. She's still pursuing *that* dream right up to the fade-out. Some people just don't know when to quit.

Attack of the Crab Monsters (1957) "Something in the air is wrong," says one of the scientists exploring a remote Pacific atoll. That something turns out to be giant crabs, mutated by the fallout from atomic test explosions. These monsters are so advanced they can actually fake the voices of the people they've just consumed. "The crab can eat his victim's brain, absorbing his mind intact and working," explains one scientists. "Once they were men, now they are land crabs!" Oh yes, and bullets pass right through them, because they are "molecularly unstable." And yet, in other ways, these jumbo prawns rank pretty low on the monster-movie evolutionary scale. Indeed, for most of the film they are represented by a single giant claw, which swipes at people from a corner of the screen. Only later do the crabs appear in all their glory, looking like deformed parade floats, with legs that never move and faces that never seem to take shape. These amazingly makeshift monstrosities are creations of the one and only Roger Corman, King of Budget-Stretching B Movies. Get used to the name. You'll be seeing it again and again.

Attack of the Eye Creatures (1965) Slimy, goggle-eyed aliens are landing their yo-yo shaped spaceships on Earth. But nobody seems to know it except a handful of amateur actors playing utterly obnoxious earthlings. Out at lovers' lane, star John Ashley and is date have run over an eye-creature with their

An oversize (but underdeveloped) crustacean chews up a screaming scientist in *Attack of the Crab Monsters.*

car. Down at the local greasy spoon, two drifters are plotting to get rich by stealing one of the spaceships. Meanwhile, out at the air force base, two sub-mental meatballs are using their satellite equipment to spy on the doings on lovers' lane. Finally, there's an old coot running around with a shotgun, chasing "smoochers" off his property. With so many subplots cluttering up the screen, director Larry Buchanan rarely has to bother showing an extraterrestrial. No matter, the comic conversations are otherworldly enough. "Nothing as ugly as that could be human," says one of the submental meatballs staring at an alien on his surveillance monitor. "Oh no?" says the other meatball. "Have you looked in the mirror lately?" No wonder we're rooting for the eye-creatures; they don't have any dialogue.

Attack of the Fifty-Foot Woman (1958) Poor, rich Nancy Archer (Allison Hayes) has a philandering husband, a bad drinking problem, and a history of nervous breakdowns. But she doesn't know what trouble is until she encounters a giant from outer space—and becomes a giant herself! For a long time, all we see is one huge plaster of Paris hand hanging over the edge of Nancy's bed. Judging from its size, her feet would have to be somewhere out in the street. But never mind the logistics. More important is the sheer

emotion that spills forth when Nancy learns that her hubby Harry (William Hudson) is out boozing with some floozy. "She's loose!" screams Nancy's private nurse, filling us in on the action the producers didn't have the budget to show. "She's tearing off the roof!" the nurse adds, keeping us updated. Finally, we get a look at fifty-foot Nancy, dimly superimposed against the night sky (and magically attired in size ninety unmentionables), on her way to find her no-good cheating husband. "She'll tear the whole town apart until she finds Harry," says the sheriff. "Yeah," agrees the goofy deputy. "And when she finds him, she'll tear *him* apart too!" Turns out the deputy is absolutely right. Hell hath no fury like a fifty-foot woman scorned.

Attack of the Giant Leeches (1959) Welcome back to the world according to Roger Corman. This time he drags us way Down South, where a backwoods slob is chasing his trampy wife into the swamp with a shotgun. Just another wallow with poor white trash? Not quite. Waiting in the water are the giant leeches! They look like under-inflated pool toys and have round diving-mask mouths, through which the faces of the actors inside can often be glimpsed. Sloshing around in the shallows like kids in a backyard pool, these suckers seize unsuspecting victims and drag them down to an underwater cave, where everyone lies around moaning and looking, well, anemic. Meanwhile, back on dry land, the yokels are hotly debating what to do. "Giant leeches!" harrumphs the sheriff, dismissing eyewitness accounts. A visiting professor, however, is more open-minded. "Maybe the proximity to Cape Canaveral has something to do with it," he hypothesizes. "They use atomic energy. Maybe this is a mutation." Well, duh, Doc! To get to the bottom of his mystery once and for all, two square-jawed deputies strap on the scuba gear and . . . dive! When they come back up, guess what comes with them? "I've been around here for years," the sheriff says, as blobs of black rubber bob to the surface. "I never saw nothin' like that before." Obviously he has never seen a Roger Corman film.

Attack of the Killer Tomatoes (1980) The killer tomatoes are just what you're afraid they'll be: bushels of juicy garden vegetables that suddenly run amok, terrorizing San Diego. They roll down the street, fly through the air, even bob like apples, attacking innocent swimmers. But exactly how they kill is never very clear. One moment they're bearing down on some unlucky victim, and next the victim is dead. This is bad enough when the tomatoes are beef-steak-size, but when they grow as big as boulders, humankind is cooked. "It's man versus vegetable," declares one pentagon-type. "Technically, sir, tomatoes are fags," says a foreign scientist. "He means tomatoes are fruits," clarifies a colleague. These are the jokes. Elsewhere in the movie, citizens are stampeding, soldiers are firing at farmland, and secret agents are trying to cut off this invasion at the roots. One agent even dresses up like a tomato, infiltrates the enemy camp and actually pulls it off—until, at mealtime, he makes the mistake of saying, "Will somebody pass the ketchup?"

All of this is obviously intended as a spoof of idiotic "Attack of" horror flicks (you know, like *Attack of the Crab Monsters* and *Attack of the Giant Leeches*). But just because it's *deliberately* bad doesn't mean it isn't...bad! In fact, in a way it's worse. It's easy to laugh at awful actors who are playing bad horror movies straight, it's not so easy when awful actors are playing it straight for laughs. As this no-talent cast makes a big show of stumbling through endless chase scenes and tomato attacks, every so often breaking into impromptu song-and-dance numbers such as "The Tomato Stomp," you start to feel as if Mel Brooks had regressed to the age of twelve and made a juvenile horror spoof, starring fans of Mel Brooks movies. The fact that it *isn't* the worst "Attack of" movie ever made is just another measure of its ineptitude. After all, these guys were trying.

The *Aztec Mummy* Movies (1959) Mexican horror films are full of cursed mummies who haunt the Aztec ruins, guarding priceless relics. Yet the stupid scientists in these movies always act surprised when they encounter one. "It's incredible! A mummy comes back to life after hundreds of years!" marvels a dum-dum doctor in *The Robot vs. the Aztec Mummy*. And, mind you, this movie is the third in the *Aztec Mummy* trilogy. Don't scientists in Mexican horror movies read the newspaper? Certainly the Aztec Mummy isn't someone you'd easily forget. Sort of a cross between the Frankenstein monster and the *Wizard of Oz* scarecrow, the Mummy is one of the crudest creatures ever to plod across a dimly lit movie frame. But he's not the only outrageous character in these movies. There's also the beautiful heroine (Rosita Arenas), who, in a former life, was an Aztec princess in love with the handsome warrior who became the Mummy. And there's the evil doctor known as the Bat (Crox Alvarado), who repeatedly tries to steal the Mummy's treasure, usually by hypnotizing someone to do his bidding.

In both *The Aztec Mummy* and *The Curse of the Aztec Mummy*, he almost succeeds, only to be (apparently) killed for his trouble. Ah, but the Bat is resilient. He bounces back for more in *The Robot vs. the Aztec Mummy*, this time with his secret weapon, the titular robot—a jerry-built tin contraption lit up by blinking light bulbs and topped by a man's head inside a space helmet. "The robot uses radium!" cackles the Bat. "He has sufficient power to disintegrate anything in the world!" Alas, the only thing that disintegrates is the robot, after the Mummy picks him up and tosses him down in a clattering heap. Having won this less-than-titanic struggle, the Mummy proceeds to strangle the Bat, presumably killing him once and for all. Then it's back to his resting place deep in the ruins, where the treasure will once again be safe and sound. But of course it had to end this way. In Mexican horror movies, Aztec mummies never die, they just rise and rise again. Stay tuned.

The Beach Girls and the Monster (1965) Coming out of semiretirement, former high-adventure hero Jon Hall (*Hurricane*) directed and starred in this black-and-white beach party, in which the title bimbos (and their surfer boys) are attacked by a cheap rip-off of the Creature From the Black Lagoon. The monster has big enameled eyes that bug out of his buckling rubber face, and he walks like a man in a monster suit. But this is okay, because he's actually supposed to *be* a man in a monster suit. Attempting to keep this secret from the audience, Hall diverts our attention with an overdeveloped family soap opera involving beach boy Walker Edmiston, his oversexed stepmother (Sue Casey), and his stuffy scientist dad (Hall himself). Dad is constantly hectoring his son for wanting to party on the beach instead of studying mutant fish in the lab. The old man just can't stand those sun-loving surfers! "I tell you sheriff, something's got to be done about them," he carps. "The boys are nothing but a bunch of loafers and the girls are little tramps! They contribute nothing to a decent society." Given this holier-than-thou vehemence we shouldn't be too surprised when the killer in the monster suit turns out to be . . . Dad! And once he gets on a roll, no one who rubs him the wrong way is safe. After he has cleaned up the beach, Daddy-O takes care of his slutty wife, who's been cheating on him all over the place. Then he kills his son's best friend, who has stumbled on Dad's fiendish secret. Finally, with the sheriff bearing down, old Dad drives his car straight off a cliff, bringing this movie—and Jon Hall's career—to a startlingly sudden conclusion. Ah, but why prolong the agony? When a thing is over, it's over.

The Beast of Yucca Flats (1961) Tor Johnson was a big, bald ex-wrestler who got a lot of work in Ed Wood, Jr., movies. From there, you'd think he'd have nowhere to go but up, but Tor stayed stuck in his beyond-bad rut with this awesomely inept entry in the nuked-out mutant genre. Johnson plays a defecting Soviet scientist on the run from sinister KGB agents, who chase him right onto an atom bomb test range. You know what happens next. Blooey! Or, to quote the cryptically cracked narrator: "Touch a button, things happen. A scientist becomes a beast." The narration is full of such off-the-wall musings, which are often the only source of entertainment as beastly Tor, looking about the same after the blast as he did before, wanders through the desert, mindlessly killing. "Killing just to be killing," says the narrator, sadly. Strangely, this desolate part of the desert seems to be crawling with tourists, who are sitting ducks for the rampaging beast. "Vacation time," says the narrator, as one doomed couple stops with car trouble. "Man and wife . . . unaware of scientific progress." What the hell is this man talking about? Who knows—but he's on a roll. Soon the local cops show up at the scene of the crime, and our narrator is right there to sift through the clues: "Man choked to death . . . a woman's purse . . . and footprints on the wasteland." Eventually, the lawmen track those footprints to the beast's hiding place and, following the narrator's advice, "Shoot first and ask questions later." That also seems to be the method director Coleman Francis used when he committed this atrocity to celluloid.

Beginning of the End (1957) The whole town's destroyed!" says a panicky cop into his radio. "Everybody died!" Actually, so far everyone has simply disappeared. But let's not quibble. This is still a job for the state police, the national guard, *and* glamour-girl reporter Peggy Castle, who tells the colonel, "A townful of one hundred and fifty people doesn't just disappear!" Packing her camera and her Doris Day wardrobe, our girl sets out for the Chicago suburbs to get to the bottom of the mystery. When she encounters a government lab where scientist Peter Graves is irradiating fruit, she knows she's onto something, well, big. Is it killer tomatoes? Wild strawberries? No, it's giant grasshoppers! Growing to the size of locomotives, the big bugs swarm across the screen, a testament to the wonders of basic superimposition. As they crawl up pictures of buildings they're so (relatively) real-looking that they put the cardboard characters to shame. Not even Graves, the nominal hero, comes off looking good here. Indeed, he spends most of this movie in the lab, working on insecticide formulas and special high-frequency signals. But at least he is eventually joined by spunky reporter Castle, who vows to stand by his side even tough the lab is at ground zero for the army's last-ditch atomic bomb. Fortunately, it doesn't come to Armageddon. Instead, Graves devises some sort of sonic mating call, luring this plague of locusts into Lake Michigan, where the stupid things drown. So ends another exercise in enlargement from Bert I. Gordon, the King of Colossal Gall.

Bela Lugosi Meets a Brooklyn Gorilla (1952) The title doesn't begin to convey the idiocy of this horror comedy, in which Lugosi actually plays second fiddle to Martin and Lewis copycats Duke Mitchell and Sammy Petrillo. Duke

A giant grasshopper the size of your thumb ambles across a snapshot backdrop in the special effects spectacle *Beginning of the End.*

looks sort of like Dino, but sings even worse. Sammy, however, looks alarmingly like Jerry, and acts even more moronic. Our heroes bail out of a USO plane onto a jungle island, where the natives all look like pot-bellied Borscht Belt comics and talk in island lingo along the lines of "bugga-bugga" and "mucky-mucky." While Duke romances the chief's Dorothy Lamour-type daughter, Sammy does comic improvisations with a chimp named Ramona. (Guess who turns out to be more of a monkey?) Every so often, the whole gang pops over to Lugosi's castle, were the mad doctor is conducting crackpot experiments in the field of evolution. Little does Duke know that the doc has designs on the chief's daughter. (Exactly *what* he has in mind for her is never made clear.)

Seeking to eliminate the competition, jealous Bela injects poor Duke with his devolution serum. "Now I can turn a man into a gorilla," Lugosi says in his best Dracula voice. Sure enough, Duke is soon hopping around inside an ape suit, which makes him a Brooklyn gorilla, even though he's from the Bronx. But no matter, in his present state he makes an even more perfect partner for simian Sammy. "What crazy thing dis?" says the native chieftain, seeing the boys arrive in the village, hand in paw. Before it can get any crazier, Lugosi shows up and shoots Sammy with a bullet meant for Duke. Oh well, better luck next time. The good news is that the whole movie turns out to have been Sammy's bad dream. The bad news is that *we* aren't dreaming. This movie actually exists! Mucky mucky!

BROOKLYN CHUMPS BECOME ISLAND MONKEYS IN A JUNGLE FULL OF LAFFS!

JACK BRODER PRODUCTIONS presents

BELA LUGOSI meets a BROOKLYN GORILLA

Introducing

DUKE MITCHELL · SAMMY PETRILLO

with CHARLITA · MURIEL LANDERS and RAMONA, THE CHIMP

Associate Producer HERMAN COHEN · Produced by MAURICE DUKE
Directed by WILLIAM BEAUDINE · Screenplay by TIM RYAN

Billy the Kid vs. Dracula / Jesse James Meets Frankenstein's Daughter (1966) "Your uncle might not like it when he finds out I'm Billy the Kid," says Billy to the pert, pretty blonde he intends to marry. "You're not Billy the Kid anymore," she reminds him. "Since coming here you're William H. Bonney." But Billy will have to turn mean again once he discovers that his bride-to-be's uncle is dead, and that the tall, gaunt stranger who says he's her uncle is really . . . Count Dracula! John Carradine creakily camps it up as the blood-lusting Transylvanian. Even creakier, however, are all those scenes where Dracula flies around as a stiff-winged bat, suspended by visible wires! As for dirty little Billy (Chuck Courtney), he looks about as deadly as the stable boy down at the livery. So what's Dracula

A vintage poster from *Bela Lugosi Meets a Brooklyn Gorilla*. Duke Mitchell and Sammy Petrillo were all too convincing as a poor chimp's Martin and Lewis. Bela Lugosi was less believable as Bela Lugosi. Paging Ed Wood!

John Carradine menaces
Melinda Plowman in this
publicity shot from *Billy the
Kid vs. Dracula.*

doing wasting his time with his puny pipsqueak? As it turns out, he's getting his butt kicked. "Your bullets can't hurt me," the count chortles as the Kid fires away from point-blank range. Then, in desperation, Billy flings his shootin' iron at the invincible vampire—and knocks him out cold!

This oddball genre hybrid was originally released with the equally unbelievable *Jesse James Meets Frankenstein's Daughter.* That's only as it should be. Both directed by William Beaudine, these films are two of a kind: They're the ultimate cheapo horror Western drive-in double feature.

Blackenstein (1973) After the surprise success of *Blacula* (1972), Sam Arkoff quickly capitalized with a follow-up batch of blaxploitative horror flix. The first (and worst) was this monstrosity, which dragged two genres down to horrifying new depths. In case you couldn't guess from the title, this movie is subtitled *The Black Frankenstein*, even though the Dr. Frankenstein figure—one Dr. Stein (John Hart)—is your basic pasty-white mad scientist. The good doctor does, however, have an African-American assistant (Ivory Stone), and she just happens to have a soldier boyfriend (Joe DiSue) who lost his arms and legs in Vietnam. Giving the boyfriend a new lease on life, the doc sews on some secondhand limbs and injects him with "massive doses of DNA." Curiously, no one questions the doctor's unorthodox methods, even after glimpsing his other patients—like the guy who has grown zebra stripes on his transplanted legs. "That's the result of an unsolved RNA injection," declares the doc, making you wonder where he got his degree, "It's part of the primeval thing . . . kind of a throwback to the jungle." But even *he* can't explain it when his new patient grows a block head, sticks his arms out in front of him, and does a shaky version of the Boris Karloff shuffle. While the monster goes on a door-to-door rampage, the movie lurches right along with him, as if the cameraman, too, has received massive doses of DNA. But of course, that's entirely possible. From the looks of this makeshift movie, the whole crew might be patients of mad Dr. Stein.

Bloody Mama (1970) Shelley Winters stars as Bloody Mama, a.k.a. Ma Barker. Along with her simpleton sons, she robs, kills, and kidnaps her way across the Depression-era South. But this clan's crime sprees are nothing compared to the way they carry on when they're hiding out. It's a toss-up which son is the sickest: junkie Robert De Niro, sadistic Don Stroud, or squirrelly Robert Walden, who comes home from prison with his S&M sugar daddy Bruce Dern. Ma loves them all not wisely but too well, giving them occasional baths and nuzzling them to her bosom. However, her weirdest love is reserved for a well-to-do hostage (Pat Hingle), with whom she has her way—while he's bound and gagged. Later, of course, she tells her boys to shoot him. They can't bring themselves to do it because he reminds them of Pa—but everyone else they encounter is fair game.

The violence in this movie is so extreme it's absurd, up to and including a final farmhouse siege involving about a billion cops. Giving it all an added twist is Mama's steady stream of daffy dialogue. "When you work with them model airplanes, you sure do get to actin' silly," she tells a goofily-grinning De Niro. Later, when De Niro ODs on some stronger drugs, she runs into the swamp where the other boys are gator hunting. "Your brother's dead," she screams at the top of her lungs. "You're playin' with alligators and your brother's dead!" This saga was directed by Roger Corman, and it's a rare one even for him. He's done cheaper ones, and cheesier ones, but seldom has he done one so seriously warped.

The Brain From the Planet Arous (1958) John Agar began his career making great Westerns with John Wayne (*Fort Apache, She Wore a Yellow Ribbon*). By the mid-fifties he was starring in B horror flicks like *Tarantula* (1955) and *The Mole People* (1956) on his way to rock bottom with *The Brain From Planet Arous.* Here, Agar plays a scientist investigating strange emanations in a desert cave. That's where he encounters Gor, a giant, evil alien brain who zaps him unconscious, then takes over his body. By the time Agar gets home, he's a changed man. His girlfriend Sally (Joyce Meadows) notices the difference right away. "The way you kissed me," she coos, all ga-ga, "it makes my toes tingle!" Soon enough, she realizes something's wrong—mostly because every two minutes Agar's doubling over in excruciating pain. She should see him when he's alone; that's when Gor likes to float back out in the open to taunt and badger Agar. "I, Gor, in your stupid body, will have power of life and death over this civilization," the evil brain brags. Oh, and by the way, Gor has a thing for Agar's girl too. "I chose your body very carefully," says Gor. "Even before I knew about Sally . . . a *very* exciting female."

Sally, however, won't be had so easily. Meeting up with Gor's good-brain counterpart, who also needs a human host, she actually considers giving *him* her body—before nominating her German shepherd George for the job instead. Can a friendly German shepherd stop an evil alien brain? Well, actually, no. In the end it's up to Agar, who waits for Gor to vacate his body, then grabs an ax and hacks the brain to death. So why didn't he just do this in the first place? Well, see, there's only this one little place where Gor's big brain is vulnerable, and Agar doesn't know where that is until Sally, who's been doing her homework on alien brains, locates the magic spot and points out the way for her guy. Only a Grade Z movie could be so laughably logical—as if a film about floating alien brains needs to make perfect sense!

The Brain That Wouldn't Die (1963) After accidentally killing his fiancée (Virginia Leith) in a car crash, genius surgeon Jason Evers lugs her lopped-off head back to his private lab—where he keeps it alive, with tubes and wires attached, in what looks like a roasting pan. "I'll get her a new body," he proclaims, after which he goes cruising sleazy strip joints and local beauty pageants. When that doesn't work, he takes to following pretty girls down the street, trying to pick them up. Unfortunately, somebody he knows always seems to happen by, inadvertently saving the unsuspecting victim. Finally the doctor finds his replacement part, a body-beautiful model whose horribly scarred face makes her an ideal candidate for a head transplant. Meanwhile, back at the lab, his fiancée's head isn't adjusting well to life without a body. Conspiring with a monstrously deformed early "experiment," she disposes of the doctor's sniveling assistant, then waits for her fiancé to return so she can harangue him about the quality of her life. "A head without a body," she keeps on saying. "A head that should be in its grave. Let me die. Let me die!" Sick of her bitching and moaning, the doc slaps masking tape across her mouth, but it's too late. She has already unleashed her monstrous friend, who kills both her and her brain-transplanting beau in a lab-wrecking rampage. Thus, the lady gets her death wish, and takes the doctor with her. As for the murderous monster, he is last seen heading toward the horizon with the scar-face model slung over his shoulder. Don't you just love a happy ending?

Bride of the Monster (1955). What made Ed Wood, Jr., the worst of the Grade Z filmmakers? In part it was his Grade A ambition. He really believed he was making something profound. The result was his increasingly infamous body of work: the most deeply convoluted claptrap ever committed to cheap film stock. *Bride of the Monster* is actually one of his more lucid efforts. That isn't to say that it makes sense, but at least its lunacy is linear. The "plot" revolves around mad doctor Bela Lugosi, who lives in the swamp in a moss-covered mansion, where he is trying to create a race of superhumans. Assisted by his big, bald helper, Lobo (Tor Johnson), the mad doctor straps down unwilling human guinea pigs and bombards them with "electrons" through a skull cap that looks like a metal lampshade. But instead of becoming superhuman, these guinea pigs invariably die, whereupon the doctor dumps them in the swamp, into the waiting tentacles of a giant octopus. A giant octopus in a swamp? Don't worry, it's rubber—although Wood does occasionally intercut a shot of a real live octopus, which looks about the size of one of Tor Johnson's hands. Along the way, Wood also inserts stock footage of snakes

Bela Lugosi scolds the one and only Tor Johnson (*right*) in *Bride of the Monster*.

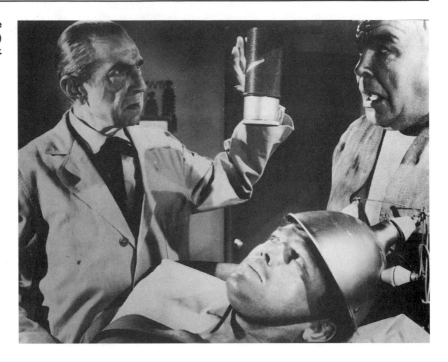

and alligators just to show that his set-bound swamp really *is* a scary place. Unfortunately nobody's buying, least of all the cast members, who cheerfully saunter through this scenario as if knowing no harm can befall them. The parade includes a feisty girl reporter (Loretta King), her cop boyfriend (Tony McCoy), and the flaky police chief (Harvey B. Dunn), who plays most of his scenes with a parakeet perched on his finger. They all converge at the mansion just in time to see the mad doctor get turned into a superhuman. (Lugosi wears Frankenstein-style platform shoes to look more imposing.) After a trash-the-lab battle with not-so-loyal Lobo, Lugosi flees into the swamp for a grand finale that features the most jarringly jumbled cross-cutting ever committed on film. What goes on out there? Who knows? The only certainty is that Lugosi ends up plunging into the water, where he wraps the rubber octopus's tentacles around him before lightning strikes and they both go up in a mushroom cloud of smoke. "He tampered in God's domain," says police chief Dunn. That epitaph pretty much sums up Ed Wood's whole career.

Cat-Women of the Moon (1954) Is there life on the moon? Only on the dark side. That's where the cat women lurk, in their black leotards and bat-wing

eyebrows. They use psychic powers to connect with the only female member (Marie Windsor) of a U.S. moon mission. Under their feline influence, she leads her fellow astronauts right into their lair, which looks like a temple left over from *Land of the Pharaohs* and is guarded by goofy giant spider puppets, which drop from cave ceilings like yo-yos. "Welcome to the moon," purrs the head cat lady (Susan Morrow). She serves the astronauts local cuisine ("Mmmm, tastes like honeydew melon," says Windsor), while the other cat girls perform seductive dances and stroke the earthmen for information about their home planet. But it's a trap! The cat women are actually planning to kill the male astronauts and hijack their rocketship to Earth—where they intend to make females the dominant sex. Only cocaptain Victor Jory is on to their plan, but he's too busy trying to woo astronette Windsor away from captain Sonny Tufts. "Who do you really love?" he implores, impassioned. "You," she answers in kind. Then they fall together in a heady swoon, while all around them the cat women scheme away. The movie was originally released in 3-D, presumably to add dimension to all those obviously painted moonscapes—but you don't need red and green cardboard glasses to look at this scenario cross-eyed.

Chained for Life (1951) In the grand tradition of circus sideshows, this shameless piece of exploitation stars real-life Siamese twin sisters as . . . Siamese twin sisters! Daisy and Violet Hilton play Dottie and Vivian Hamilton, a vaudeville singing act who get roped into a publicity stunt that will romantically link Dottie with a suave sharpshooter named Andre. Not surprisingly, Andre's arrival causes problems for two sisters who've always done *everything* together. "Come on Viv, we have a date," says Dottie, as they powder their noses. "No, *you* have a date," says Viv. "If I have a date, you have a date too, my dear," answers Dottie. They both have a date all right—with destiny. It turns out Andre is playing Dottie for a fool, letting her think he loves her, then skipping out on their wedding night. Incensed at the indignity, Viv picks up one of Andre's guns and shoots him dead—right on stage! This leads to a sensational murder trial, in which both sisters face life sentences for the crime of only one. Such cruel fate! Such awful irony! In the end, trying to fob off this freak show as a philosophical discourse, the judge stares into the camera and asks us to search our souls for the righteous verdict. To which we should reply: Guilty! Guilty to all concerned! It's perverse enough watching Dottie and Viv get paraded around, doing their joined-at-the-hip sideways shuffle for sheer novelty value. But what makes it worse is that these sisters are identically awful actresses. And they can't even sing! To watch them lip synching sappy love ballads with matching forced smiles is to cry out What next? Bearded ballerinas? Two-headed calves jumping through hoops? Some producers will do anything for a buck.

College Confidential (1960) It's Steve Allen as you've never seen him! He's a small-town sociology professor who conducts a personal survey on campus sex habits. And if you think that's questionable casting, wait'll you see Jayne Meadows (*Mrs.* Steve Allen) as an ace reporter, not to mention Mamie Van Doren as a prominently featured member of the student body. They're all thrown together in a tawdry little plot that finds the progressive professor's best intentions twisted into a trumped-up morals charge. One look at Steverino playing it straight and you just know he couldn't possibly be a dirty old man. But that doesn't prevent a truly bizarre public hearing from being held in the local general store and attended by such real-life gossip columnists as Walter Winchell, Earl Wilson, and Sheilah Graham, who are covering the event as if it were the Scopes Monkey Trial. This media circus hardly needs any added attractions, but they're here, in the form of heavyweight champ Rocky Marciano as a dimwit deputy sheriff and country singer Conway Twitty as a college boy who cruises around with Mamie in his roomy convertible. Oh yes, he also warbles the title song. Produced and directed by Albert Zugsmith, *College Confidential* was hyped as a sequel to his earlier, funnier *High School Confidential* (1958). But this one takes place in an entirely different world. In fact, it's in a world all its own. Spending time on this campus is like being in the Twilight Zone.

The Cool Ones (1967) The go-go sixties get completely misconstrued in this clueless musical comedy. But under all the clatter, this is really just your basic, timeless boy-meets-girl story. He (Gil Peterson) is a fading teen heartthrob; she (Debbie Watson) is a starry-eyed dancer. They fall in love on their way to a featured slot on the TV dance show *Whiz Bam*, which is sort of like the actual sixties show *Shindig*—if *Shindig* had been a Lawrence Welk production. Given that the two leads sing and dance like rejects from Up With People, *Whiz Bam* would seem to be exactly where they belong. Just when this idiocy is becoming unwatchably wretched, along comes Roddy McDowall as a supercool, star-making agent from England. Suddenly things become perversely fascinating. McDowall wears a mod haircut and leather pants and calls everybody Luv; Watson invents a dance called the Tantrum and calls everybody Ding-a-ling; and Peterson keeps his Bobby Rydell hairdo from budging and tells Watson, "Hey, I'm tuned in and I like the program." All this plus sixties novelty act Mrs. Miller (the poor woman's Kate Smith), who waddles out from backstage in a seamstress smock to yodel "It's Magic" while the crowd goes wild in mock ecstasy. Finally, it feels like the sixties!

The Creeping Terror (a.k.a. *The Crawling Monster*) 1964) Picture a moldy old carpet thrown over some plastic shrubs, with vacuum cleaner hoses dangling from its head—and visible human feet! This is the Creeping Terror, a people-eating alien that crash-lands near a sleepy town and crawls around the countryside scarfing up fishermen, picnickers, and heavy petters in the park. These victims invariably stay put whenever attacked, patiently waiting for the slow-moving terror to drape itself over them and suck them into its folds. Once captured, they often must help the Terror ingest them by kicking their feet off the ground and pushing themselves all the way in. Ai-eee! As if this epic home movie weren't shaky enough already, it comes to us minus most of its soundtrack, which director Art J. Nelson somehow managed to misplace. To compensate, Nelson overdubbed many scenes with a narrator who sounds like he came from an army training film. Here's how he calmly paraphrases one heated exchange following the latest terror attack: "The sergeant, a shaken man, returned babbling about what had happened. Colonel Caldwell, realizing the full danger of the situation, decided that he had only one means left to stop the monster: grenades! Now Professor Bradford made a drastic move. Acting on his superior authority, he forbade Caldwell to destroy the creature. The colonel, more concerned with saving lives than advancing science, told Bradford to go to hell." With summaries like that, who needs dialogue—especially when what little remains is way out of synch with the actors and sounds like it's coming from across the field. *The Beast of Yucca Flats* has got nothing on this Triple Z terror.

Devil Girls from Mars (1954) Her name is Nyah. They call her the Devil Girl from Mars. But in her shiny black cape and matching skull cap, she looks like Mrs. Darth Vader. By any name, however, she's trouble. Accompanied by her clanking robot, who resembles a walking refrigerator, she barges into a lonely pub in the Scottish Highlands. She's imperious, she's impervious, and she's taking male prisoners. Mars needs men! Patricia Laffan keeps a campy straight face as the no-nonsense Nyah, but the rest of the cast behave as if they were in a dinner theater production of an Agatha Christie mystery. The cross-section of humanity includes a crusty professor, a cynical reporter, an escaped convict, and a world-weary model. But they're such a blandly blithering bunch that you aren't surprised when they respond to the invasion by sitting down to tea. Needless to say, a devil girl from Mars stands out in this crowd—especially when she starts bragging about her "paralyzer rays" and her "perpetual motion chain reaction beam." And wait'll you see her disappearing act into the fourth dimension! "So there *is* a fourth dimension," the professor remarks, matter-of-factly. Coming from such a two-dimensional character, that's quite a statement.

Dinosaurus (1960) Shades of Jurassic Godzilla! While blasting in the harbor of a tropical resort, developers unleash two dinosaurs from underground deep freeze. Deep freeze in the tropics? You bet—and it gets dumber. Before you

can lose count of the monster movie clichés, they've become intertwined with another old story: There's a caveman awake on the island too. His primitive makeup makes him almost as hokey as the poorly-matched, special-effects monsters. But at least these beasts are more animated than the generic human cast, which includes a rock-jawed hero, a feisty red-haired heroine, a seedy villain in a Panama hat, a comic relief guy named Dumpy, and a sappy little kid named Julio, who befriends the brontosaurus. "I never had so much fun in my life," he says, riding on the back of his newfound friend. He has almost as much fun with the caveman, for whom he fixes breakfast in a heartwarming scene that bonds them for life. To the kid, the caveman is some kind of hero; to us he's more like a running joke. He encounters a shortwave radio and hits it with an ax. He sees his own reflection and hits it with an ax. He meets the seedy villain and . . . throws a pie in his face! Nothing like a Neanderthal to keep things nice and loose.

Dracula vs. Frankenstein (1971) The showdown you've always been waiting for takes place not in some gloomy Carpathian castle, but in a seedy, seaside carnival. That's where old wheelchair bound Dr. Frankenstein (J. Carrol Naish) runs a two-bit freakshow while conducting experiments on headless young women in his basement lab. The ancient Naish looks positively embalmed as the cellar-dwelling doctor. Meanwhile, Lon Chaney, as his ax-wielding idiot helper, grins, grunts, and cuddles his puppy, as if he thinks he's still playing Lenny in *Of Mice and Men*. He's so gentle that the doctor has to give him an injection to drive him berserk enough to chop off women's heads. Just when you think things couldn't get any worse, along comes Dracula (Zandor Vorkov), who shows up with spaced-out eyes and a satanic goatee, sporting a ring that shoots deadly lightning bolts. Ever the vampire, Dracula has exhumed the remains of the original Frankenstein monster—which the doctor obligingly revives and sets loose. "It will be a bloodbath such as the world has never seen," declares Dracula.

And that's not the half of this movie. There's also a Vegas showgirl (Regina Carrol) looking for her missing sister, an overage hippie (Anthony Eisley) who puts up the showgirl at his "pad" and romances her during long walks on the beach, and some younger hippies who frolic at the amusement park when they aren't running off to "the big protest." "What are we protesting tonight?" says one girl. "I don't know," says her boyfriend. "But I bet it's fun." Add Russ (*West Side Story*) Tamblyn as a sleazeball biker-gang leader and Jim (*Dallas*) Davis as the local sheriff, and you've got more characters than hack director Al Adamson can handle. Trying his best to kill them all off, Adamson zaps Eisley with Dracula's lightning bolts, crashes Naish's wheelchair into a guillotine (which sends the old geezer's head rolling across the screen), and builds to a grand finale which finds Dracula dismantling the lumbering monster. "I'll destroy you piece by piece, as Dr. Frankenstein created you," Dracula says. However, the old boy gets so carried away that he stays out after sunrise and winds up a pile of ashes. This movie falls apart every which way it can.

Eegah (1963) A real live caveman is wandering around the Palm Springs desert. It's Richard "Jaws" Kiel of James Bond movie fame—and he's the best actor in the cast! When the big lug meets the ditzy teen heroine (Marilyn Manning) on a lonely desert highway, it's love at first sight. He throws her over his shoulder and carries her off to his cave—where he has already imprisoned her bumbling scientist dad. Our two captives take turns humoring the caveman until help can arrive. However, things get strange when, to pass

Richard Kiel grinds his choppers as a modern-day caveman in *Eegah.*

the time, the heroine gives her dad a shave and Eegah has to have one too. (Oh well, it's one way to get rid of a phony beard.) Finally, the grooming period is over and the heroine's dorky boyfriend (Arch Hall, Jr., son of the director) rides to the rescue in his dune buggy. Somehow outwitting the caveman, the dork frees the ditz and her dad, loads them into the dune buggy, and burns rubber back into town. Eegah follows, of course, setting up the inevitable clash with modern civilization. Unfortunately, on Arch Hall Sr.'s budget, civilization is reduced to a country club pool party, where the dorky boyfriend and his band are playing songs that set back rock and roll at least one million years. Is it any wonder Eegah goes nuts? "A large man or giant is creating a disturbance," reports a radio dispatcher, sending a task force of two whole cops to pump Eegah full of lead. Only then does it occur to us how truly tragic this ending is. With Eegah floating face down in the pool, our ditz is now stuck with her dune buggy dork, who sings like he thinks he's Ricky Nelson and actually says things like "Wowee wowee wow!" It's enough to make a girl scream "Eegah!"

Empire of the Ants (1977) Borrowing a page from *Them,* director Bert I. Gordon unleashes giant ants against defenseless—but deserving—humans. Most deserving of all is Joan Collins, here rehearsing her *Dynasty* act as a man-eating real estate diva hustling resort island condominiums. Little does she know that radioactive waste has turned the island's ant population into mammoth mutants! Get ready for some bitchin' screams, as Joan and her prospective condo buyers get swarmed by superimposed ants twice their size. For close-ups, ingenious Gordon employs huge, hairy puppets which are vigorously shoved toward the victims, who accommodatingly cringe on the ground. The ants just keep on coming, and the people drop like flies. The title credit says that the movie was based on a story by H. G. Wells. If so, it sure took a lot of liberties. Like, for instance, an ensemble of soap opera characters who all seem to be escaping bad debts or bad marriages; a bitch-queen leading lady who gets increasingly helpless as the ants close in; and a back-water hamlet whose traumatized townsfolk are psychically enslaved to these superants. "Don't you see, we mustn't disobey them," says a suddenly mellow Joan after getting zapped by the queen ant's mind control mist. Then she toddles off to join the other slaves at the sugar refinery, where they all toil away to satisfy the giant ants' sweet teeth. Only Bert I. Gordon could have thought of this. But, of course, if he hadn't, Roger Corman would have.

Faster Pussycat! Kill! Kill! (1966) Russ Meyer generally confined himself to sleazy, softcore sex comedies stacked with chesty women. But he aimed for supercult status with this surreal trashfest starring supervixen Tura Satana (*Astro-Zombies*) as the leader of a tough gang of go-go girls. After a hot night's dancing in their cages, these go-gos are too revved up to quit. So they dress up in shiny leather, jump into their cars, and drag race into the desert. Trouble, however, is just around the bend. Crossing paths with an innocent couple, the girls emasculate the guy by making fun of his wheels. "You could time that heap with an hourglass," says one girl. "Did someone mention my figure?" quips another. These chicks are fast with their tongues, too. But when they play too rough with the guy and accidentally kill him, they're forced to abduct his hysterical girlfriend and head for the nearest shack along the highway. There, they meet their match in an ornery old sidewinder and his two slob sons. "You girls a bunch of nudists or are you just short of clothes?" drools the old man. When the girls give him more trouble than he bargained for, he gets even uglier, railing against the world, especially women. "They let 'em smoke and drive. They even put 'em in pants. And whaddya get? A Democrat for president!" This guy is asking for it and boy, does he

Sensationally sizzling ad art from *Faster, Pussycat! Kill! Kill!* The actual movie more than delivers as promised.

get it. In fact, nearly everybody gets it here, spitting and snarling and wallowing in the sand until they kill each other off. When a director like Russ Meyer tries to outdo himself, he has nowhere to go but over the top.

Firemaidens of Outer Space (1955). "Hey, I wonder what we'll find on Jupiter's thirteenth moon," says one member of a laid-back space team. But even Flash Gordon would do a double take if he saw who's living up there. They're the descendants of the last citizens of Atlantis—and they're all girls! All, that is, except one lone patriarch ruler, who holds our space explorers hostage until they agree to kill a poor imitation of "the Thing." Unfortunately, the boys have trouble concentrating on their task, since the girls all wear chiffon minidresses and dance around harem style to the familiar refrain of "Stranger in Paradise." Shaking free of this enthralling display, our heroes make short work of the unscary monster, survive a strange-but-silly fire sacrifice, and head back to Earth with a bevy of fire-maidens in tow. "But we were promised husbands," says one of the maidens being left behind. "Don't worry," says the head space explorer, "we'll be sending expeditions." How much can one moon stand? This comically casual British space opera shows why our allies never got into the space race: Their idea of space travel was just another holiday in the colonies!

Flesh Feast (1970) "Imagine," says the pretty young lab assistant. "We'll be striking the first blow against the aging process." Hah! That's what she thinks! Little does she know that her boss, diabolical doctor Veronica Lake (yes, Veronica Lake) is only pretending to perfect her fountain-of-youth formula— so she can lure Adolf Hitler out of hiding, strap him to a table, and kill him by letting maggots eat his face! "I've been working for years developing, breeding, and conditioning these maggots," she declares. This is one dedicated mad doctor. While she makes her final preparations, various undercover agents, Nazi war criminals, and sinister South Americans skulk around the plywood sets, reciting absurd dialogue with absolutely no clue how silly they sound. That's to be expected from no-talent, no-name actors, but what is Veronica Lake doing here? Since this was her first film in almost twenty years, it would be easy to say she didn't know what she was getting into. But she knew, all right. She produced the damn thing! At times it also sounds as if she improvised her own dialogue. "It's so warm today; my hands are so sticky," she says, filling an embarrassing lull while she struggles into a pair of rubber gloves. Meanwhile, the pretty lab assistant stands idly by, all but tapping her foot and looking at her watch. If you have fond memories of Veronica Lake as a forties femme fatale, her presence in this movie is not a pretty sight. Even if you never heard of Veronica Lake, her presence in this movie is still not a pretty sight.

Frankenstein Conquers the World (1966) Eye-boggling doesn't begin to describe the sights you'll see when the Frankenstein monster goes to Japan and makes like . . . Godzilla! The fun begins during World War II when the Nazis ship the living heart of the monster (here known simply as Frankenstein) to their Japanese allies for safekeeping. Wouldn't you know it—the A-bomb drops and the heart is lost in all the confusion. Years later, however, a youthful monster turns up, gets caught, and immediately starts sprouting to colossal proportions. While token American scientist Nick Adams tries to prevent authorities from destroying Frankenstein, the monster runs amok, tossing toy boats out of the water and kicking over the usual model-train-set villages. At the same time, out of nowhere, *another* monster appears. He looks like a reptilian reject from a Gamera movie, and he, too, wrecks miniature sets. At one point, he attacks a farm and destroys a stable full of plastic horses, which fall over without losing their premolded shapes. Not to be outdone, Frankenstein hunts down a stuffed wild boar and picks up an unfortunate scientist who is really a Ken doll. The movie practically flaunts these flamboyantly bogus non-effects, and the idiotically dubbed dialogue is just as inescapable. "It's weird," says one scientist, surveying the ruins of still another village. "Why don't we see anyone? What happened to everybody who was hurt or killed?" "I think I know what happened," says a fatalistic soldier. "Frankenstein got hungry and they were just available." Considering what we've seen, that's as good an answer as any.

Frogs (1972) Frogs on the front porch! Snakes in the chandeliers! Geckos in the greenhouse! Patriarch Ray Milland's private island is overrun, and he's hopping mad! The invasion takes place on his birthday weekend, with his whole clan gathered to kiss his ring and stab each other in the back. Also on the premises is rugged outdoorsman Sam Elliott, who informs Milland, "You've gone overboard with the pesticides and poisons." In other words, the frogs are hopping mad too. While the humans act out their low-rent *Cat on a Hot Tin Roof,* all sorts of creepy crawlies encroach, picking off party guests one by one: A cottonmouth takes out Granny; lizards gang up on a sleazeball son-in-law; an alligator gobbles up poor Joan Van Ark. Unfortunately, the movie's budget dictates that we not actually *see* too many of the gory details. More often than not these critters seem to kill by the power of suggestion. Nevertheless, dead is dead. But does Big Daddy get the hint? Not a

Tina Carver barks up the
wrong tree monster in *From
Hell It Came.*

chance! "I'm going ahead with the celebration just as planned," he sputters. "I'm not going to let a couple of deaths spoil the day's schedule." When last seen he's partying all by himself, with roughly a million frogs leading the final charge. Rip it!

From Hell It Came (1957) His name is Kimo (Gregg Palmer), and he used to be the son of a South Seas island chieftain. But then the local witch doctor had him killed for hanging around with white men, and now Kimo's spirit has returned—in the form of a cardboard tree that sprouts fully grown from his grave! The natives call this tree man Tabonga, believing him to be a voodoo legend come back to life. But Tabonga is actually the result of good old-fashioned radioactive fallout from nearby A-bomb tests. What else could create a movie monster so utterly ridiculous? Uprooting himself to seek revenge on his killers, Tabonga grows a pair of stumpy legs and lumbers around the island wearing a mean old scowl like you might see on one of the scarier Muppets. "I just saw the Tabonga!" says a hysterical native woman. "Well, how do you know it was Tabonga?" asks the witch doctor. "Because it looked like a tree and it had eyes and hands!" replies the woman. Actually, Tabonga doesn't have hands, but branches—which he uses to sweep up a pretty blond scientist (Tina Carver) and carry her around the island. God knows what gnarly fate might await her, if not for her boyfriend, the Great White Doctor (Tod Andrews), who takes aim at a knife stuck in the tree man's trunk and, with one lucky shot, drives the blade deep into Tabonga's . . . heart? When last seen, the mahogany monster has toppled into quicksand, where he quickly sinks—taking this movie with him. Timber!

The *Gamera* Movies. Gamera is a giant, nuclear-powered turtle who flies like a Frisbee, with flames shooting out his leg holes. Is it any wonder that he's beloved by Japanese school boys everywhere? Created by a rival studio to cash in on the Godzilla craze, this terrible terrapin starts out second rate and gets sorrier with each sequel. Although in his first film (*Gamera the Invincible*, 1966) he's your basic bad monster, he reforms in time to protect Japan from even more improbable monsters—like the laser-breathing lizard in *Gamera vs. Barugon* (1966), or the spear-headed monstrosity in *Gamera vs. Guiron* (1969). Compared to these cheesy-looking creatures, Godzilla looks like a dinosaur from *Jurassic Park*. But just as cheesy are the assorted alien chicks who always seem to be poking their pretty noses into the poky action. The good ones tend to dress like Supergirl, while the bad ones—who like to shave little boys' heads and eat their brains—generally favor slinkier attire. Good or bad, they provide a perfect complement to all those live-action cartoons trying to pass as monsters. These batty space babes are like Japanese Barbie dolls magically come to life.

The Giant Claw (1957) It's just another day in the wild blue yonder, until a UFO comes along and starts plucking air force planes out of the sky. It flies so fast that radar can't detect it, yet when fighter jets are dispatched, they somehow get a good gander at what turns out to be . . . a giant, goofy bird! What's so goofy about it? Try big bulging eyes, an outrageous plume, an elongated os-

Gamera crumples a speeding locomotive like a Lionel train, in a typical tantrum from the *Gamera* movies.

trich neck, and heavy-duty wires that hold it aloft, occasionally flapping its creaky wings. "I've seen some mighty big chicken hawks back on the farm, but this one takes the cake," says one pilot. "I'll never call my mother-in-law an old crow again," cracks another. Everybody's a comedian here, including costar scientists Jeff Morrow and Mara Corday, who engage in playful battle-of-the-sexes banter while putting their heads (and lips) together to defeat the monster. "Being flip doesn't help," scolds the exasperated general, during one zingy exchange. Ah, but he's wrong. When it comes to would-be wit, few Grade Z bombs are more unintentionally funny than this giant turkey.

The Giant Gila Monster (1959) The Giant Gila Monster isn't really so giant; he's just your regular-size reptile, peacefully crawling around a scale model landscape. Meanwhile, in another part of the editing room, cars are veering off the road and people are looking up, screaming in terror, as if the gila monster had some sort of connection to them! Since this kind of cine-magic can only go so far, the movie is overloaded with plot complications involving its teenage hero (Don Sullivan), a singing auto mechanic with a crippled little sister and a French girlfriend on the verge of deportation. Someday our hero will be rich and famous and solve everybody's problems. In the meantime, he attempts to save the movie by singing some cornball songs at the local sock hop. This is exactly the sort of thing that drives giant gila monsters crazy. The next thing you know, the creature has crawled out of the underbrush to attack dancing teenagers. Not to worry. Switching to his Steve McQueen-in-*The Blob*-mode, our junior hero loads up his hot rod with nitroglycerin and sends it zooming into the belly of the beast. The resulting bonfire looks like a book of matches that have all gone up at once. At least it's true to scale.

Girls Town (1959) It's reform school for hot number Mamie Van Doren after she violates parole, gets involved in a brawl, and narrowly escapes being charged with a local punk's murder. But a girls' home run by nuns may as well be prison for a gal like Mamie. "This pad spooks me," she sneers the second she arrives. After that, it's one long-running battle with nuns and fellow inmates alike. Spouting hilarious hipster dialogue, Mamie sends this Albert Zugsmith camp classic into orbit. She really doesn't even need the help of a supporting cast that includes Mel Tormé (yes, Mel Tormé) as a too-cool tough guy who calls girls "baby chick," or Paul Anka (yes, Paul Anka) as a teen heartthrob who sings the title song as well as a heartfelt "Ave Maria." To be sure, these guys steal their share of scenes, but ultimately they can't compete with Mamie's gum-cracking, hip-snapping, platinum blond trash queen, who calls the police chief "Daddy-o" and the other girls "dirty skags," and only gets boring when her heart of gold starts to show through. Before this overcooked melodrama is done, Mamie will have saved her roommate from a drug overdose, sobbed at the sound of Anka's "Ave Maria," and rallied her fellow inmates for a free-for-all slugfest against the hot rod punks who've abducted her little sister. Now, no fifties juvenile delinquent film was complete without a moralistic message, but this is ridiculous!

Glen or Glenda? (1953) Director Ed Wood also plays the title role in this case history of a closet transvestite. The movie is narrated in pseudo-clinical terms by a reassuring "psychiatrist." But leave it to Wood to augment the psychoanalysis with an out-of-the-blue appearance by—Bela Lugosi! Lurking in the shadows of your basic haunted house, Bela intones ominously about the dark forces of fate while thunder and lightning whip up a storm outside. So is this *Glen or Glenda?* or *Dr. Jekyll and Mr. Hyde?* Actually, it's both—and more!

With the narrator's psycho-babble in one ear and Bela's ordinary babble in the other, we follow Glen's progress from a teen who borrows his sister's dress for a Halloween party ("Go ahead," says his mother, "you always did look better as a girl.") to a seemingly normal man engaged to marry perky Barbara (Dolores Fuller). "Those fingernails have got to go," says Barb, holding Glen's hand. "My goodness, they're almost as long as mine. Maybe even prettier. We'll have to paint them sometime, just for the fun of it." Little does she know what she's letting herself in for. But lest we become equally horrified, the psychiatrist periodically pops back in to digress about men's fashion handicaps (bet you didn't know that wearing tight fedoras causes baldness) and ancient anthropology (bet you also didn't know that in primitive tribes the males were the flashier dressers).

When modern psychiatry can no longer explain, back comes Lugosi to intone, "Bevare! Bevare of the big green dragon who eats little boys!" The dragon is presumably in the head of tortured Glen, whose nightmares about being tempted by the devil finally drive him to spill his guts to fiancée Barb. Will she understand? She does better than that! After a head-holding, hand-wringing initial reaction that redefines *sturm und drang*, she removes the angora sweater that Glen has "always admired" and holds it out to him, in the ultimate gesture of support. With a girl like Barb behind him, Glen finds the inner strength to shed his girlish alter ego and become a regular guy. Not even scary old Bela can put a damper on this happy ending.

As always, Wood was completely in earnest with this flabbergastingly free-form, cinematic excursion. In fact, this was probably his most personal film. But then this was a guy who wore angora sweaters, high heel pumps, and pretty pink panties himself—while directing! Is it any wonder that *Glen or Glenda?* was his one-from-the-heart?

The *Godzilla* Movies: When Godzilla nuked Tokyo in 1955, he blazed the trail for many like-minded monsters—among them such legends in their own right as Mothra and Rodan. These monsters have certainly had their moments (let us not forget the Thumbelina-sized, twin singing pixies who lived on Mothra's island). But when it comes to massive appeal, Godzilla wins, tails down. Is it any surprise that his studio saw fit to bring him back in over a dozen sequels? Unfortunately, these sequels get sillier and sillier, as increasingly absurd behemoths spew forth from the bowels of the earth (or some-

Godzilla scores a direct hit on the ersatz Kong in the one and only *King Kong vs. Godzilla.*

times outer space) to challenge Godzilla's title as King of the Monsters. These gargantuan grudge matches always follow the same pattern: first an hour or so of slow buildup, in which scientists and generals bore us to tears with badly dubbed technobabble, then a final half hour of hit-or-miss monster mashing, performed by lead-footed men in baggy rubber costumes.

Now, this is bad enough when the aberrations are three-headed dragons (*Ghidrah the Three-Headed Monster*, 1965) or jumbo shrimp (*Godzilla vs. the Sea Monster*, 1966) or giant blobs of toxic waste (*Godzilla vs. the Smog Monster*, 1972). But when Godzilla takes on King Kong, in *King Kong vs. Godzilla* (1963), he doesn't just trash his own image. He brings down the great ape, too. Of course, this isn't *really* Kong. This is just another guy in a moth-eaten monkey suit. But since such a "monster" is obviously no match for mighty Godzilla, the filmmakers even things up by striking Kong with a lightning bolt that gives him an extra charge. "Kong has been electrified!" blurts a typical Japanese citizen, from the sidelines. Meanwhile, in the main event, King Kong and Godzilla punch, kick, bob, weave, throw big cardboard rocks, and even clap with glee when they score a direct hit. This will become standard behavior in future Godzilla sequels, peaking with the quintessential

Destroy All Monsters! (1969), in which Godzilla, Mothra, Rodan, and a half-dozen others team up against three-headed Ghidrah *plus* an all-female race of spangle-suited aliens from "one of the many planets between Mars and Jupiter." Still to come will no doubt be even more Godzilla movies, but they'll never get any nuttier than this.

Hercules in New York (1970) As the title suggests, this isn't just another torsos and togas epic. In fact, it seems to be someone's idea of a joke: Hercules gets booted off Olympus by Zeus, only to land in modern day Manhattan, where shady wrestling promoters turn him into a top attraction. Are we laughing yet? Wait, there's more. None other than Arnold Schwarzenegger (billed originally as Arnold Strong) makes his movie debut here, ridiculously dubbed to sound exactly like Steve Reeves. And though he has the title role, top-billing goes to another Arnold—none other than Arnold Stang! Are we laughing *now*? Stang plays a sniveling little twerp who befriends our beefy hero and shows him how to take a bite out of the Big Apple. Needless to say, it's Schwarzenegger who does all the heavy lifting. See Herc drive a chariot down the middle of Broadway! See Herc fight an escaped bear who is really an amateur stunt man in mangy fur. See Herc team with Atlas and Samson in a cloddishly choreographed free-for-all against half the New York mafia. So where did Atlas and Samon come from? Why ask? Considering this movie's concept of dramatic license, a better question might be: Where is mighty Ursus?

High School Confidential (1958) Transfer student Russ Tamblyn arrives at his new school, cigarillo in mouth, calling his pretty teacher "Doll" and his principal "Baldy." By the end of the week he's the leader of the local tough-guy gang—and reaping the benefits of their booming marijuana business. Believe it or not, the action is even hotter at home, where Tamblyn lives with his "aunt," (Mamie Van Doren), who slinks around the kitchen in skintight sweaters and comes on to her nephew against the refrigerator. "Stop treating me like a saint," she purrs, crawling up the front of his shirt. "Relatives should always kiss each other hello and goodbye." Somehow Tamblyn tears himself away to be with kids his own age, including a cute little blonde (Diane Jergens) who's hooked on Maryjane. "I'm dying to blast, but I'm clean," she tells Tamblyn. "Are you holding?" As it turns out, he isn't. In fact, he's really an undercover cop assigned to bust this hopped-up high school

IT'S TREMENDOUS!!
IT'S STUPENDOUS!!
IT'S FUN!!

HERCULES IS COMING TO TOWN!!

see him topple two-ton newspaper rolls!

see him thunder through Times Square!

see him toss tough men like toothpicks!

see him subdue a mammoth, ferocious bear!

FILMED ENTIRELY IN NEW YORK!

HERCULES IN NEW YORK
IN EASTMANCOLOR
ARNOLD STANG — ARNOLD STRONG
"MR. UNIVERSE"

He's going by the name Arnold Strong. But guess who that big guy in the toga really is.

dope ring. Surprise! You have been watching a typical fifties antireefer film. Or, as the narrator puts it, "an authentic disclosure of conditions in our high schools today." But since this exposé was produced by Albert Zugsmith, (*Girls Town*), it comes to us overloaded with fistfights, shoot-outs, drag races, and hyperbolic hipster slang—like one cool chick's pseudo-beat rant in a swingin' jazz joint. "The future is a drag, man," she says in a world-weary drone. "The future is a flake." All this plus Jackie Coogan as a Mr. Big drug lord, and Michael Landon as a high school football captain who's so square he's cubed. The fifties didn't come much flakier than this.

Hillbillies in a Haunted House (1967) Hard-up country crooners team with washed-up, fright-night stars in this horribly comic horror comedy. Ferlin Husky plays pickin', grinnin' Woody Wetherby, who is traveling with his girl-friend Boots (Joi Lansing) and his faithful companion Jeepers (Don Bowman). En route to a Nashville "jamboree," the trio gets caught in a rain-storm and seeks refuge in an abandoned mansion in the woods. Little do they know that the place is haunted—not just by ghosts, but also by enemy agents. (On top of everything else, this movie is a would-be spy spoof!) While Basil Rathbone, John Carradine, Lon Chaney, Jr., and some guy in a gorilla suit rattle around in the shadows, our country cousins try to make themselves at home. Whenever the action flags, Ferlin whips out his guitar and warbles a song, with echo-chamber effects so tinny they give new meaning to the term *canned music*. As an added attraction, some other country singers stop by to do a few numbers. When all else fails, somebody turns on a television and there is Merle Haggard, singing still *more* country songs. But at least while this haunted hootenanny is going on, the cast doesn't have to stand around, hands in pockets, drawling moronic dialogue—which isn't to say that we're entirely spared. "It's a weird-wolf!" says the submental Jeepers, glimps-ing a furry, fanged face in a closet. And he's not "imaginatin'" either! Despite this plethora of plot possibilities, the story wraps up after about an hour, then moves on to that Nashville jamboree, where still more second-rate country singers take their turns performing. It doesn't matter how many Grade Z movies you've seen. Nothing can prepare you for this hee-haw horror show.

The Horror of Party Beach (1964) What happens when rotting skeletons in a sunken ship get doused in radioactive waste? They become the horrors of Party Beach! They climb ashore somewhere on Long Island to attack would-be surfers and bikers, who are doing the Swim and the Monster Mash to er-satz sounds of the sixties. While the Del-Aires perform "The Zombie Stomp," the real monsters are stomping one deserving little slut who wanders too far from the party. It's possible these creatures are driven crazy by bad music, since they later wipe out a slumber party where the girls are gathered round in an off-key sing-along. Or maybe the monsters just don't like girls having fun, since their next victims are three tight-skirted Brooklyn chicks who get a flat tire on their T-Bird convertible. Whatever their motivation, these killers have the citizens *scared*. "It's voodoo!" says the local professor's stereotypical black maid. "They're zombies!" says the professor's pretty teenage daughter. Of course, the professor has a more rational explanation. After rambling on about protozoans, parasites, and animal-plant mutations, he finally sums it all up: "They're like jellyfish." Actually they're more like cheap rip-offs of the *Creature From the Black Lagoon*, with plastic seaweed hanging from their arms, plastic eyes that roll in their sockets, and fish-face mouths that seem to be full of foot-long hot dogs. They're much, much goofier than the monster from *The Beach Girls and the Monster*, and that is indeed unfortunate—because these guys are supposed to be for real!

Hot Rods to Hell (1967) Two more Golden Age movie stars bite the dust in this hopelessly square message movie about manhood and safe driving. Dana Andrews visibly grits his teeth as a family man recovering from a near fatal auto accident. Still road-shy, he lets wife Jeanne Crain man the wheel as they motor through the desert toward a new start for the whole family. Just when life is looking good again, some teens in souped-up cars come around the bend and run them off the road. Why, one feisty blonde (Mimsy Farmer) even tosses a beer can! "What kind of animals are those?" seethes Andrews. The fact that those chino-clad "animals" all look as threatening as Wally Cleaver seems to have escaped his notice. Even so, their reign of terror might have been more exciting if the movie didn't spend so much of its running time inside an ultra-fake car interior, with a steering wheel the size of a Mack truck's and enough leg room to install a recumbent exercise bike. Inside this mobile prison, Andrews grips the wheel in fear, Crain grows increasingly hysterical, and the kids screw up their faces in various grimaces because they never got acting lessons. Finally, the family makes it to a seedy motel in the middle of no place—where Andrews's teenage daughter (Laurie Mock) gets the forbidden hots for one of those aforementioned animals. Just what old Dad needs to regain his macho confidence and take on those hot rodders from Hell! Anybody for a game of chicken?

I Was a Teenage Werewolf (1957) Just before becoming Little Joe Cartwright, Michael Landon paid his dues in this vintage drive-in creep show. As a mad-at-the world teen named Tony, he starts out like just another rebel without a cause. ("People bug me," he barks to a friendly cop.) But then the local mad scientist (Whit Bissell) gives him an experimental serum, and turns him into . . . a teenage werewolf! It doesn't happen any too soon either, because elsewhere in this movie more well-adjusted teens are attending impossibly clean-cut parties, where they play bongos and sing songs like "Eeny Meeny Miney Mo." No wonder Tony turns teen wolf and tears some classmates to shreds. But you know, even with that chintzy Lon Chaney mask, he's really no worse as a werewolf than he was as a hotheaded punk. Maybe that's why the towns-folk seem to take it in stride when they discover a wolfman in their midst. Indeed, only the mad scientist seems unable to accept the fact that he has created a monster. "This is America," he sputters, "not the Carpathian Mountains!" Right then and there, you know he's gonna get it. Nevertheless, Whit Bissell will soon return in *I Was a Teenage Frankenstein* (1957), in which he pulls Gary Conway out of a car wreck and rebuilds him into a monster. Once a mad scientist, always a mad scientist.

The Incredible Two-Headed Transplant (1971) The minute we see Bruce Dern's lab full of two-headed monkeys and rabbits, we know it's only a matter of time before he tries transplanting a human head. Right on cue, a homicidal maniac escapes from the asylum and shows up on the doctor's doorstep. Little does this psycho know that Dern's lab assistant (Berry Kroeger) is handy with a shotgun. Blam! Now, how to clean up the mess? How about sewing the splattered psycho's head onto the healthy body of the retarded handyman? "We've got two perfect specimens," the lab assistant practically drools, "a retarded man who's of no use to anyone and a homicidal maniac who'll be dead in a minute anyway. Such an opportunity may never come again!" Yeah, it's not every day that you can put a moron and a maniac together in the same body.

Dern performs the amazing operation with all the verve of a dentist doing a root canal. (Remember, this was the laid-back seventies.) Somehow though, the two-headed man wakes up anyway, and his conversations with himself are, well, one of a kind. "Who are you?" says the moron. "I'm your brother," says the maniac. "I don't have a brother," says the moron. "You do now," says the maniac. "My neck hurts," says the moron. "*Our* neck hurts, stupid," says the maniac. No wonder their neck hurts—if you had to do all your close-ups with your chin on another actor's shoulder, your necks would hurt too. Nevertheless, these two stick together, staggering across the countryside, killing as they go. To the rescue comes future *America's Top 40* host Casey Kasem, as a Dern colleague who smells a rat in the lab and alerts the authorities. "Man," whistles a deputy, checking out what's left of the lab after the transplant has broken out. "The doc must have been brewing some of that Jekyll and Hyde joy juice in here." Jekyll and Hyde joy juice? Ah, that explains everything.

The Incredibly Strange Creatures Who Stopped Living and Became Mixed-Up Zombies (1963) Directed Ray Dennis Steckler, calling himself "Cash Flagg," is also the star of this self-made mess. But you've got to give him credit: He's a schlockmeister who's not afraid to be *in front of* the camera when he makes a fool of himself. Steckler-Flagg plays Jerry, a deadbeat who wanders into a carnival sideshow, gets lured backstage by an exotic dancer, and gets hypnotized by her fortune-teller sister into stabbing a less exotic dancer at a nearby nightclub. After that, Jerry's a ticking time bomb. Every time he sees a spinning object he snaps, and once more turns into a mindless murderer. And that's not the half of this equally mindless runaround, which pads its eighty-two-minute running time with various singers, dancers, and stand-up comics, who perform their routines unabridged while we impatiently wait for the real action to start.

Fortunately, these amateur-hour rejects are madman Jerry's victims, which means that as their ranks thin, the action can't help but pick up. Even so, things don't really get going until the fortune-teller throws acid in Jerry's face, turning him into the latest addition to her private collection of carnival freaks. "Take him back and put him with the rest of the little pets," she orders her brutish henchman Ortega. Unfortunately, Ortega bungles the job, allowing the freaks to break free and run wild through the carnival. It's sheer pandemonium! It's panic on the midway! The crowd screams, the cops open fire, and lurching actors with Movie Makeup 101 faces start dropping like flies. Presumably, this is what Steckler meant by incredibly strange creatures who stopped living and became mixed-up zombies. Or maybe he was referring to audiences who actually paid money to see this movie. You'd *have* to be incredibly strange to want to do something like that.

King Dinosaur (1955) A strange planet suddenly pops up in our solar system—so naturally a two-man, two-woman space team rockets off to investigate. When they get there, they discover a place a lot like our lovely Pacific Northwest. Can you blame them for lolling around like two couples on a weekend camping trip? "So what are the plans for tomorrow?" says one astronette, nibbling on what looks like an hors d'oeuvre. The casual chitchat, however, quickly turns to screams when the space team finds a volcanic island full of alligators, iguanas, and armadillos, all badly blown up to look like dinosaurs. Why, one lethargic lizard even stands up on his hind legs impersonating a Tyrannosaurus rex. From the way he arches his back, it looks like he's being held in place by an offscreen human hand. It also looks like it hurts. To put him and all the other dinos out of their misery, the astronauts set aside their picnic lunches long enough to plant an atomic bomb, jump into an inflatable raft, and let the island blow sky-high. Watching the mushroom cloud from, oh, half a mile away, the space team sheds a tear for paradise lost (or something like that), then heads for home. The solar system is once again safe from free-floating planets full of dinosaurs. The people who made this movie, however, are still out there somewhere.

Konga (1961) What we have here is a typically British low-budget horror show: scene after scene of anal retentive build-up eventually collapsing in a heap of pure trash. At the center of it all is pompous professor Michael Gough, who returns from a whole year missing in the jungle with a miraculous discovery: A growth serum that can turn Venus-Flytraps into man-eaters! When he tests this stuff on his adorable pet chimp Konga, the screen gets wavy, the images blur, and presto! Konga becomes a killer gorilla! Obeying the professor's commands, the ape eliminates a disapproving dean, then a competitive colleague, and then the professor's young rival for a pretty coed's affections. Later, the professor's wife gets jealous and pumps Konga full of enough serum to make him King Kong–size. Literally going through the lab roof, Konga grabs a doll that looks like Michael Gough and heads for a six-foot replica of Big Ben. Meanwhile, the jumbo flytraps have trapped the pretty coed in the professor's greenhouse and are merrily chomping away. What a little shop of horrors! And yet the true villain here is Michael Gough, who gives such a supercilious performance that we find ourselves wishing him dead even before he plans his first murder. He is certainly more offensive than poor shaggy Konga, as played by the usual man-in-an-ape-suit—who tries several ways of walking like a gorilla, but never walks the same way twice. You know a King Kong copycat is in king-sized trouble when he has to share the spotlight with a bunch of plastic man-eating plants.

The Loves of Hercules (1960) Back before Arnold Schwarzenegger, studs like Steve Reeves and Gordon Scott made whole careers out of playing mythical musclemen in cheapo Italian imports. Sixties audiences couldn't get enough of these togas-and-torsos epics; the resulting demand for Herculean heroes also made stars of such unlikely names as Alan Steel (*Hercules Against the Moon Men*), Ed Fury (*Samson Against the Sheik*), and Mark Forest (*Mole Men Against the Son of Hercules*). Somehow, though, the good times didn't extend to poor Mickey Hargitay, who plays a particularly muscle-headed Herc in *The Love of Hercules*. Mickey may be a former Mr. Universe, but he can't hold Steve Reeves's loincloth. Hell, he has enough trouble holding his own with his leading lady, his real-life wife Jayne Mansfield! Then again, who wouldn't? As if she didn't already have an unfair advantage, Mansfield makes double trouble by appearing in a dual role—in two different wigs! Black-haired Jayne is an innocent damsel in distress; titian-haired Jayne is the evil queen doing the distressing. Put the two together and there's absolutely no reason to be looking at Mick. Along with this scene-stealing bombshell, Hargitay's ersatz Herc also must contend with talking trees, an overweight cyclops, and a three-headed dragon that looks like a float in a Chinese New Year's parade. Conveniently, this scary monster sticks out all three necks, and patiently holds that pose while Hargitay labors mightily to chop at least one head off. It was never like this for Gordon and Steve.

Manos, The Hands of Fate (1966) What happens when a fertilizer salesman decides to sink his savings into making a movie? What else? He produces horse manure! That's the only way to describe this ragged slab of used film stock, directed by would-be horror hack Hal P. Warren. Using a bare minimum of camera setups, Warren tells the sad story of a vacationing family that wanders off the main highway and winds up in the midst of a weird Satanic cult. Shot somewhere outside of El Paso, Texas, the movie is mostly confined to two cramped rooms in a desert shack where the husband, wife, and little girl huddle close together, while a seemingly brain-damaged cretin named Torga shuffles back and forth, making vague references to someone called "the Master" and putting his filthy paws all over the pretty missus. Whenever

Torga is out of the room, the other actors stand around looking at each other as if they didn't know what to do. But this isn't really surprising, considering the cluelessness of their first (and only) time director, whose "style" reminds you of a home movie-maker who has left his camcorder running after he has left the room. Somehow Warren manages to pick up the pace toward the end, when a bevy of the Master's "wives," all draped in white sheets, wake from a trance-like slumber and start wrestling each other to the ground in a frenzy of mutual jealousy. At 'em girls!

Marihuana (1936) The original anti-pot propaganda movie, in which a group of fun-loving party kids fall under the influence of a big-time underworld drug trafficker, who promptly destroys their lives. It all starts out so innocently with a party at the bad guy's beach house. Never mind that this pinstripe-suited, pencil-thin-mustached sleazeball is so obviously a gangster that Eliot Ness would have shot him on sight. The kids think he's "just a pretty grand person to know." But while they're swilling his booze he puts out a dish of funny looking cigarettes, which, for some reason, the girls all scarf up like candy. One puff and they're a bunch of laughing ninnies! One whole cigarette and they're jumping out of their clothes and running down to the beach. That's the end of the innocence. Before you know it, one girl has drowned, another has gotten pregnant and her boyfriend has gone to work running drugs for Mr. Big. But on his first day on the job he gets shot by the cops, so it's up to his girl to fend for herself. She gives up her baby and becomes a pot pusher who specializes in weaning her customers onto the harder stuff. Pretty soon the nation's drug problem is out of control, as shown in a stunning montage that consists of anonymous hands making drug transactions and newspapers blaring their headlines in end-of-the-world size type. WAVE OF BRUTAL CRIMES LINKED TO MARIHUANA SMOKING, says one, summing up the movie's message. THE DRUG HABIT IS EXPENSIVE AND THE USEFULNESS OF THE VICTIM IS GONE, announces another, in case we *still* don't get it. The whole thing ends with our hardcore pusher girl masterminding the kidnapping of her own sister's daughter—only to discover that the child is actually hers! Realizing what a mess she's made of her life, she collapses and dies from an overdose of heroin—and heartbreak. As still another headline says, NARCOTICS BRING RUIN! After witnessing this spectacle, who among us would argue?

Tommy Kirk (*right*) and a fellow Martian interrogate an unidentified Earthling in *Mars Needs Women.*

Mars Needs Women (1968) Tommy Kirk heads the all-male contingent from the planet Mars which delivers a simple message to the U.S. Air Force. "You won't believe it," says the decoder to the colonel in charge. "We've checked and double-checked. The message is: Mars needs women!" And Mars means business! When the air force denies the request for females to help repopulate their planet, Kirk and company dump their space suits (which look like wet suits equipped with stereo headphones) and don sports coats and ties, to infiltrate Middle America. "These ties serve no functional purpose," complains one Martian, struggling into his disguise. "The red planet abandoned the use of ties fifty years ago, as a useless male vanity." Kirk and company say these lines with comically deadpan faces. Meanwhile, director Larry Buchanan (*Attack of the Eye Creatures*) treats the material like it's real science fiction or something. Unfortunately, Buchanan is undermined by a no-talent cast, special effects that seem better suited to *My Favorite Martian*, and dialogue that just keeps getting goofier and goofier. "All lovely, built like goddesses and unmarried," muses the colonel, trying to solve the mystery of the missing Earth girls. "Now there's got to be a pattern here someplace." Sorry, sir. There isn't.

Mesa of Lost Women (1952) Set in the dusty southwestern desert, this cheapie comes equipped with a nonstop score of Flamenco guitar-strumming that'll have you fully jangled within the first half hour. It's almost as annoying as the windbag narrator, who prattles on about "our race of puny bipeds with monstrous egos" (you know: we humans) until the plot at long last kicks in. And what a plot it is! We take you now to the mountain hideaway of mad scientist Jackie Coogan (in fake goatee and eyebrows), who's been messing with spider nervous systems and human growth hormones until he has produced a bevy of barefoot beauties with Cleopatra haircuts, four-inch fingernails, and the killer instincts of black widows. How're you gonna keep 'em up on the mesa after they've tasted human blood? One spiderwoman named Tarantella is especially hot to trot, performing a hip-whipping dance of death at the local cantina. The real action, however, is back on the mesa, where some plane crash survivors sit around the campfire waiting to be sucked dry by the spiderwomen and their giant pet tarantula. At one point, the horror gets so intense that a snooty rich man's mistress (Mary Hill) stumbles through the cactus, making a complete mess of her wardrobe. "Oh look," she spits. "This skirt's ruined. And so is this heel!" Oh well, what can you expect from a shrew who made her entrance back at the cantina, declaring "What a dump!" like some sort of Grade Z Bette Davis? What a dump indeed.

Message From Space (1978) Of all the lame-o *Star Wars* rip-offs that showed up in the late seventies, there was none quite like this absurdity, made in Japan. We never have any doubt where the movie's inspiration came from: The plot involves an evil conquering empire, a refugee rebel princess, and some daredevil dogfight pilots. But as an added attraction, it also features Vic Morrow as a jaded star fleet general who sits around brooding and drinking booze while his pint-sized robot chirps, "Master, don't get smashed. We must find a place to crash tonight." The dubbed dialogue is full of such clunkers, while the costumes seem variously borrowed from a samurai film, a toxic waste cleanup crew, and a summer stock production of *Yankee Doodle Dandy*. Needless to say, the disjointed outer space dogfights are a sight to behold. While watching them, you may be reminded of the last time the dog knocked over the Christmas tree.

Monster-a-Go-Go (1965) "What you're about to see may not even be possible within the narrow limits of the human mind." That is *Monster-a-Go-Go*'s opening voice-over warning, which hardly prepares us for what we're really about to see: an unfinished mutant-on-the-loose film, complete with filler footage spliced in at random by schlock impresario Herschell Gordon Lewis (*Blood Feast, 2000 Maniacs*). The result is beyond our comprehension, all right. In fact, it's downright incoherent. The mayhem begins when the first manned spaceship returns to Earth mysteriously *un*manned. A top secret team of NASA scientists naturally investigates, which leads to endless scenes of helicopters landing and men wandering in fields with "geiger counters" that look like blow dryers. Occasionally they stumble over a dead body, which they take back with them for tedious testing. "Actually, there was no blood," says one astute scientist, reporting his findings. "That accounts for the shriveled effect."

The thing doing the shriveling is a nine-foot mutant who used to be six-foot astronaut. While he's stalking the countryside, the concerned authorities are sitting in their offices, discussing the potential danger. At one point one of them makes a sound like a telephone ringing, then picks up the receiver. Think of the money Lewis must have saved on sound effects! Later, however, he blows his budget, sending over a dozen bit players in trucks on an all-out manhunt. After a breathtaking scene in which they all struggle into their radiation-proof suits, they are finally ready for the climactic battle. Alas, it never comes. After all, this is an *unfinished* movie, remember? Instead of providing an ending, Lewis has simply added more cryptic voice-over narration suggesting that the monster is still out there somewhere. As for the "A-Go-Go"—there isn't any! No discotheques, no dancers, no white vinyl boots, no nothing. Either they never existed or Lewis simply forgot to splice them into his final cut. Somewhere on the cutting room floor there may be a very interesting movie lying around. And it probably makes at least as much sense as the one Mr. Lewis actually released.

Nabonga (a.k.a. *Gorilla*) (1944) Legend has it that deep in the jungle there lives a white witch who talks to animals, scares natives silly, and kills off any safaris that dare to enter her domain. But that's no white witch. That's fifties songstress Julie London in a jungle print sarong, Max Factor makeup, and a fresh flower stuck into her fluffy perm. She crashed in a plane with her father when she was just a tyke, and ever since she's been living with Nabonga (a.k.a. Samson), the guy-in-a-gorilla-suit who protects her and her fortune in jewels. When hero Buster Crabbe comes looking for the lost treasure, Julie acts as though he's the first white man she's ever set eyes on. (Then what was

Dad?) "I like to look at you," she tells Crabbe in wide-eyed wonderment. "You're not exactly hard to look at yourself," Crabbe replies, keeping one nervous eye on Nabonga. It goes on like this forever, until finally some bad treasure seekers crash their way through the twelve square feet of backlot jungle to jeopardize innocent Julie. It's Nabonga to the rescue!

This essential slice of Hollywood jungle lore was directed by Sam Newfield, whose other expeditions included *Jungle Siren*, starring Crabbe and Ann Corio as yet another Sheena-style jungle queen; and the one and only *White Pongo*, starring absolutely no one you've ever heard of plus a guy in a fleecy white gorilla suit—as if your basic Nabonga black wasn't silly enough.

The Navy vs. the Night Monsters (1966) A military plane carrying strange plant specimens crash-lands at a tropical naval base. The next thing you know the island is crawling with mobile man-eating shrubs with big rubbery leaves. They blend right in with the lush fake foliage and rear projection backdrops, making it very hard for the sailor heroes to find them. And that doesn't leave very much for the sailor heroes to *do*. Mostly, this cast of TV has-beens, (including Anthony (*Hawaiian Eye*) Eisely and Billy (*Father Knows Best*) Gray,) sit around wondering exactly what's out there. Every so often an expendable swabby or night nurse wanders down to the dark end of the soundstage. Then suddenly there's an offscreen scream and you know the rubber shrubs have claimed another victim. Since there are relatively few such horrible deaths, acting commander Eisley and fellow officer Edward Faulkner have plenty of time to fight it out over head nurse Mamie Van Doren, here almost unrecognizable in a sensible haircut, navy-issue uniforms, and a performance so bland you'd think she was trying to remain incognito. Who can blame her? In a movie in which even the monsters remain incognito, it's probably best just to quietly put in your time and take an early discharge. And discharge is the word. As this shockingly uneventful thriller builds to its anticlimax, Mamie and her costars are simply shunted to the sidelines while some stock-footage fighter planes supposedly drop napalm on a field full of oil barrels disguised with tree branches. These are the night monsters, and this is how they are conquered. Over and out.

Night of the Ghouls (1959) Ed Wood strikes again, this time with a nightmare-of-living-dead so compelling that he can't always keep his mind on it. Narrated by the not-so-famous clairvoyant Criswell, who pops up from a coffin to introduce the proceedings, this movie does a free-form rumination on various social ills (juvenile delinquency, traffic fatalities, etc.) before settling down to tell the story of "strange doings at the old house at Willows' Lake." Responding to reports of ghosts wandering the grounds, police lieutenant Dan Bradford (Duke Moore) rushes off to investigate. Barging into the old house, he meets a mystic host in a ridiculous satin turban who leads him back into the dark shadows, to a room where the mystic holds seances for the bereaved. Of course, the fellow is a fake, preying on rich, grieving widows. So imagine his surprise when real ghosts and ghouls rise up from their graves. But before they do, we are treated to a silly seance sequence featuring bad overactors in white sheets and sound effects so phony they don't even seem to interest, much less frighten, the people gathered around the table. As an added treat, old Tor Johnson emerges from the depths, reprising his role as Lobo—Bela Lugosi's assistant in *Bride of the Monster*. Yes, folks, Mr. Wood intended this movie as a sequel to his earlier "masterpiece." He has even brought back a minor comic relief character, Officer Kelton (Paul Marco), who figures much more prominently here, cowering in his squad car and firing away at things that go bump in the night. "Monsters, space people, mad doctors," he whines at one point. "They didn't teach me about such things at the police academy." And wait'll he sees the black-caped Vampira-type in the rhinestone tiara. Strange doings indeed.

Night of the Lepus (1972) Attempting to stem a rabbit population explosion, the world's stupidest scientists (Stuart Whitman and Janet Leigh) inject the bunnies with an experimental hormone without even knowing what the side effects will be. The next thing you know the countryside's crawling with giant cottontails. Just how giant are they? That depends on which miniature set they're trashing. Sometimes they look no larger than a horse, sometimes they seem bigger than a full-grown triceratops. Maybe they just grow fast. One thing's for sure—they eat a lot. And somehow they've acquired a taste for people. "They're heading this way, killing as they come!," says one frantic radio report. Silly rabbits. They don't even know they're not supposed to eat meat. Rory Calhoun and DeForest Kelley are among the endangered humans in this cavalcade of cheesy special effects, which ends when the rabbits are herded onto electrified train tacks and barbecued into oblivion. They say it tastes like chicken.

Plan 9 From Outer Space (1959) Some say this is the worst movie anyone ever
made. Certainly it's the worst movie Ed Wood ever made. And nobody but
Wood could have made it. The lunacy begins with a portentous introduction
from our old friend Criswell, the clairvoyant. "Greetings my friends," Criswell
reads from his cue card. "We are all interested in the future because that's
where you and I are going to spend the rest of our lives." While we're still
mulling over the meaning of that statement, Wood hits us with the heavy-
duty special effects, in the form of UFOs flying over Hollywood Boulevard.
Actually, they're only hubcaps, superimposed on a pseudo-sky, but that's one
of the more clever cinematic illusions in a movie so technically inept that day
often turns into night within a single scene. Under the circumstances, it's no
surprise when such Halloween figures as Bela Lugosi, Tor Johnson, and
Vampira start emerging from their graves in the San Fernando Cemetery. As
it turns out all these phenomena are connected, as part of the aliens' Plan 9—
a diabolical plot to conquer Earth by resurrecting dead bodies.

Speaking of dead, that's what became of Lugosi after only a few days' filming. Instead of reshooting Lugosi's scenes, Wood simply replaced him with an
obviously taller double (reportedly Wood's chiropractor), who lurks from
shadow to shadow with a cape drawn over his face to conceal the fact that
he's *not* Bela Lugosi. Needless to say, it's hilarious, but no less funny are the
aliens, who sit around their saucer dressed in Buck Rogers satin while looking down their noses at the inferior earthlings. "All you of Earth are idiots,"
sneers the alien leader. "Your stupid minds! Stupid, stupid!" Such goofy dia-

logue is delivered with appropriate zeal by hambone thespians who have absolute-zero talent. As they throw themselves into scenes that seem to have been scripted on the spot, Criswell keeps piping up on the sound track, trying to explain what's going on. It's no use. Finally, he reappears onscreen to sum it all up: "My friends, you have seen these incidents based upon sworn testimony. Can you prove it didn't happen?" As always, it is impossible to argue with the logic of Ed Wood.

Prehistoric Women (1950) This is a tale of "romance when the world was young." So says our omnipresent narrator, setting up the love story of a prehistoric woman and her primitive man. Tigri (Laurette Luez) belongs to a lost tribe of man-hating tree dwellers. Engor (Allan Nixon) is one of the clean-shaven cave people. The romance gets off to a rocky start when Tigri and her girls ambush Engor's hunting party, pelting them with stones. Quickly prevailing, the women capture the men, drag them into the treetops, and convert them into personal slaves. "What type of women are these, who attack men and live in trees?" asks the indignant narrator. Just call them tigers in lipstick! "Hah!" says Tigri (practically her only dialogue) as Engor cringes fearfully at her feet. Of course, this can't last for long. Caveman that he is, Engor eventually reverses their roles and turns Tigri into a pussycat. Along the way he also discovers fire while banging two rocks together. "He doesn't understand it," the narrator explains. "But he knows this new discovery has the power to inflict injury." Soon enough, Engor has the chance to test this new weapon, using a torch to save Tigri from a duck rigged up to look like a pterodactyl. For her part, Tigri also does some innovating, as we witness when she executes a perfect swan dive into a jungle pool. "Strangely enough, the swan dive was invented before the swan," comments the narrator. But not, it seems, before the duck in the pterodactyl costume.

Prehistoric Women (1967) No, this *isn't* a remake of the 1950 nonclassic (see above). In fact, the ladies in this movie *aren't* really prehistoric, even if they do seem to be dressed in Raquel Welch's wardrobe from *One Million Years B.C.* Retro fashions aside, they're actually a tribe of raven-haired Amazons who live in an isolated backlot jungle where they worship a rhinoceros god and keep blond women as slaves. When a not-so-great white hunter (Michael Latimer) stumbles into this party, the sultry Amazon queen (Martine

Beswick) summons him to her private cave to be her personal love toy. Having just watched her impale a spirited slave girl, our upright (uptight?) hero says thanks but no thanks. "I am the queen, I will not be denied," she seethes, unfurling her shiny black whip. And so off he goes into bondage with the rest of the males.

But you can't keep a good man in chains forever, nor can you oppress a whole race of women just because of the color of their hair. Once the blond slave girls get tired of dancing during the queen's dinner hour, they throw off their inhibitions, join up with the men, and revolt! It's a good thing too, because those dance routines they've been doing make them look like third-grade girls on their first day of ballet class. However, this is not the silliest sight to be found in this movie. That booby prize goes to a blatantly bogus rhino who shows up at the end, looking like the latex statue that he is, to charge the Amazon queen and run her through with his horn. The fact that he's quite obviously rolling on wheels—at about one mile per hour—doesn't help his credibility much. Of course, if he'd been moving any faster he'd have crashed right through the walls of this claustrophobic studio set. When you're working in Grade Z movies, you've got to work within your limitations.

Queen of Outer Space (1958) Already a little punchy from a prolonged, pre-credit prologue, a four-man spaceship crew crash-lands on Venus—where they are promptly taken prisoner by gorgeous females in Flash Gordon finery. The guys are so busy ogling these babes they aren't even fazed when the masked Queen of Venus imprisons them as spies. "Twenty-six million miles from Earth and the dolls are just the same," cracks the flight crew Casanova. He doesn't understand that they're doomed—unless Zsa Zsa Gabor, the planet's only rational woman (huh?), can outfox her queen and set the men free. Gabor is an artificial wonder in her floor-length chiffon and blindingly blond hair. Never once changing her expression—or the tone of her voice—she nimbly negotiates palace intrigue, then leads the men on the lam through a ridiculously overripe jungle of fake foliage. She never even breaks a high heel! Not even a giant spider puppet, left over from *Cat Women of the Moon*, can cramp her style. But what of the man-hating queen (Laurie Mitchell)? After all, she *is* the title character. Alas, she's not all she's cracked up to be. Turns out she's just bitter because her once-beautiful face was disfigured during the heat of battle—against the men of Venus! Suddenly it's clear! This is a good, old-fashioned, interplanetary war between the sexes. And all, it seems, is fair. "I don't think you're a tyrant," says mission commander Eric Fleming. "I think you're just a woman who's been hurt." Then he rejects her in favor of Zsa Zsa. The fifties had a long way to go.

Radio Ranch (1935) Singing cowboy Gene Autry had many strange adventures, but none came close to this genre-bending mind-blower, originally released as *The Phantom Empire*, a twelve-part serial. *Radio Ranch* is the standard condensed edition, cut by a full two-thirds for release as a feature film.

MANKIND'S FIRST FLIGHT TO **VENUS** --the Female Planet!

QUEEN OF OUTER SPACE

COLOR *by deluxe* CinemaScope

starring ZSA ZSA GABOR

with ERIC FLEMING · LAURIE MITCHELL · LISA DAVIS

But eighty minutes is more than enough to leave you disoriented for days. The story starts out conventionally enough . . . that is, for a Gene Autry movie. Our hero is carrying on as usual, dressed in his Tom Mix duds and ramrodding a modern day ranch, from which he does a daily radio broadcast. He tells stories, sings songs, and joshes with teenage sidekicks Frankie (Frankie Darro) and Betsy (Betsy King Ross). But things get weird in a hurry when a "vicious party of research scientists" shows up at the ranch looking for a fortune in radium. Unwittingly, these dastardly treasure hunters arouse the underground civilization of Murania, whose queen (Dorothy Christie) will stop at nothing to protect her world. The Muranians are an odd-looking bunch. In their brocaded vests, Elizabethan collars, bullet-head helmets, and Batman capes, they promenade around their futuristic city, behaving as though they'd feel more at home in a Buck Rogers serial.

However, since this is Gene Autry's show, they're stuck with *him* as a nemesis. "We must capture Gene Autry," says the queen, voicing what will become an obsession before her reign is over. Meanwhile, the radium-hunters are plotting Gene's demise, comic relief ranch hand Smiley Burnette is playing harmonica and falling out of haylofts, and Frankie and Betsy and their Junior Thunder Riders are bailing Gene out of one scrape after another so he can hightail it back to Radio Ranch for his two o'clock broadcast. "If we miss it, we'll lose our contract!" exclaims ever-conscientious Gene, several times. Eventually he'll take on even more dire challenges in the depths of Murania—where he contends with the queen-who-must-be-obeyed, her bumbling guards, the rebel underground, and, last but not least, the very crudest, silliest, tin can robots any movie ever put on screen. Next to this, *Radar Men From the Moon* looks like *2001*.

Rat Pfink à Boo Boo (1966) "In a world populated by quite a few billion souls," introduces our narrator, "there are bound to be some who would seem to stand out from the rest." That's one way of describing Rat Pfink and Boo, costumed crimefighters who are obviously modeled after Batman and Robin, but who actually behave more like Yogi and Boo Boo. Rat Pfink is really rock star Lonnie Lord (Vin Saxon), who "carries his guitar everywhere because he never knows when he'll be asked to play a song." Boo Boo is really gardener Titus Twimbly (Titus Moede), who may be a moron, but is probably just acting like one. Lonnie spends his spare time in his secret identity singing twangy tunes in primitive precursors of music videos. Titus toils away day after day, raking the same front lawn. But when three deadbeat hopheads kidnap Lonnie's girlfriend, it's no more Mister Nice Geek. "This is a job for you-know-and-who," says Lonnie. Then he and Titus jump into a closet and crash around for a while before finally emerging as our heroes. Rat Pfink sports a make-shift cape and tights, topped off by a woolen ski mask with pompom. Boo Boo is even sillier, wearing what look like modified kiddie PJs, complete with tiger-striped booties and matching cap with floppy ears that have little blinking lights on the end. Chasing after the bad guys, Boo Boo drives a motorcycle while Rat Pfink stands in the sidecar, hands on hips. "After them, Boo Boo," he commands, reminding his companion to stop at all stop signs and look both ways. Needless to say, these superheroes have all they can handle with the three kidnappers, who fight them off during several klutzy free-for-alls in nondescript backyards, and lead our heroes on a never-ending chase through shady suburban streets. "Hi-Yo, Boo Boo!" Rat Pfink exclaims, taking to his sidecar, again and again. As a superhero, he is nothing if not unrelenting. This addle-brained adventure was written, directed, and photographed by Ray Dennis Steckler, the auteur who gave us *The Incredibly Strange Creatures Who Stopped Living and Became Mixed-Up Zombies*, as well as other abominations such as *The Lemon Grove Kids Meet the Monsters.* One thing you can say about his movies: They always live up to their titles.

Reefer Madness (1936) It helps to be high while viewing this classic cautionary tale, which reveals the ravaging effects of marijuana: "The *real* Public Enemy Number 1." The giddiness begins with some stern words from the movie's moral voice, high school principal Dr. Albert Carroll, who lectures parents and teachers on the far-reaching consequences of smoking the evil weed. Why, did you know that under the influence of marijuana, one young boy killed his whole family with an ax? Nothing so awful actually happens in this movie. Ah, but that's the point. The insidious weed can get you in all sorts of ways. Teenage Jimmy (Carleton Young) tokes up, drives his car too fast, and runs down a pedestrian. His sister Mary (Dorothy Short) unwittingly smokes a reefer and gets so high she can't fight off a manhandling lowlife. Mary's boyfriend Bill (Kenneth Craig) gets so fired up that he runs to Mary's rescue and fights the lowlife for a gun, which accidentally goes off and kills poor Mary.

All of this takes place in a sleazeball couple's apartment, where clean-cut kids are unconscionably converted into craven addicts who Bogart cigar-sized joints, make Harpo Marx-type faces, and laugh like blithering idiots. But don't worry, in a movie like this, sleazeballs always get their due. While poor Bill stands trial for murder, the dope dealers make the mistake of harboring Mr. Manhandler, who is cracking under the pressure. Sucking down reefers two at a time, he tells his piano-playing girlfriend "Play faster! Faster!" before going completely bonkers and beating one dope dealer to death. Later, in court, the D.A. pronounces the manhandler "hopelessly, incurably insane, a condition caused by the drug marijuana." Now do you understand why they call it Public Enemy Number One? Hell, between this movie and its same year counterpart, *Marihuana,* you'd think it was the root of *all* evil.

Riot in Juvenile Prison (1959) The Ditman Hall Reform School for boys is having a hard time. The student body is out of control and the guards have resorted to Gestapo methods. After an attempted breakout in which several boys get mowed down, the governor hits on a drastic solution: He turns Ditman Hall into the first *coed* reform school! "I've seen harebrained ideas before," sputters warden John Hoyt, "but I've never seen anything like this."

But nobody listens—and boy, will they be sorry. No sooner are the girls bumping and grinding off the bus than the sexual tension gets so thick you could cut it with a switchblade. Especially troublesome is teen temptress Dorothy Provine, a platinum blond stripper's daughter whose vamping in the lunchroom stirs up more than one male libido. "Hiya, tall, dark, and delinquent," she purrs to Method punk Scott Marlowe. All things considered, rioting seems a reasonable response. Yet it isn't until the experiment fails and the girls are transferred back out that all hell really breaks loose, in a revolt that make Attica look like a lunchroom food fight. No wonder juvenile delinquency was such a problem in the fifties. With reform schools like this, how could a guy help himself?

Riot on Sunset Strip (1967) The time: 1967. The place: Sunset Strip. The street is just crawling with kids carrying picket signs, so prepare yourself for sixties social commentary—in the unfortunate form of a fifties message movie. "These are not dangerous revolutionaries," explains the all-knowing narrator. "These are teenagers on a peaceful night, with nowhere to go, nothing to do, no goal in life." What to do about the youth problem? One uptight Mr. Businessman suggests barber shears. "After we've grabbed a few goldilocks boys and fixed them up with crew cuts, I bet they'd take to the hills," he chuckles. "And what about a few baths?" chimes in another pillar of the community. "And maybe some shoes!" Like adults in any decade, they don't have a clue. But then, neither do the kids, especially dumb blonde Mimsy Farmer, whose cop father (Aldo Ray) and drunk mother have provided her with a broken home. Staying out after curfew, she goes to clubs and dances to bands so god-awful that you almost understand what grownups have against rock and roll. One night, at a party, she even drinks some spiked diet soda. The resulting freak-out is a high-camp piece of modern dance, which peaks with Mimsy on all fours violently whipping her hair on the floor. Later she passes out and half the boys at the party have their way with her. Then it's her cop daddy who does the freaking out, beating up several of the partygoers in the hospital waiting room. "Call the orderlies," cries a nurse. "What have I done?" cries Dad. What he *hasn't* done is provoke the titular riot, which never actually happens. Instead, all we get is a half-assed protest. "We want peace not police," shouts one demonstrator. "Hey, that rhymes," says his girlfriend. Where is the tear gas when you really need it?

Robot Monster (1953) A movie of such surpassing awfulness that it rivals *Plan 9* as the worst of all time. Conceived as an end-of-the-world nightmare, it's such a disorienting experience—from its scrambled narrative to its junkyard props to its absurdly primitive special effects—that it almost works in spite of itself. The first time you see it, you might think you're hallucinating! The story begins innocuously enough with a nice boring family picnic. But suddenly lightning is flashing, then dinosaurs are fighting, and then Robot Monster— a fat guy in a gorilla suit wearing a deep sea diving helmet—emerges from a cave and turns on a bubble machine that is supposed to be some sort of doomsday device. He's trying to kill our picnicking family since they represent the last survivors on Earth. But his death ray isn't working because they've invented a vaccine with the help of a handsome scientist who has joined up with them. Frustrated, Robot Monster tunes in the survivors on his view screen to engage them in rambling dialogues about why they must die. When not talking to Robot Monster, the survivors busy themselves, trying to build a counter weapon. Sometimes tempers grow short, as when the handsome scientist takes exception to the pretty eldest daughter's haughty attitude. "You're so bossy you ought to be milked before you come home at night!" he barks. Nevertheless, they decide to get married, end of the world or not.

Meanwhile, Robot Monster, unable to kill off these people, has become riddled with self-doubt. It doesn't help when the little brother of the family comes around to rub it in. "You look like a pooped-out pinwheel," he taunts, apropos of who-knows-what. At about this point, you decide for sure that you're rooting for Robot Monster to wipe out what's left of the human race. Alas, it is not to be. This is all just a dream, remember? *Robot Monster* was written by a man named Wyatt Ordung, and taken much too seriously by its director, Phil Tucker, who reportedly was so depressed by the reviews of his movie that he contemplated suicide. In the end, of course, there was no need. In terms of his career, he'd already pulled the plug.

Santa Claus (1959) Here comes Santa Claus, Mexicali-style. And wait'll you see how the North Pole looks from south of the border. It's a garishly bright, two-dimensional toyland, where children from all around the world serve as Santa's helpers. So whatever happened to elves? Gone the way of all North Pole stereotypes. In their place, however, are other stereotypes: The little African kids have bones in their hair, the Middle Eastern kids dress in harem-

He's a deep-sea diver with UHF reception! No, he's a guy in a cheap gorilla suit! No, he's . . . Robot Monster! Can you blame George Nader and Claudia Barrett for being terrified?

wear; the South American kids look like Carmen Miranda and her band; and the kids from the United States wear cowboy hats. Each group of munchkins gets to sing its own Christmas song, in full ethnic dress. The cumulative effect is like sitting through a bizarro version of "It's a Small World, After All." And what of Santa? Why, he's a jolly-to-the-point-of-demented old coot who sits in his bargain-basement workshop, operating gadgets that enable him to see you when you're sleeping. "Let's look into the little rich boy's dreams," Santa says, while onscreen the kid unwraps two huge presents containing . . . his parents! "A dream is a wish that the heart makes," Santa explains, leading us at long last to the movie's plot—in which a red-faced devil with shiny plastic horns pops up from Hades to invade kids' sugarplum visions and turn them bad. When he messes with one little poor girl's head, he goes too far. It's Santa to the rescue! Jumping into his sleigh, drawn by fake white reindeer,

St. Nick charts a course for planet Earth. What? You didn't know Santa lived in outer space? It doesn't matter. What counts is that he eventually makes it to Earth, where he out-foxes the devil, restores the yuletide spirit to one little rich boy and one little poor girl, and still has time to deliver all his presents—with timely help from Merlin the Magician. Yes, Virginia, there is a Merlin in this movie—but there is no Comet or Cupid or Donder or Blitzen or even a Mrs. Claus. No wonder Santa keeps all those kids around. The North Pole can be a very lonely place—especially when it's in outer space.

Santa Claus Conquers the Martians (1964) This is the movie that proves that American hacks can trash Santa Claus every bit as badly as Mexicans. And they do it by sending Santa even farther into space. The travesty begins when Martians kidnap the jolly old elf, along with two cute kids. Since this was meant as a children's movie, everyone agreeably flies to mars, laughing all the way. Once they get to the angry red planet, Santa spreads yule tidings to emotionally underprivileged Martian kids. Later, a goofy grown-up Martian who'd rather be an elf helps Santa escape from the clutches of an extraterrestrial Scrooge. All of this plays like a local TV kiddie show, and it looks like one too. The Martians wear green leotards and rabbit ear antennae, the kids wear sappy, self-conscious smiles, and Santa wears a glaze-eyed look of bemusement, just like your grandfather used to wear after too much Christmas cheer. Other highlights include a robot who looks like the Tin Man, a polar bear who is really a giant teddy bear, and Pia Zadora, in green-face, as a good little Martian girl. All together now: Ho, ho, ho!

The *Santo* Movies. Batman and Superman pale next to Santo, the superhero of some fifty Mexican adventures, filmed from the late 1950s through the early 1980s. A champion wrestler in a culture that reveres them, Santo (playing himself) dashes across the screen in his silver mask, shiny cape, bare chest, and flabby belly, ready to battle "evil wherever it exists." Neither man, nor machine nor monster is any match for this overweight avenger, who pads his movie plots with full-blown, interminable wrestling exhibitions, then leaps from the ring to answer the S.O.S. of endangered citizens. Out of his fifty or so escapades, only a handful have made it across the border. But if you've seen one *Santo*, you've seen them all. In *Santo vs. the Vampire Women* (1961) he takes on lovely lady bloodsuckers who drape themselves in white

The same year as *The Carpetbaggers*, Joseph E. Levine also released *Santa Claus Conquers the Martians.* That kid in the funny spacesuit (*upper right-hand corner*) is a young Pia Zadora.

robes like refugees from *Lysistrata*. In *Santo in the Wax Museum* (1963) he plows through armies of wax figures brought to life by a mad scientist. And in *Santo Against the Zombies* (1961) he battles . . . zombies!

Throughout his illustrious crime-fighting career, Santo has also grappled with witches (*Santo Attacks the Witches*, 1964), ghosts (*Santo vs. the Ghost of the Strangler*, 1967), and famous movie monsters (*Santo and Blue Demon vs. Dracula and the Wolfman*, 1967). Whatever the challenge, Santo prevails. The authorities can only stand by, thanking God that Santo is on their side. "There he goes," says one admiring policeman in *Santo Against the Zombies*. "He always does the same thing. Never waits around. Never expects to be thanked. I wonder who he really is. That's a good question. Who knows the answer?" And who knows why audiences clamored for half a hundred of these films? Indeed, the formula proved so durable that it served not only the *Santo* series, but also various copycats, the most blatant being *Neutron*, another wrestling champ who took off his shirt and put on a mask to fight evildoers free of charge. Neutron's mask is black instead of silver, and he has a chiseled chest that his role model can only dream about. But he can never play better than second fiddle to Santo: the original off-the-wall masked avenger Mexican wrestler. Viva El Santo!

Sex Kittens Go to College (1960) Mamie Van Doren is back on campus—and this time she's on the faculty! Once again working for producer Albert Zugsmith (*High School Confidential, College Confidential*), she plays Dr. Mathilda West, a statuesque stunner selected by a robot named Thinko to become the new head of the science department. Mathilda is actually a stripper—but she has an IQ of 298. What's the difference to a robot? "You can't blame Thinko," cracks college P.R. man Martin Milner to the flustered dean. "How could a machine know we wouldn't like somebody who looked like Mamie Van Doren?" And that's about as witty as this would-be campus farce ever gets. More often, its concept of laughs is to let Mamie go around apparently oblivious to her own attributes, while football heroes fall down at her feet and old hams like Louis Nye and Jackie Coogan do vertebrae-rattling double takes. "You make every woman in the world feel positively flat-chested," pouts student sex kitten Tuesday Weld. "You're a menace, that's what you are."

The real menace, however, is the supporting cast, which also features John Carradine as a horny biology professor, Vampira as a geeky lab assistant named Etta Tootle, and Mijanou Bardot (Brigitte's little sister) as a man-eating exchange student. They're all thrown together in a free-for-all finale that also includes various gangsters, firemen, and fringe faculty members, not to mention Thinko, who blows all his circuits during a striptease dream sequence. Putting a merciful stop to this stupidity, Mamie douses everybody with a fire extinguisher, then leaves town in a hook and ladder truck, accompanied by future husband Milner and a chimp named Voltaire. The lesson to be learned here: Don't ask Al Zugsmith to do comedy. He's a lot funnier when he sticks to so-called dramas. *Girls Town*, anyone?

She Demons (1958) The definitive bad movie about a mad doctor on a desert island with a live volcano and many beautiful women. Strapping Irish McAlla (the original Sheena) stars as one of four pleasure cruisers who get shipwrecked on that unchartered isle. She's a haughty heiress who's beside herself because her crew couldn't salvage her wardrobe. "You might have at least thought to save me a pair of toreador pants," she snaps at future love interest Tod Griffin. But her lost leisure-wear will be the least of her worries when she and her companions discover they're not alone! "Real crazy," says "Oriental" hipster Victor Sen Yung (*Bonanza's* Hop Sing). "These footprints go in a circle. Maybe the natives here are getting on this rock 'n' roll kick." Pretty soon they meet the natives: a scantily clad group of girls who sashay around the campfire like Las Vegas chorines. The reason could be that they're being played by a troupe called the Diana Welles Dancers. In any case, they're not nearly so frisky when they get rounded up by a Nazi war criminal (Rudolph Anders), who is trying to create a new face for his disfigured wife. "Jumpin' won tons!" says hipster Sen Yung—and he hasn't even seen how beastly the native girls look after the Nazi doctor is finished with them. Don't look now, but Irish is his next victim—and she hasn't a thing to wear! Just in time the volcano blows, deluging the doctor in bubbling lava and sending our survivors scurrying for safety. As rear-projected boulders tumble down around her, Irish has a revelation. "Now I know what an empty, self-centered person I've been," says the formerly haughty heiress. Rarely has such a beautiful girl weathered such a ridiculous situation with so much ripe dialogue—and so little acting talent.

The Sinister Urge (1960) Some nut is killing pretty girls and dumping them in the park. Who would do such a thing? According to Ed Wood, it's the work of a man who has lost control after gazing upon too many dirty photographs. Yes folks, welcome to the world of smut picture purveyors. They prey on the weak, sex-starved minds of society's perverts. "Some characters will steal or kill just to get this stuff," says chief of detectives Kenne Duncan, making like Jack Webb in *Dragnet*. "The smut picture racket is worse than kidnapping or dope peddling, and can lead to the same place: the morgue. Show me a crime and I can show you a picture that could have caused it."

To stop this horribly horny epidemic, Duncan and his partner Duke Moore work around the clock to break up the local smut syndicate, which is led by a brassy blonde (Jean Fontaine) in skintight silver lamé pants and stiletto heels. "Let's see those legs," she commands a poor girl who thought she was auditioning for a legit movie producer. "And when I say, 'Let's see those legs,' I mean from your toes right up to your hat." Tough broads like this need tough underlings—and this broad has got 'em. Even the pretty models who double as distributors are hard as nails, as we see when four girls in their summer dresses shove ice cream in the face of a soda jerk-smut dealer who owes them back payments. Like Detective Duncan says, "Pornography. It's a nasty word for a dirty business." But somebody's gotta do it.

Swamp Women (1955) In this Roger Corman classic of budget-stretching badness, Beverly Garland leads a bunch of tough broads on a prison break. Next stop: the bayou, where the ladies plan to pick up a fortune in stashed diamonds. Along the way they also pick up innocent sightseer Mike Connors and his date, and hold them hostage for an endless canoe trip through the backwater. Of course, the main reason it seems so interminable is that Corman has padded the journey with mile after mile of travelogue footage featuring mostly banyan trees and Spanish moss. Sure it's atmospheric—if you like the smell of rotting vegetation—but if it's action you want, you'll have to wait until Day 2 (or is it Day 3?), when Connors's date is eaten by an alligator. Mind you, Corman's budget isn't big enough to actually show the gator attack. Instead, he sort of implies it. One minute the poor girl is thrashing around the water, the next, there's a shot of a gator swimming somewhere in a hurry. And then the next, the girl is gone and Connors is in the water, flailing way with a knife in the gator's general direction. Thankfully, Connors survives this attack. In fact, he recovers so completely that he's soon making passes at his various captors, all of whom have taken knives to their prison-issue blue jeans and turned them into short-shorts. "I want to cut mine a little shorter," says the peroxide blond swamp woman. These broads are so darn brazen that it's only a matter of time before they break out in catfights, which inevitably end up in the water so their blouses can get soaked and cling to their curves. Things overheat to a climax when Garland and the gals discover that one of them is actually an undercover police-woman. Now the wet fur really flies! All Corman has to do is let the camera roll. Everybody back into the swamp!

Teenage Caveman (1958) Like Victor Mature in *One Million B.C.*, Robert Vaughn is a beardless caveman. But that's okay, because he's a *teenage* cave-man—even though he looks at least thirty years old. In any case, this isn't *re-ally* the Stone Age; it's actually some sort of postapocalyptic world in which the survivors wear animal skins and live in caves, yet still retain some vestiges of their distant, civilized past. Ah, so *that* explains the barber-shop haircuts, the biblical-epic dialogue, and Vaughn's meaningful, method-actor pauses. "I wonder how many strange things there are beyond the river," he muses, jut-ting his bare chin in the river's direction. Being (ahem) an impetuous youth, he wants to see what's out there for himself. The clan elders, however, forbid such a quest, explaining that beyond the river there are "shadows deep and cold," and "dirt that eats men," and a "god who gives death with its touch." But, of course, that's where all life's answers are. It's also where the teenage caveman will encounter stock-footage dinosaurs borrowed from—you guessed it—*One Million B.C.*! Yet another cost-cutting hack job from the Roger Corman hit machine.

Teenage Devil Dolls (1952) This is the case history of a teenage junkie, as nar-rated by the cop who witnessed the whole sordid story. And you can't help but listen to what he says—because his is the only voice you're going to hear in this movie. Coming on like gangbusters, our no-nonsense narrator tells the tale of bad girl Cassandra (Barbara Marks), who hooks up with a bunch of punks, takes one whiff of marijuana, and completely ruins her life. It's all the fault of her "much married mother," who never gave Cassandra the love a teenager needs. Can you blame the girl for smoking reefer and cackling like a lunatic? There goes college! In lieu of higher education, Cassandra finagles a June wedding to a go-getter named Johnny. Alas, the primrose path proves thorny. "Cassandra was ill-prepared for the adjustments and responsibilities of married life," the narrator comments, as we watch her tearing Johnny's clean shirts off the clothesline and throwing them on the ground. Next thing you know *she's* on the ground, overdosing on Seconals. "The junkies call them goofballs," the narrator informs us, "and Cassandra was about as goofed up as the physical limitations of the human body can stand." And so the downfall goes, as Cass descends from selling reefer to "the teenage bop crowd," to smoking up all her inventory, to becoming a pathetic heroin addict. At her absolute pits, she and her dope-dealing boyfriend can be found foaming at the mouth as they slowly dehydrate in their desert hideout. Don't you just hate when that happens?

Teenagers From Outer Space (1959) Wearing what look like leftover costumes from *Rocky Jones, Space Ranger*, a team of teenage aliens lands on Earth to unleash a horde of giant man-eating lobsters. Conscientiously objecting, one young fellow (director Tod Graeff) goes AWOL into the nearest all-American town, where he meets a pretty girl named Betty (Dawn Anderson) and her goofy old granddad. "Where are you fellas from anyway?" asks Gramps, as more teenage aliens start showing up. "I don't believe I've seen uniforms like yours before." Wait'll he gets a load of those giant lobsters, which appear as silhouettes superimposed on the screen. But at least they stay in character, which is more than you can say for Harvey B. Dunn as Gramps—who can be seen reciting his lines, then doing a hasty exit stage left, dropping his Gramps act before he can even get out of camera range. It should probably come as no surprise that Dunn was also a member of Ed Wood's stock ensemble. Just goes to show: You can take a bad actor out of Ed Wood movies, but you can't take Ed Wood out of a bad actor.

The Terror of Tiny Town (1938) Producer Jed Buell's idea of a joke was to populate this "rootin', tootin' drama of the great outdoors" with "an all-midget cast." And then to make it even more attention-getting, he decided to do it as a musical! When the citizens of Tiny Town break out in a chorus of "Laugh Your Troubles Away," it's just like listening to the munchkins sing. But even more amazing (or amusing, if you're Jed Buell) is the sight of this vertically challenged ensemble struggling through the conventions of the Western genre. They don't walk through saloon doors, they walk *under* them.

The poster for *Teenagers From Outer Space.* Don't laugh, those x-ray special effects were visionary in their day.

They don't ride palominos, they ride Shetland ponies. And actually, they don't *ride* so much as hang on for dear life. Even out of the saddle, life is an uphill struggle, as one poor old coot discovers when he hauls himself up the

The "All-Midget" cast from *Terror of Tiny Town* heads for a showdown.

front steps of the barber shop. Later a whole posse takes on a similar challenge to get to the sheriff's office. This sort of sight gag is typical of director Sam Newfield's comic approach, which is to scale down most of the set decoration to little people size, so that the occasional full-size prop—like the beer mug that engulfs one thirsty midget's face in a flood of suds—will pay off with giant-sized yuks. Newfield is the man who gave us *Nabonga* and *White Pongo*, so nothing he does should surprise us. But he's really outdone himself this time. Small wonder he wasn't run out of town.

They Saved Hitler's Brain (1963) Vic and Toni are seventies secret agents investigating the murder of a government scientist. Everything's dragging along drearily enough, when suddenly they are catapulted into the footage of a 1963 thriller. Yes, this is another of those incomplete old movies filled out with newer footage shot well after the original stuff. Yet few such cut-and-paste jobs have been as mismatched as this one. Vic and Toni are practically caricatures of seventies fashion: Vic has long sideburns and a droopy Sonny Bono mustache; Toni dresses like one of the Brady Bunch. Meanwhile, the men they're chasing wear sixties style suits with narrow lapels and short-brim hats, and drive around in cars of 1950s vintage. Are there three different movies stitched together here? Who can say for sure? But no sooner do we shake the disorientation than Vic and Toni are killed off and Phil (Walter

Stocker), a 1960s CIA man, takes over the case. Confused? The fun's just beginning. Accompanied by his ditzy wife (Audrey Caire), Phil pursues the Nazi war criminals who have kidnapped his scientist father-in-law and hustled him off to South America—where Hitler's living head is hiding out, preserved in a glass jar connected to wires and gauges. Phil, however, doesn't know about Adolf yet—he thinks he's chasing run-of-the-mill Nazi war criminals. Meanwhile, his wife goes duty free shopping and idly wonders whatever happened to her father. Just when things couldn't get any more absurd, who should show up but Phil's wife's hipster sister, who was also kidnapped by Nazis but is now just hanging out, dancing at the local Calypso Club. Don't worry, it gets weirder. The plot also includes shady South Americans with bad South American accents, mysterious Germans with bad German accents, and a Texas billionaire with the worst accent of all. "Will you tell us what this is all about and how you fit into this rat race?" says Phil to the billionaire. The answer, like everything else here, is giddily garbled. Suffice to say that this is all about Adolf, who, of course, is still trying to conquer the world. While his head sits in its jar squawking out orders, the intrigue stumbles toward a climactic low-speed chase in the hills—where Phil single-handedly foils the Führer's plan by tossing grenades at the Nazis, who stand around their cars like ducks in a shooting gallery. Eventually, Hitler's car gets hit, and the old boy's head goes up in flames, slowly melting before our eyes like the wax figure it is. Vic and Toni did not die in vain.

The Thing With Two Heads (1972) The very silliest two-headed transplant movie ever made. But with Ray Milland and Rosey Grier as the two heads, how could it miss? The fun begins when genius Milland perfects his transplant technique just in time to escape his own decrepit body. Alas, he lapses into a coma before he can approve the volunteer who will receive his head. When Ray wakes up, he's sharing the massive frame of pardoned death row convict Rosey. Now it's Ray who feels imprisoned, and wouldn't you know it—he's a lifelong bigot! "Is this some kind of joke?" he sputters, holding one black hand in front of his face. As a matter of fact, the movie does play Milland's dilemma for laughs—although most of the time we're laughing at it instead of *with* it. What other response can there be as Rosey makes his break from the science lab, taking reluctant Ray with him on a cross-country chase. (In the long shots, Milland's head, which usually sits on Grier's sizable

Don Marshall, Roosevelt Grier, and Ray Milland in *The Thing With Two Heads.* Is that self-loathing on Milland's face or does he just have a cramp in his neck?

shoulder, is replaced by what looks like a spare skull from Madam Tussaud's museum.) While cops and other concerned officials try to catch up, Ray and Rosey scramble over hill and dale. But they don't get along any better as they go along. In fact, these deformed defiant ones argue so incessantly that they finally start hitting each other in the face. Why, it's almost like watching a dog chase its own tail. Eventually, still on the lam, they arrive at the home of Rosey's old girlfriend (Chelsea Brown), who handles the reunion with comical cool. "You get into more shit," she says, shaking her head. "Do you have two of anything else?" Throughout this ordeal, Milland makes sourpuss faces as only a leading man who ended up starring in this and *Frogs* could make them. "Don't touch me," he barks when Rosey playfully pats his head. You have to feel sorry for the man.

The Trip (1967) What was the Summer of Love like for someone on LSD? Roger Corman dares to show us in this cinematic trip (written by one Jack Nicholson). Peter Fonda plays a slick TV commercial director who drops a tab with buddies Bruce Dern and Dennis Hopper. "You got to do just exactly like they say," coaches Dern. "Turn off your mind and relax and just float down the stream." Yes, you've heard that line before, in the Beatles' song "Tomorrow Never Knows"—but that was a far more psychedelic experience than this journey to the center of Peter Fonda's mind. Between cheesy kalei-doscopic light shows, our day-tripper wanders around Dern's house hallucinating all sorts of acid-etched clichés: He is chased by mysterious horsemen on a Big Sur beach. He is frolicking with a naked girl in a field of flowers. He is watching himself make love to his wife. "Everything's familiar, but I feel separate," he marvels, as pictures of Lyndon Johnson and Timothy Leary float before our eyes. Whenever Fonda freaks out—or simply falls in the swimming pool—Dern steps right in to help him make sense of it all. Then it's back to more flashy lights and scary painted faces, as Fonda gives Dern the slip and flees into the night. "Incredible," he says, watching the clothes tumble inside a laundromat dryer. Incredible isn't the word.

Trog (1970) In her final film, Joan Crawford dons dowdy lab coats of different colors to play an anthropologist who meets . . . the missing link! Actually, it's a prehistoric troglodyte who shows up in the English countryside, surprising the hell out of some local spelunkers. That's when Dr. Joan comes in, taking control for the good of science—only to conduct a series of experiments that are unlike science as we know it. Sometimes she treats the troglodyte like a nursery school child, teaching him the alphabet with pretty colored blocks. Other times, she acts as though she's training a new puppy. "Let's see if he'll fetch the ball," she says to her assistant. "Here, Trog! Good boy!" It's quite a scientific breakthrough all right, but some people aren't impressed—among them a big bad local official (Michael Gough), who snarls, "Kill it first. Then study it." He pretty much gets his wish when Trog escapes, wreaks havoc on the countryside, and gets blown away by the usual battalion of pea-brain soldiers. Dr. Joan can only stand there in her dowdy lab coat and wonder what might have been. She should be wondering why she even bothered. Yet another star from Hollywood's golden years gets lost in the Grade Z abyss.

Untamed Youth (1957) Mamie Van Doren goes to prison! She and Lori Nelson play singing sisters who make the mistake of hitchhiking through one of those Deep South cracker towns that doesn't cotton to vixenish vagrants. Sure enough, the girls are promptly hauled in and sentenced to hard labor on a local cotton farm. The place is run by a sadistic ramrod (John Russell) who feeds the inmates dog food and works their manicured fingers to the bone. "I hate tramps—male *or* female," he sneers. But he especially hates females. Does this

"Here, Trog! Good Boy!"
Joan Crawford tames a
savage troglodyte in the
tawdry *Trog*.

crimp our singing sisters' style? Not on your life! Shaking off those cotton-pickin' blues, they team up with some other musically-minded inmates to turn this caged-women picture into a rock and roll revue. It's not exactly *Jailhouse Rock*. In fact, it's not like anything you've seen before. Applying some serious torsion to her torso, Mamie sings no less than four showstoppers, including something called "Oobala Baby" and something else called "Go Go Calypso," the movie's big finale—in which Mamie, now safely in Hollywood, dolls herself up like a saucy señorita to lead a bunch of conga-playing chorus boys. Another triumph of sleazy showmanship from the one and only Al Zugsmith.

The Viking Women vs. the Sea Serpent (1957) Norse legend, Roger Corman's way. Abby Dalton leads the beautiful Viking women across a stormy sea in search of their missing men. They find them all right, in a distant land where the men are enslaved by—gasp!—a dark-haired tribe! The dark-haired women are wanton bitches; the dark-haired men are just plain bitchy. Worst of all is the chieftain's sissy son, who has an embarrassing tantrum when Abby saves his butt during a wild boar hunt. "A girl!" he bleats. "A girl had to save a Grimault warrior! My father will never forgive me!" Later, still smarting, he challenges Abby to an arm-wrestling match, which she tries her best to lose, but can't because he's so wimpy. But the real test for her and the Viking

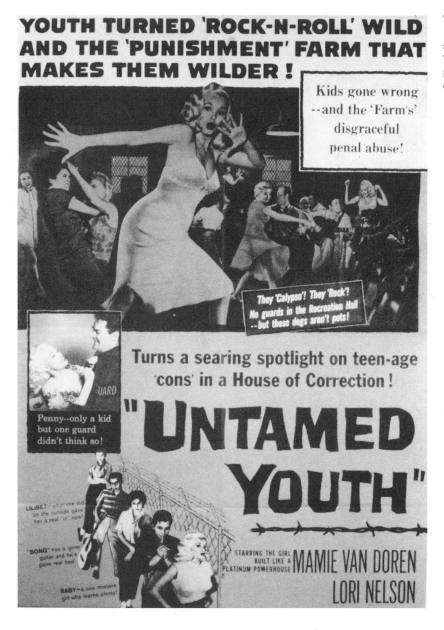

YOUTH TURNED 'ROCK-N-ROLL' WILD AND THE 'PUNISHMENT' FARM THAT MAKES THEM WILDER!

Kids gone wrong --and the 'Farm's' disgraceful penal abuse!

They 'Calypso'! They 'Rock'! No guards in the Recreation Hall --but these dogs aren't pets!

Penny--only a kid but one guard didn't think so!

Turns a searing spotlight on teen-age 'cons' in a House of Correction!

"UNTAMED YOUTH"

LILIBET—what she did on the outside gave her a real 'in' now!

"BONG" has a gone guitar and he's gone real bad!

BABY—a one-mistake girl who learns plenty!

STARRING THE GIRL BUILT LIKE A PLATINUM POWERHOUSE MAMIE VAN DOREN
LORI NELSON

This overstuffed poster for *Untamed Youth* did get some things right: Mamie Van Doren *was* a platinum powerhouse, and she *did* endure penal abuse!

women is how to keep their Anita Ekberg makeup intact after being thrown into slavery. They don't get much help from the Viking men, who all look like *Beach Party* bleach boys and fight like . . . Viking women! Meanwhile, the Viking women all fight like cats—especially among themselves. The chief

Viking man Brad Jackson (*right*) stares down Grimault chieftain Richard Devon (*left*) while Viking women Abby Dalton (*far left)*) and Susan Cabot (*third from left*) look on, in *Viking Women vs. the Sea Serpent*.

antagonist is Corman's stock villainess Susan Cabot (*Sorority Girl*), who plays the brunette black sheep of the Viking clan. "Are you all right?" she innocently asks, after cutting loose a mast that nearly decapitates Abby. "Ooh, she gives me the creeps," says another Vikette, using slang that puts her a thousand years ahead of her time. But it's true, bad Susan *is* creepy. Indeed, she's lots creepier than the titular sea monster, who only appears in two scenes: one at the outset when he nearly sinks the Vikettes, and one at the climax when he apparently swallows up a boatload of Grimault warriors. In both instances, he looks like something you'd see on a kiddie ride at Disneyland.

Village of the Giants (1965) Prepubescent science geek Ronny "Opie" Howard cooks up a formula that makes a giant out of anything that eats it. Get ready for the Invasion of Colossally Awful Special Effects. A huge house spider takes over the basement while Tommy Kirk and his girlfriend fight it off with bug spray. A pair of jumbo ducks shake their tailfeathers at a discotheque while the Beau Brummels rock band tries to act astonished. Then a bunch of bad teens, led by Beau Bridges and Tim Rooney, slurp down the stuff, bust out of their clothes, and start copping giant-sized attitudes. "Wait'll my old

A drake the size of a dromedary takes the discotheque dance floor in *Village of the Giants.*

man gets tough with me again," sneers one punk, pounding his fist into his hand. Next thing you know, they're ready to take on the whole adult world. "It's *our* world now," declares Tim Rooney. Just in time, little "Opie" comes up with the antidote—but not before Johnny Crawford makes the ultimate heroic gesture, hanging off a giant blond bimbo's banner-sized bra while waiving an ether-soaked towel under her nose. Yet another cheapie from Bert I. Gordon, this one also includes such highlights as the bad teens doing the Frug in the middle of a mudslide, then later the same bad teens doing the same dance steps, this time as giants . . . in slow motion! You can't say old Bert didn't give you your money's worth.

The Violent Years (1956) Ed Wood only wrote the script for this loony look at juvenile delinquents—but the "actors" couldn't have played it with more campy panache if Wood had directed them himself. The stars of this show are four teenage bad girls (none of whom looks a day over twenty-nine). At home, they're all sugar and spice, but once their parents go out, these hellcats hit the streets! Packing pistols in their pretty plaid skirts, they stick up gas stations and shoot it out with cops. One night, for variety, they head for lovers' lane, where they waylay a young couple, tying up the girl with her own dress and dragging the boy into the woods to "criminally assault" him.

"These fool kids," says one cop, to which his partner clarifies: "These aren't kids, they're morons." But, of course, it's really the parents' fault. All wrapped up in careers and country clubs, they've given their daughters everything . . . "everything but love," says one repentant mother. Yes, that's the problem, all right. "I don't care about money," explains the hellcat leader (Jean Moorehead). "There's plenty of that at home. It's the *thrill* that gets me. The thrill of the chase!" She gets her chase, all right, driving her getaway car right through a plate glass window. Later, in prison, she dies during childbirth, and justice is somehow served—but not before a judge delivers two long sermons abut parenthood, religion, family values, and everything else good and true. Ed Wood, Jr., strikes once again.

Viva Knievel! (1977) Evel Knievel plays himself—as he'd like you to believe he really is. Between death defying, self-promoting motorcycle stunts, he visits crippled children and miraculously cures them, takes on a ring of ruthless drug smugglers, and makes a real woman out of feminist photojournalist Lauren Hutton. "I'm just a man doing my own thing," he tells her. "Are you a woman . . . or a Ms?" Judging from this and other lame one-liners, Evel apparently had a hand in the screenplay, too. The man does everything! But he also gets help. Indeed, for a typical made-on-the-run drive-in movie, this vanity vehicle has more than its share of famous names—including Gene Kelly as a boozy mechanic; Red Buttons as a sleazy promoter; and Leslie Nielsen, Cameron Mitchell, Dabney Coleman, and Marjoe Gortner as various slimy villains. It's a veritable who's-who of has-beens and never-quite-weres—except, of course, for Evel. He's in a class by himself. "That's me, Super Evel," he says to his crippled-kid fan club. So who are we to argue?

Voyage to the Planet of Prehistoric Women (1968) In 1965, Roger Corman bought a Russian space movie called *Planet of Storms*, then used its footage as the framework for an epic he called *Voyage to the Prehistoric Planet.* The Russian film told the story of a space team's trip to Venus, where they encounter a desolate landscape, angry dinosaurs, and hungry man-eating plants. To this rather decent scenario Corman added new footage (directed by Curtis Harrington), which consisted mostly of professor Basil Rathbone monitoring the action and barking orders into a microphone from his moon-based command center. Corman's cinematic sleight-of-hand worked so well that three years later he used the Russian footage again for *Voyage to the Planet of Prehistoric Women*—which replaced the Rathbone footage with a new plot thread (directed under a pseudonym by Peter Bogdanovich) featuring Mamie Van Doren as the leader of a tribe of Venusian vixens. Sporting seashell bikini tops and shimmery skirts that look like cheap motel drapes, these platinum blond space babes sure do spice up the splice. But Corman's attempt to put them on the same planet as the Russians proves to be a bit of a reach. It's one thing to have Basil Rathbone periodically piping in from millions of miles away. It's another to have Mamie Van Doren, in her D-cup clamshells, traipsing over poorly matched terrain. One look at her and you know she isn't from the same movie. It's even more obvious that she isn't prehistoric—even if she does idolize a pterodactyl from the original Russian footage. Corman has tried to recreate that flying reptile for some key scenes with Mamie and the girls, but the closest he can come is a limp lump of monster effects that already looks extinct. As usual, Corman didn't know how to quit while he was ahead. (Author's note: Neither *Voyage to the Planet of Prehistoric Women* nor *Voyage to the Prehistoric Planet* has any connection to *Women of the Prehistoric Planet*, or to the previously discussed *Prehistoric Women* movies, which of course have no connection to each other. Sometimes there's less to a title than meets the eye.)

The Wasp Woman (1960) Right from the start, you can tell what kind of experience this is going to be: The opening credits for *The Wasp Woman* unfold against a backdrop of . . . bees! Leave it to Roger Corman to stretch a budget in the wrong direction. And wait'll you see the Halloween mask the title character wears. She looks like a pinheaded version of Al Hedison in *The Fly*. It all starts when cosmetics tycooness Susan Cabot hires a weird scientist who claims that the queen wasp's royal jelly can reverse the aging process. The boss lady craves eternal youth—and now she shall have it! But she can't be satisfied looking five years younger. N-o-o-o! She has to inject a megadose of "enzyme extract" against the warnings of the weird professor. After that, of course, there's no turning back. One minute she's a waspish woman, the next she's the Wasp Woman—a bloodthirsty she-creature who jumps out from behind furniture to sink her teeth (or whatever) into unsuspecting employees. Unfortunately for her, this insect lady hasn't sprouted wings. If she had, she wouldn't have to plummet to her death after being pushed out the window by leading man Fred Eisley. Oh, such stinging irony!

Wild Women of Wongo (1959) On the prehistoric island of Wongo all the women are beautiful and all the men look like couch potatoes. Meanwhile, on the island of Goona, all the men are handsome and all the women look like couch potato sacks. When the Wongo women save a Goona male from being speared by jealous Wongo men, the girls are banished from their village. What else can they do but set sail for Goona? It's Kismet! Set against a backdrop that looks like Coral Gables, the movie has all the primitive impact of *Where the Boys Are*. The way those Wongo women brandish their spears, they're definitely not in danger of breaking any nails. Still, they do have their moments. Encountering some Goona hunks swimming in a lagoon, one Wongo girl beckons, "Come out and we'll cook you a meal." When the boys demurely decline, the girls pull out their lassoes and reel 'em right in! For added comic relief there's also a big red parrot who sits in a tree, commenting on the comings and goings. "Take it easy, take it easy," he croaks during one Wongo catfight. Maybe he's worried that these wild women will ruin their carefree perms.

The Wild World of Batwoman (1966) Batwoman (Katherine Victor) is just what she sounds like: a campy female counterpart to a legit superhero. But she doesn't stop there. All decked out in feathers and faux fur (with a bat tattoo on her bosom) she presides over a bevy of Batgirls, nubile bimbos in bikinis who loll around Batwoman's split level pad, smack dab in the suburbs. Their poolside oath: "We the girls who are dedicated to Batwoman fight against evil with all sincerity." These girls are just itchin' for action, and boy do they get it. During the course of this movie Batwoman and her babes must contend with a masked archvillain named Ratfink, a mad scientist and his "happy pills," a stolen "atomic eavesdropping device," a lot of shady feds, and some slimy mole men who live in the caves at the beach. The mole men are actually "borrowed" footage from the fifties schlock shocker *The Mole People*, but these recycled monsters are the least of Batwoman's worries. Much harder to handle are the Batgirls themselves, after they get into the happy pills and start flailing around like demented go-go dancers. Following their lead, the rest of the cast collides at the mad scientist's lab, where everyone runs around and around in circles, until the whole movie flies off its axis in a frenetic climax. When last seen, the Batgirls are dancing around the pool, having the time of their lives—without a happy pill in sight. Just a bunch of fun-loving girls, fighting evil with all sincerity.

The *Wrestling Women* Movies. Their names are Loreta Venus (Lorena Velazquez) and the Golden Ruby (Elizabeth Campbell)—but you can call them the Wrestling Women. Coming from the same studio as Santo, they're similar . . . but different. Like Santo, they're self-appointed crimefighters who also wrestle (tag team-style) during endless bouts in the ring. Unlike Santo, however, they don't wear silly superhero costumes. They do just fine in tight sweaters and tighter Capri pants, which they wear while punching out bad guys in clunky slapstick action scenes. These girls never rip a seam, never even muss a single teased hair. But that's not to say they don't have all they can handle against enemies every bit as way out as Santo's foes. In *Wrestling Women vs. the Aztec Ape* (1962) they battle a mad scientist, an ape with a transplanted human brain, and a muscle-bound lady wrestler named Vendetta. But that's tame compared to *Wrestling Women vs. the Axtec Mummy* (1965), which pits them against a latter day Fu Manchu and his jujitsu sisters, who are after an Aztec treasure guarded by—you guessed it—another of those infernal Aztec mummies! Though not as cartoonishly cheesy as Santo, the Wrestling Women are still plenty funny, especially when their dialogue gets dubiously dubbed for English language prints. "She got lost in the pyramids," says a comic relief sidekick, reporting his girlfriend's disappearance. "The mummy will have her for supper!" "Oh, the poor kid," says Lorena, as if she's just learned that a casual acquaintance has spilled guacamole on her best party dress. Such grace under pressure will stand the girls in good stead over several further adventures, up to and including *Wrestling Women vs. the Murdering Robot* (1969). Yet somehow, the Wrestling Women haven't attained the legendary stature of Santo, and one wonders why. They're weird enough, they're wild enough, and they're pretty, too. No matter how silly their situation, they always stay kinda cool. The world of Grade Z movies could use more gals like Loreta and Ruby.

Zontar the Thing From Venus (1968) If John Agar hit bottom with *The Brain From Planet Arous*, he scraped it in this space invader dirge, directed by Larry (*Mars Needs Women*) Buchanan. How bad is *Zontar*? Bad enough to be a lousy remake of a Roger Corman cheapie called *It Conquered the World*. In other words, it doesn't get much worse! The horror begins when NASA scientist Anthony Houston tries to warn colleague Agar of an alien invasion. It turns out Houston has inside information because he's been conducting regular ham radio chitchats with the alien invader. They're even on a first name basis! Explains Houston: "Although his name is untranslatable to any known Earth language, it would sound something like . . . Zontar!" Hunkering down in the standard cave hideout, the unseen Zontar begins his conquest by shutting down all power, then sending out robotized bat creatures to implant mind control devices in people's necks. "I saw a funny looking boid," says one of the comic relief G.I.'s who wander around the outskirts of the movie. Meanwhile, his buddy is musing, "Hey, I wonder how this power failure will affect my wife's big mouth!"

All these yuks don't make it any easier for our hero Agar, who ends up riding around for help on a bicycle while the action is taking place elsewhere. The robotized bats attack community leaders. Citizens panic and stampede. Society as we know it grinds to a halt. Worst of all, Houston zealously converts to Zontar's cause, leaving behind his Barbie doll wife (Patricia DeLaney) who promptly flips out. "You listen and listen good," she harangues Zontar over the ham radio. "I hate your living guts for what you did to my husband and my world. I'm gonna kill you!" Sure enough, she grabs the nearest pistol (in this movie, everybody has one), then heads for Zontar's hideout to pump him full of holes. Poor girl, she never has a prayer! But at least she draws Zontar out into the open, where he reveals himself to be a bat-winged humanoid covered with melted multicolored candlewax—you know, just like a chianti bottle in a cheap Italian restaurant. Somehow, this drippy looking creature withstands the assault of conventional weaponry. It is left to a grief stricken Houston to destroy the monster who killed his wife, zapping Zontar with a laser gun powered by "plutonium ruby crystals." All Agar can do is stare at the smoldering aftermath and sadly shake his head. Wouldn't you? Zontar may not have conquered the Earth, but he did wreck what was left of Agar's movie career. Into the black hole poor John went, joining Joan Crawford, Ray Milland, Jon Hall, and the rest. They all live on, of course, in glorious infamy. So do their movies.

INDEX